Apple Pro Training Series

# Sound Editing in Final Cut Studio

Jeff Sobel

Apple
Certified

Apple Pro Training Series: Sound Editing in Final Cut Studio
Jeff Sobel
Copyright © 2010 by Peachpit Press

Published by Peachpit Press. For information on Peachpit Press books, contact:

Peachpit Press
1249 Eighth Street
Berkeley, CA 94710
(510) 524-2178
Fax: (510) 524-2221
http://www.peachpit.com
To report errors, please send a note to errata@peachpit.com.
Peachpit Press is a division of Pearson Education.

**Apple Series Editor:** Serena Herr
**Project Editor:** Stephen Nathans-Kelly
**Production Coordinator:** Kim Wimpsett, Happenstance Type-O-Rama
**Technical Editor:** Robert Brock
**Technical Reviewer:** Christopher Phrommayon
**Copy Editor:** Dave Awl
**Compositor:** Maureen Forys, Happenstance Type-O-Rama
**Media Producer:** Eric Geoffroy
**Indexer:** Jack Lewis
**Cover Illustration:** Kent Oberheu
**Cover Production:** Happenstance Type-O-Rama

ISBN 13: 978-0-321-64748-1
ISBN 10: 0-321-64748-3
9 8 7 6 5 4 3 2 1
Printed and bound in the United States of America

# Contents at a Glance

# Table of Contents

# Getting Started

Welcome to the official Apple Pro Training Series course for Sound Editing in Final Cut Studio!

This book is a comprehensive guide to audio editing and sound design with Final Cut Pro 7 and Soundtrack Pro 3. It aims to broaden your skills as a post-production expert.

The book uses real-world footage—including a montage from the hit TNT series *Leverage* and a beautiful HD trailer for the documentary *One Six Right*—to demonstrate the software features and practical techniques you'll use every day. While you work through the exercises, you'll learn not only the many audio editing, mixing, recording, and sound design features in both Final Cut Pro and Soundtrack Pro, but also how to perform those tasks in real-world situations.

Whether you're an expert or a newcomer to the Final Cut Studio suite, this book will teach you how to use Final Cut Studio as an integrated package to produce professional audio and sound design. So let's get started!

## The Methodology

This book takes a hands-on approach to learning the software. The lessons are project-based and designed to teach you the techniques and workflows used by audio engineers to correct and improve sound in the video post-production environment. Every exercise aims to get you performing professional-quality sound editing in Final Cut Pro and Soundtrack Pro as quickly as possible.

Each lesson builds on previous lessons, methodically introducing the interface elements and guiding you through their functions and capabilities until you can comfortably use the standard workflows of both applications together.

The lessons are self-contained, so if you're already familiar with these tools, you can go directly to a specific section and focus on that topic. However, each lesson is designed to support the concepts learned in the preceding lesson, and newcomers to audio editing should go through the book from start to finish. The first five lessons, in particular, teach basic concepts and are best completed in order.

## Course Structure

The book follows the workflow of audio post-production, starting with the completed video edit in Final Cut Pro, sending the project to Soundtrack Pro for correction and sweetening, and then returning to Final Cut Pro for output.

You'll begin by covering mixing basics in Final Cut Pro and will learn when its tools are all you need to meet your goals. Then you'll bring the Final Cut Pro project into Soundtrack Pro using the "round-trip" workflow, where you'll learn the basics of editing sound in Soundtrack Pro, and then complete the round-trip and return the project to Final Cut Pro.

Once you've learned the essentials of audio post-production in the two applications, you'll focus on Soundtrack Pro and learn the techniques and tools audio engineers use while following a real-world post-production workflow. The lessons are grouped into the following categories:

### Sound Editing and Mixing Basics, Lessons 1–2

The first two lessons cover the basics of sound editing and mixing in Final Cut Studio. You'll use the tools in Final Cut Pro extensively to sweeten and correct levels, and then send to Soundtrack Pro. You'll use Soundtrack Pro's noise reduction process to eliminate unwanted background sound, and then complete a mix of the project. Finally, you'll return the project to Final Cut Pro for final output.

### Getting to Know Soundtrack Pro, Lesson 3

This lesson provides an overview of the Soundtrack Pro workspace. You'll explore the application's four panes, and also learn playback techniques, track controls, and the round-trip process back to Final Cut Pro.

### Fixing Audio Files, Lesson 4

This lesson focuses on fixing common problems in audio files, including clicks and pops, as well as unwanted background noise. As you work through the exercises you'll further explore the Soundtrack Pro workspace and utilize scripts to automate repetitive tasks.

### Editing in Frequency Spectrum View, Lesson 5

Soundtrack Pro contains a specialized editing interface for adjusting the frequency content of audio clips. In this lesson you'll learn detailed use of the Frequency Spectrum view as well as general audio concepts.

### Working with Dialogue, Lessons 6–8

In a typical post-production workflow it's common for the audio editor to not only correct and sweeten the production sound, but to record new sound for the project as well. In these lessons you'll learn to record audio in Soundtrack Pro. You'll employ all of Soundtrack Pro's tools to finesse the audio clips in the project, including nudging, time-stretching, and using ambient noise prints. You'll also use the Multitake Editor to perform automatic dialogue replacement (ADR) and make a perfect composite take to replace bad production dialogue audio.

### Spotting Sound Effects, Lesson 9

Most sound effects heard in a video or film are added in post-production. This lesson will cover the techniques used to spot sound effects to the Timeline, find sound effect audio files on your system using the Bin and the Browser, create three-point edits, and utilize the Multipoint Video HUD (heads-up display).

### Scoring Using Loops, Lesson 10

This lesson will teach you how to create an original score for your project even if you have little or no musical skill. Using the Apple Loops included with Soundtrack Pro, you'll select and arrange music loops on the Timeline, set tempo and musical key, use markers to conform the music to onscreen events, and crossfade to create smooth transitions between musical passages.

### Mixing and Conforming Multitrack Projects, Lessons 11–12

Completing the workflow started in the previous lessons, you'll produce a finished mix of the dialogue, sound effects, and music tracks you've created. You'll learn to create submixes and to apply real-time effects, and then send the finished mix back to Final Cut Pro. In the final lesson, you'll learn how the Final Cut Studio workflow helps you to handle changes to the video edit made after audio post-production has begun.

## Using the DVD Book Files

The *APTS: Sound Editing in Final Cut Studio* DVD (included with the book) contains the project files you'll use for each lesson, as well as media files that contain the video content you'll need for each exercise. After you transfer the files to your hard drive, each lesson will instruct you in the use of the project and media files.

## Installing the Sound Editing Lesson Files

On the DVD, you'll find a folder titled SoundtrackPro3_Book_Files, which contains individual subfolders for each lesson in the book. Each subfolder contains a lesson file (either a Final Cut Pro or Soundtrack Pro project file) and a Media folder containing all the clips required for that lesson.

1 Insert the *APTS: Sound Editing in Final Cut Studio* DVD into your DVD drive.

2 Drag the SoundtrackPro3_Book_Files folder from the DVD to the top level of your hard drive to copy it there. The Media folders contain about 6 GB of media in total.

3 Eject the DVD before beginning the lessons.

Each lesson will explain which files to open for that lesson's exercises.

**Reconnecting Broken Media Links in Soundtrack Pro**

In the process of copying the media from this book's DVD, you may break a link between the project file and the media file. If this happens, the next time you open a project file, a window will appear saying that the application can't find a file and asking you to reconnect the project files. Reconnecting the project files is a simple process. In Soundtrack Pro, follow these steps:

1   In the Can't Find File window, click the Find File button.

2   Navigate to where the SoundtrackPro3_Book_Files folder resides on your hard disk, and then go to the specific Media subfolder.

3   Using the File Browser, in the appropriate Media subfolder, select the media file you wish to reconnect.

4   Click to select the Use Selected Path to Reconnect Other Missing Files checkbox.

5   Click the Choose button to reconnect all the media for that project.

6   Repeat steps 2 through 5 until all project files have been reconnected.

**Reconnecting Broken Media Links in Final Cut Pro**

To reconnect media files in Final Cut Pro, follow these steps:

1   Click the Reconnect button.

    A Reconnect Files dialog opens. Under the Files To Connect portion of the dialog, the offline file is listed along with its possible location.

2   In the Reconnect Files dialog, click Search.

    Final Cut Pro will search for the missing file. If you already know where the file is located, you can click the Locate button and find the file manually.

3   After the correct file is found, click Choose in the Reconnect dialog.

4   When the file is displayed in the Files Located section of the Reconnect Files dialog, click Connect.

5   Repeat steps 2 through 4 until all the Final Cut Pro project files are reconnected.

## System Requirements

Before using *Apple Pro Training Series: Sound Editing in Final Cut Studio,* you should have a working knowledge of your Macintosh and the Mac OS X operating system. Make sure that you know how to use the mouse and standard menus and commands; and also how to open, save, and close files. If you need to review these techniques, see the printed or online documentation included with your system. For the basic system requirements for Final Cut Pro and Soundtrack Pro, refer to the Final Cut Studio documentation.

## About the Apple Pro Training Series

*Apple Pro Training Series: Sound Editing in Final Cut Studio* is both a self-paced learning tool and the official curriculum of the Apple Pro Training and Certification Program.

Developed by experts in the field and certified by Apple, the series is used by Apple Authorized Training Centers worldwide and is also the market-leading series for self-paced readers who want to learn Apple Pro applications on their own. The lessons are designed to let you learn at your own pace. Each lesson concludes with review questions and answers summarizing what you've learned, which can be used to help you prepare for the Apple Pro Certification Exam.

For a complete list of Apple Pro Training Series books, see the ad at the back of this book, or visit www.peachpit.com/apts.

## Apple Pro Certification Program

The Apple Pro Training and Certification Programs are designed to keep you at the forefront of Apple's digital media technology while giving you a competitive edge in today's ever-changing job market. Whether you're an editor, graphic designer, sound designer, special effects artist, or teacher, these training tools are meant to help you expand your skills.

Upon completing the course material in this book, you can become an Apple Certified Pro by taking the certification exam at an Apple Authorized Training Center. Certification is offered in Final Cut Pro, Motion, Color, Soundtrack Pro, DVD Studio Pro, and Logic Pro. Apple Certification gives you official recognition of your knowledge of Apple's professional applications while allowing you to market yourself to employers and clients as a skilled, pro-level user of Apple products.

To find an Authorized Training Center near you, go to www.apple.com/software/pro/training.

For those who prefer to learn in an instructor-led setting, Apple offers training courses at Apple Authorized Training Centers worldwide. These courses, which use the Apple Pro Training Series books as their curriculum, are taught by Apple Certified Trainers and balance concepts and lectures with hands-on labs and exercises. Apple Authorized Training Centers have been carefully selected and have met Apple's highest standards in all areas, including facilities, instructors, course delivery, and infrastructure. The goal of the program is to offer Apple customers, from beginners to the most seasoned professionals, the highest-quality training experience.

## Resources

*Apple Pro Training Series: Sound Editing in Final Cut Studio* is not intended as a comprehensive reference manual, nor does it replace the documentation that comes with the applications. For comprehensive information about program features, refer to these resources:

▶ The Reference Guide. Accessed through the Soundtrack Pro Help menu, the Reference Guide contains a complete description of all features.

▶ Apple's website: www.apple.com

# 1

| | |
|---|---|
| Lesson Files | Lesson Files > Lesson 01 > 01_SoundEditingBasics.fcp |
| Media | One Six Right and Golfer |
| Time | This lesson takes approximately 75 minutes to complete. |
| Goals | Sweeten dialogue to improve clarity and tone |
| | Use normalization to set the peak level of a clip |
| | Control dynamic range using compression |
| | Reduce noise using Soundtrack Pro |
| | Perform equalization to finesse frequency levels |
| | Remove hums caused by electrical interference |
| | Add ambience and sound effects to bring a scene to life |
| | Perform sub-frame audio adjustments |
| | Integrate music into your sequence |

# Lesson **1**
# Sound Editing Basics

Working with audio involves many of the same tools used in cutting video, but it requires a different mindset. Aside from the obvious difference of focusing on hearing instead of vision, sound carries a subtler element of the production than images. Sound conveys the emotional tone of a scene, whether it's through music or the inflection of spoken words. If seeing is believing, then hearing is feeling.

Because of this fundamental difference, some people tend to excel at editing and mixing sound, whereas others are perfect picture editors. Hollywood understands this and has traditionally hired specialists to handle sound editing tasks. Increasingly, however, the picture editor is asked to do at least a large portion of the sound work herself. If you're put in this situation, understand that you'll need to change your perspective to excel at sound editing and focus on feeling more than meaning.

## Understanding the Sound Editing Process

Although some sound work is done in tandem with the video edit—such as finessing timing or splitting edits—the bulk of sound editing tasks are generally deferred to the end of the process, after picture has been locked. Picture editing is an iterative task; you cut and review and cut and review, and continue refining and finessing the edit until everyone agrees that it's done (or that the air date is upon you).

Cutting sound is much less amenable to repetitive tweaking. Each fade and filter is tied to a specific point in time, and trimming a clip by even a few frames can undermine the intended result of an effect.

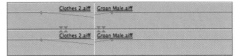

Fade before trim                                    Fade after trim

In the figure above you can clearly see that trimming the clip after the fades were applied resulted in truncating the fade. The fade will need to be rebuilt to restore its intended effect. If the clips are then trimmed again, the fades will have to be rebuilt a third time, and so on.

By delaying sound editing until the picture is finished, each sound clip can be faded, filtered, and mixed to perfection once and only once.

Generally, sound elements are divided into three categories: dialogue, effects, and music. These three categories are also referred to as *stems*. Working with each involves different techniques and requires different tools. This lesson takes you through each of these categories and teaches you the essential tasks required to make the best use of them.

## Cleaning Dialogue

*Dialogue* is any spoken language used in your program, including interviews, narration, singing, and character dialogue. With rare exceptions, dialogue is meant to be clearly heard and understood by the listener. Unfortunately, the realities of production often result in poorly recorded dialogue that must be cleaned, or *sweetened*, to improve its clarity.

Final Cut Pro and Soundtrack Pro provide a wealth of tools specifically designed to address common dialogue problems. Mastering these tools can help you create better-sounding audio.

Let's review the basic components of sound before delving into details about how to adjust them. Think of an audio signal as a specific frequency transmitted at a specific amplitude. In more common parlance, this means a given *pitch* at a certain *volume*. When you're adjusting audio, you're typically adjusting the frequency or the amplitude (or a combination of the two). If you can identify an issue as a frequency problem or an amplitude problem, you'll likely resolve it more quickly.

> **MORE INFO ▶** The Soundtrack Pro User Manual contains an excellent resource for learning about the nature of sound and the terminology commonly used when talking about it. For more info, refer to "Appendix B: Audio Fundamentals" in the Soundtrack Pro User Manual.

## Normalizing Audio

You make amplitude adjustments all the time by adjusting the volume (or *gain*) of an audio clip. Such adjustments modify the level uniformly across the entire clip. *Boosting* the volume makes a sound louder, but if you go too far, the loudest sections will distort, or *clip*. *Attenuating* quiets the sound, but when overdone, the quietest audio may become inaudible.

Deciding how much to adjust a clip's level can be tricky. First of all, some pitches can seem louder than others—even at equal gain settings—and original recording conditions can vary enormously, so each track may need individual settings.

*Normalization* is an automatic process that adjusts a clip's gain so that its loudest points are at a level that you determine. This may require either boosting or attenuating the signal. Normalization is a way to quickly create a relatively uniform gain structure across a range of clips (provided that they were all recorded in similar environments).

Let's begin by normalizing a sequence from *One Six Right,* director Brian J. Terwilliger's documentary about the Van Nuys Airport (www.onesixright.com).

**1**   In Final Cut Pro, open Lesson Files > Lesson 01 > **01_SoundEditingBasics.fcp.**

**2**   Play the first few clips of the *1. Normalize* sequence.

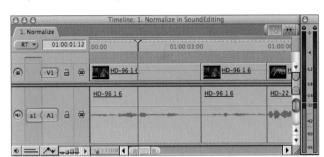

Pay particular attention to the levels in the audio meters. You'll notice that the average level of the first two clips is about −32 dB, and the loudest point hits about −26 (where the speaker says "realization").

**3**   Position your playhead over the first clip in the sequence.

**4**   Choose Modify > Audio > Apply Normalization Gain.

The Apply Normalization Gain dialog appears.

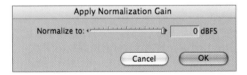

Setting the level to 0 dBFS (decibels full scale) attempts to place the loudest point in your clip at maximum volume without distorting it. However, because sound waves are so variable, it's very difficult to guarantee that some brief peaks won't break the barrier and create pops or clipping. For this reason, it's much safer to lower the slider by a few decibels.

**NOTE ▶** If the audio was clipped during the recording process, lowering the level will not fix the distortion that occurred.

**5**   Set the Normalize slider to −8 and click OK.

**6**   Play the sequence again and observe the audio meter.

Now the whole clip plays much louder.

**7**   Double-click the first clip (**HD-96 1 6**) and, in the Viewer, click the Filters tab.

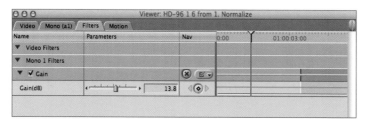

When you add normalization gain, a Gain filter is automatically applied to the clip, and Final Cut Pro calculates the proper setting to achieve normalization. Adding normalization gain to a clip with the Gain filter already applied does not add a new filter, it simply resets the filter's settings to create a new normalization goal.

Because the setting is applied as a filter, you can still use the level controls to remove a pop, create a fade-in or fade-out, or further modify the overall volume level of the clip. You can also remove the normalization by removing the filter.

**8**   In the Filters tab, select the Gain filter and press Delete.

The clip is returned to its original state.

## Normalizing a Group of Clips

In the real world, normalization is typically performed on a group of clips to create a seemingly uniform volume, regardless of discrepancies in the audio levels of the individual shots.

1  Working with the same project as in the previous exercise, play the whole sequence, paying special attention to the audio levels.

2  Press Command-A to select all of the clips, and then choose Modify > Audio > Apply Normalization Gain.

3  Set the slider to −12 and click OK.

4  Play the sequence.

Now the levels have been unified to an acceptable dialogue level.

NOTE ▶ See Lesson 2, "Sound Mixing Basics," for more information on volume settings.

## Controlling Dynamic Range

Because most clips contain a variety of loud and soft sections, simple level adjustments such as normalization are often not enough to control the apparent volume of the clip. Our perception of volume is based on the *average* level of an audio passage, not the peak level. The difference between a clip's quietest audio level and its peak level is called *dynamic range*. A clip with a wide dynamic range has both very quiet and very loud parts. A clip with a more limited, narrower dynamic range plays at a largely uniform volume. Controlling the dynamic range is one of the most important tasks in setting up a good mix.

A wide dynamic range can intensify the emotional impact of a scene, but too much dynamic range can make it difficult to set a proper audio level. For example, imagine a shot where someone intermittently whispers quietly and yells loudly. If you set the level high enough to hear the whispers, the yelling will peak and distort. If you lower the level so the screams aren't too loud, the whispers will become inaudible.

Fortunately, you can *compress* the dynamic range to bring the peak level closer to the average level of the clip.

**1**  Open the *2. Compression* sequence and play it.

This sequence repeats the same clip three times. The first version is unadulterated, the second has been normalized, and the third will be used to demonstrate the Final Cut Pro Compressor/Limiter filter.

**2**  Select the third clip and choose Effects > Audio Filters > Final Cut Pro > Compressor/ Limiter.

**3**  Double-click the clip to open it into the Viewer, and click the Filters tab.

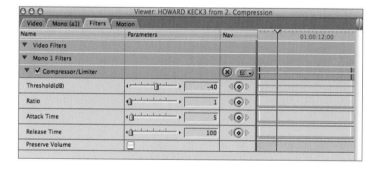

**NOTE ▶** To compress the dynamic range, you must define the target maximum level using the Threshold(dB) slider and define how aggressively the area above that level is reduced using the Ratio slider. The other two sliders—Attack Time and Release Time—affect how quickly the effect is applied and removed. You can ignore them for now.

The best way to apply Final Cut Pro audio filters is to adjust them while looping playback, so you can hear in real time how the filter changes affect the clip.

**4** In the Timeline, position the playhead over the third clip, and then press X to mark the clip, setting an In point at its beginning and an Out point at its end.

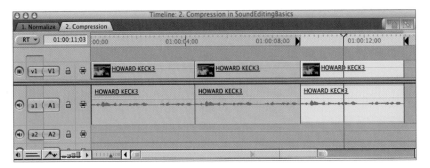

**5** Choose View > Loop Playback (or press Control-L).

**6** Press Shift-Backslash (\) to Play In to Out (from the In point to the Out point).

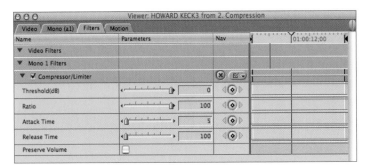

**7** In the Filters tab in the Viewer, raise Threshold(dB) to 0 dB and Ratio to 100.

Because you set Ratio at its highest value (100), the effect of the filter will be plainly apparent, but not until you lower Threshold(dB) to the level of the actual audio in the clip.

If you look at the audio meters while the clip plays, you can see that the average level is around −30 dB, but some of the quieter words are as low as −40 dB, and some of the loudest are as high as −23 dB.

Your goal is to reduce that dynamic range using the Compressor filter so that the quietest and loudest parts all occur at roughly the same level. This is done by attenuating the loud parts until they're the same volume as the quiet parts. Once that's done, you can raise the overall level to whatever volume you prefer.

**8**    Lower the Threshold(dB) slider slowly and listen carefully.

You should begin to hear an effect when you near –30 dB. The further you go, the quieter the whole clip seems to be. If you watch the audio meters, you can see the dynamic range being reduced.

**9**    Set Threshold(dB) to approximately –42 dB.

**10**    Lower Ratio to 1.

At a ratio of 1, the filter has no effect, but you can raise it slowly until you achieve your desired effect.

**11**    Select the Preserve Volume checkbox.

When this checkbox is selected, the gain is increased to compensate for the amount of applied compression. The result is that the more compression you apply, the louder the clip.

**12**    Drag the slider to slowly raise Ratio from 1 to 4.

You can now hear how significantly the compression is affecting the clip.

**13**    Set Ratio to 2.

**14**    Play the entire sequence.

The difference between the second and third clips may seem subtle at first, but it's very significant. Watch the meters as the clips play. In the second clip, the level ranges from –24 to –6; in the third clip, it ranges from –18 to –12. Although the clips appear to have a similar "loudness," the second clip is much closer to peaking. If you added some music or sound effects, it would be nearly impossible to avoid some spikes that would clip and distort.

**NOTE** ▶ The two clips have a similar apparent loudness in spite of the third clip's lower peak level because our ears evaluate volume based on a sound's average level, rather than by a sound's peak level. This is why we can increase the perceived volume of a clip by lowering its peak level via compression. Compression raises the average level of a sound.

## Separating Signal from Noise

Another basic sound concept is the difference between *signal* and *noise*—that is, the distinction between the recorded sounds you *want* people to hear and the extraneous elements that were incidentally recorded. In a dialogue track, the signal is obviously the voice, and the noise is any sound other than the voice. This could be environmental noise, such as traffic or an air conditioner, or it could be people talking or clanking dishes in the café where your interview was recorded.

Ideally, the signal is significantly louder than the noise, but sometimes poor recording technique will leave you with a track that contains similar volume levels for both signal and noise.

If the noise is isolated to audio frequencies that don't overlap with much of the signal, you can attenuate the unwanted frequencies, rendering the desired frequencies easier to hear (see "Removing Hums" later in this lesson). If, however, both signal and noise span across the frequency spectrum (the most common scenario), you need to use a tool such as a noise gate.

A *noise gate* attenuates sections in which the audio is relatively quiet, such as the moments between your talent's words or sentences when the background noise can be heard. The result is a reduction in noise level that leaves the signal unaffected. This is, in effect, the opposite of a compressor, and in fact this type of filter is often called an *expander*. Final Cut Pro has an Expander/Noise Gate filter that can accomplish this effect, but by sending the clip to Soundtrack Pro we gain access to several additional expanders, as well as a specialized feature built expressly for the removal of unwanted noise.

1   Open and play the *3. Background Noise* sequence.

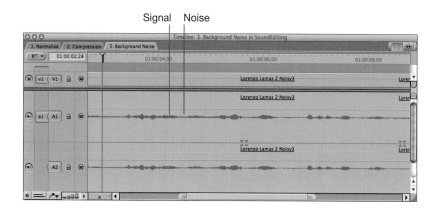

This clip obviously has quite a bit of background noise that is reducing the clarity of the interview subject's dialogue. You can even see this in the waveforms.

2   Select the clip and choose File > Send To > Soundtrack Pro Audio File Project.

A dialog appears, asking for a new filename.

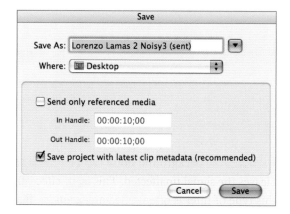

**NOTE** ► For this exercise, you can save the file to the desktop, but in the real world, you would want to save this file to your Final Cut Pro Documents folder or wherever you store Final Cut Pro project files.

**3**   Keep the default clip name and checkbox settings and click OK.

> **NOTE** ▸ This procedure enables you to keep the audio from the original clip unchanged and use Soundtrack Pro to modify a duplicate copy that you're naming and saving here. Final Cut Pro will automatically put this new, modified version of the clip and its audio into your sequence when you return from Soundtrack Pro. This process is referred to as *roundtripping*.

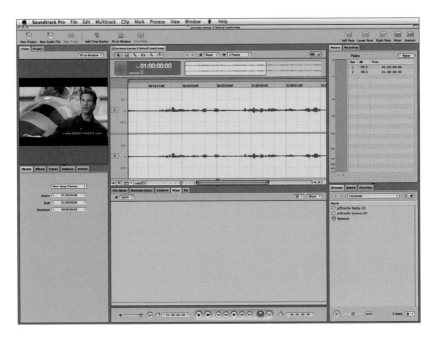

When you click OK, Soundtrack Pro opens automatically with the selected clip loaded into a new project. Soundtrack Pro has a variety of tools that remove background noise, but the noise reduction feature yields the best results with the least effort. To use this feature, you'll specify a *noise print,* a section of audio used to identify the frequency and amplitude of the offending sounds, and then use the Reduce Noise command to control how much noise to eliminate.

**4**   In Soundtrack Pro, drag in the green area of the clip display to select a portion of the audio where the waveform appears basically flat.

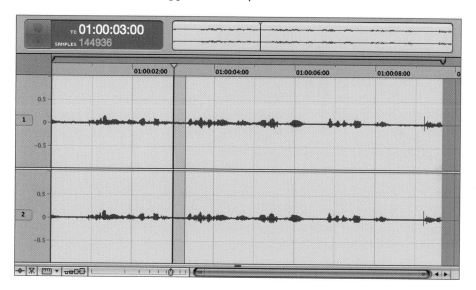

The longer the section you choose as a noise print, the more effective noise reduction will be. Near the end of the clip, there is a good section to use.

**5**   Press the spacebar to play the selected section.

By default, the playback will loop. Make sure you haven't accidentally selected part of a word. When you're sure you've selected only the background noise, press the space-bar to stop the looping playback.

**6**   Choose Process > Noise Reduction > Set Noise Print.

**7**   Click anywhere in the green area of the audio clip to deselect the section of the clip.

This allows you to apply the noise reduction to the entire clip. If you made a different selection before step 8, you would be applying the noise reduction only to that new selection.

**8**   Choose Process > Noise Reduction > Reduce Noise.

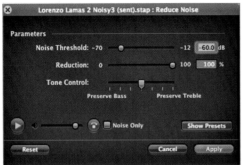

The Reduce Noise window appears. This works similarly to the Compressor filter in Final Cut Pro. The Noise Threshold setting identifies the peak volume level of the noise. The Reduction slider determines how much to attenuate that noise. The Tone Control allows for a small degree of frequency adjustment.

**9**   Click the Preview Play/Pause button and adjust the volume slider to a comfortable level.

**10**   Drag the Reduction slider all the way to 100%.

This allows you to easily hear the results of the effect.

**11**   Select the Noise Only checkbox to hear only the sound that you're eliminating.

Selecting this checkbox can be very helpful to ensure that you aren't accidentally removing too much of the signal along with the noise.

**12**   Deselect the checkbox again to turn off Noise Only.

**13**   Adjust the Noise Threshold slider until you can hear the effect of the filter; then back it off slightly and begin to adjust the Reduction slider.

**14**   When you're happy with the results, click Apply.

**NOTE** ▶ Remember, the goal is not to remove all background noise, but to improve the clarity of the signal by reducing the noise. Also note that noise reduction works quite well on some clips and not so well on others. If the signal-to-noise ratio is too low (that is, the signal and noise are at similar volumes, and/or the signal and noise frequencies are very similar) you may not be able to eliminate the noise. In those cases, your best course of action is to re-record the track.

**15** Press Command-S to save your work.

**16** Choose File > Close Project.

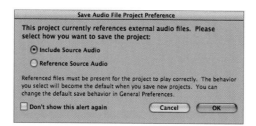

The Save Audio File Project Preference dialog appears, asking whether you want to embed the audio file into the Soundtrack Pro document, or to reference the original clip.

**17** Select Include Source Audio, and click OK.

When you return to Final Cut Pro, the audio will be updated automatically.

## Controlling Audio Frequencies

Almost everyone has some experience modifying audio frequencies on home or car stereos using an *equalizer* (EQ) or just a tone knob. If the low frequencies (or *bass*) are too loud, the thumping vibrations can overpower the more delicate high frequencies (or *treble*). On the other hand, if the treble is too loud, the sound can be piercing or "tinny." Most audio sounds best when the frequencies have been balanced or equalized. This is done by boosting or attenuating the frequency levels individually.

The most familiar tool for adjusting audio frequencies is a 3-band EQ, which lets you independently control the high, mid, and low frequencies. Adding more "bands" or control points allows more customized shaping of the sound.

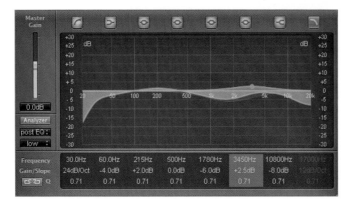

The Soundtrack Pro Channel EQ

**TIP** ▶ Because audio mixing is additive, it's generally better to attenuate the frequencies you don't want rather than boost the ones you do.

1   In Final Cut Pro, open and play the *4. Equalization* sequence.

This is a typical audio track that can be improved with some minor EQ work. Final Cut Pro has a few equalization filters, but those in Soundtrack Pro have more intuitive interfaces.

2   Select the clip and choose File > Send To > Soundtrack Pro Audio File Project.

3   Save the new audio file to the destination of your choice.

4   In Soundtrack Pro, choose Process > Effects > EQ > Channel EQ.

The Channel EQ window opens.

The horizontal scale represents frequency, and the vertical scale represents amplitude. To equalize your sound, simply click the horizontal frequency line and drag it up or down.

**5**   Click the Play button to preview your changes in real time, and then experiment with changes to the equalization graph.

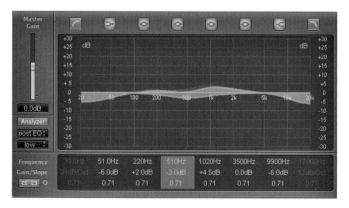

There are no "correct" settings. This figure represents one possible approach.

## Correcting Highs and Lows

One of the other common frequency-related tasks is the elimination of very low or very high frequencies, to remove a low rumbling from poor mic handling or the high whining sound of the transport system in some tape-based cameras.

A High Pass filter eliminates the lower frequencies, allowing everything above a designated pitch to *pass through* unaltered. A Low Pass filter does the opposite, removing sounds above a specified frequency.

Both Final Cut Pro and Soundtrack Pro have pass filters; however, there are also roll-off buttons built into the Channel EQ that perform a similar service by adding a steep reduction of the lowest and highest frequencies.

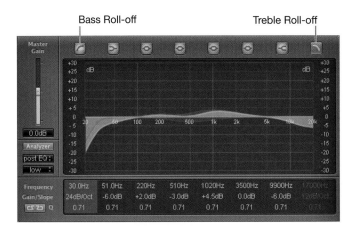

1    Click the Bass Roll-off button.

The low frequencies are eliminated from the clip.

2    Click Apply to add the effect to the clip, and then save and close the project to return to Final Cut Pro.

## Removing Hums

Some noise doesn't fit so neatly at the top or bottom of the frequency spectrum. For example, the hum introduced by electrical interference has a very specific frequency based on the rate of the alternating current. In the United States, the interference manifests as a 60 Hz hum.

To eliminate this sort of noise, you can employ a parametric equalizer, which boosts or attenuates frequencies within a definable and graduated range.

Because that 60-cycle hum is so common, both Final Cut Pro and Soundtrack Pro have filters specifically designed to remove it. Soundtrack Pro's filter is more advanced, so let's use it to fix this clip.

1   Open and play the *5. Hum* sequence.

    That familiar noise is impossible to miss.

2   Select the clip and choose File > Send To > Soundtrack Pro Audio File Project. Keep the default settings and click Save as you did before.

3   Click the Analysis tab in the left pane.

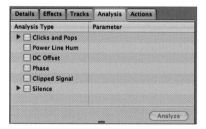

4   The settings in this tab represent six common issues that Soundtrack Pro can identify and automatically fix. Select the checkbox next to Power Line Hum.

**5**   Click the Analyze button. Soundtrack Pro analyzes the audio clip and highlights the waveform in red anywhere the problem is detected. Because the hum exists through-out the entire clip, the whole waveform has turned red.

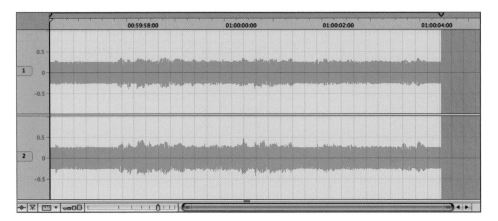

Look once more in the Analysis tab and you'll see that hum has been identified as a problem. In this part of the tab you can clearly see the type of problem, where in time the problem starts, its duration, and on which channels the problem is occurring, as well as the problem's status (Fixed or Not Fixed).

**6**   Click the Fix All button at the bottom of the Analysis tab.

Soundtrack Pro quickly processes the clip to remove the hum. You'll notice the wave-form is much thinner now that the hum has been removed.

**7**   Play the clip to verify that the hum has indeed been removed and the dialogue has been left untouched.

**8**   Press Command-S to save your work.

**9**   Choose File > Close Project.

When you return to Final Cut Pro, the audio will be updated automatically.

## Integrating Sound Effects

One of the signature aspects of professional filmmaking is the painstaking attention paid to sound. Amateur editors often don't realize that the audio recorded on the set is only a starting point. Production microphones are specifically engineered to record human voices, and directional shotgun mics and close-mounted lavaliere mics do very little to record any of the other complex elements—such as footsteps, hand props, and ambient noise—that make up the environmental sound of the scene.

Proper sound design requires reconstructing all of these elements and even adding sounds that weren't there at all. Almost everything that moves on screen requires a corresponding sound element. This includes titles and graphics, as well as objects and actions within a shot. In the real world, almost nothing that moves is silent (and if it does, it scares us). If a car drives by outside the window, a failure to include its sound will subtly pull your audience out of the story.

Sound design is a very important creative task; the sounds you choose can have an extraordinary impact on the feelings a scene evokes. For example, putting the sounds of children playing behind an interview subject can give a subtle cue to the audience that he is friendly and active in the community. Replacing that background sound with the deep hum of a walk-in freezer will make him seem less friendly and less connected to the world around him.

And this brings up an important point. Sound design is not reserved just for narrative, dramatic films. Documentaries, corporate training videos, and wedding videos are immeasurably improved by thoughtful sound design.

1   Back in Final Cut Pro, open and play the *6. Sound Effects* sequence.

   Let's bring this scene to life by adding a variety of sound effects. Your first task is to identify where sound elements should be added. This process is called *spotting*.

2   Play the sequence again, and think about what sounds could be added.

3   While the sequence plays, press M to add markers wherever a sound might go.

Obviously, the impact of the golf club hitting a golf ball needs a sound, but there's quite a bit more to be added. As the sequence opens, the man rubs his hands on the golf club grip and rocks his legs back and forth; during the swing, his clothes move; at the end of the swing, his foot scuffs the ground; and then, of course, he walks away.

Every one of those elements needs a sound effect to make the scene feel truly real. Final Cut Studio comes with a huge library of sound effects for this purpose. You can browse and preview those sound effects in Soundtrack Pro, but to save time, you'll find a group of them already imported into a bin in the project.

## Constructing Ambiences

In the world of sound effects, it's very common to combine multiple sounds to create a single "effect," or, in this case, an ambience. One trick to combining ambient sounds is to pay attention to the frequencies used in each element. If too many sounds use the same frequencies, the result will sound muddy and vague. If, however, you combine some low-frequency sounds with some highs, both will be clearly audible and the sound will feel more defined.

**1**  In the Browser, expand the Golf Sounds bin.

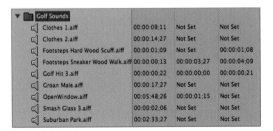

This bin contains all of the sounds used in this project. In addition to the clothes, footsteps, and golf hit, there are some tracks that can serve as an ambience track.

**2**  Open and play Golf Sounds > **OpenWindow**.

**3**  Set an In point anywhere after the initial fade-in has completed (about 2 seconds in).

4   In the Timeline, set the a1 audio target track to track A3.

5   Press End to bring the playhead to the end of the sequence, and then press O to set an Out point.

6   Press Home to move to the head of the sequence, and then press F10 to overwrite the ambience track into the sequence.

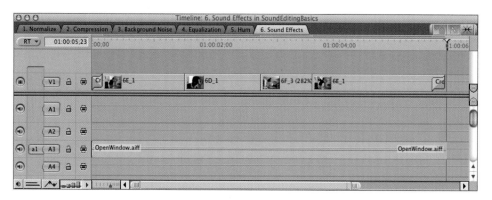

Although this element helps to establish the environment, there's room for improvement. It sounds more natural than absolute silence, but because it's so constant, it doesn't give much sense of place or texture.

The **OpenWindow** sound has a nice mid-to-low frequency hum to it (along with a higher-frequency hiss that you may or may not decide to remove using a Low Pass filter). To add something without muddying the sound, it would have to either be very low-pitched or very high-pitched.

7   Open and play **Suburban Park.aiff.**

This sound provides more of a sense of place and time of day (there are birds sing-ing, not crickets chirping) and, conveniently, those bird sounds are high-pitched and won't compete with the audio frequencies in the **OpenWindow** shot.

**8**    In the Timeline, set the a1 target to track A4 and the a2 target to track A5.

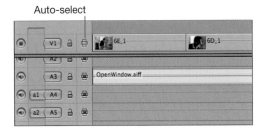

**9**    Click the Auto Select control for track V1 to disable it.

**10**    With the playhead positioned anywhere over **OpenWindow**, press X to set In and Out points at the head and tail of the clip.

**11**    Press F10 to edit the **Suburban Park** clip onto tracks A4 and A5.

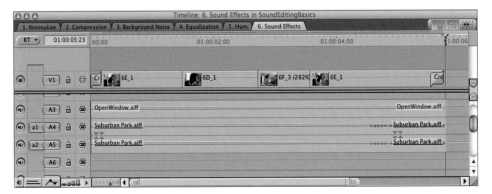

**12**    Play the sequence.

The birds add a nice touch, but those chirps at the end are overpoweringly loud. We don't want to suggest that our golfer has a sparrow caged in his living room. It would be better if we could find a section of the bird track without those loud chirps.

**13** In the Timeline, double-click the **Suburban Park.aiff** clip to open it into the Viewer.

Be sure you see the sprocket holes in the Viewer scrubber area to confirm that you're editing the version from the sequence.

**14** Press Shift-Z to zoom the entire length of the **Suburban Park** clip to fit in the Viewer.

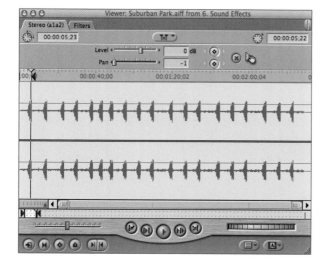

The waveform clearly shows where the loud chirps occur. If you have any doubt, play the clip and watch the playhead move through the waveform.

**15** Shift-drag the Out point until the In and Out points are safely located between loud chirps (after the second chirp and before the third).

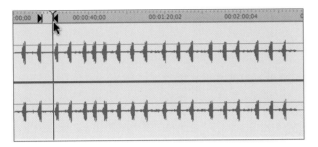

**TIP** ▶ Holding down Shift locks the In and Out points together, allowing you to perform a slip edit, just as you would when using the Slip tool in the Timeline.

**16** Play the sequence to hear how your ambience is taking shape.

Of course, it will be critical to set the relative levels of these two clips, but as long as they're not overpowering now, you can defer that task until the rest of the sound effects have been laid in.

## Editing Subframe Audio

The next step is to add the sound of the golf club hitting the ball. Such a task is often as simple as dropping in a sound effect that lines up with the correct frame in the sequence. Often, however, the cue point of a sound effect does not occur at the very start of the clip. There may be a moment of silence before the sound is heard, or there may be a passage that precedes the portion of the sound that needs to be synced such as a door creaking before it slams shut. In these cases the audio clip needs to be placed more precisely than simply syncing it to the video frame.

**1** Open and play **Golf Hit 3.aiff**.

If you zoom in, and position your playhead over the moment of impact, you'll see that the actual sound occurs midway through the frame.

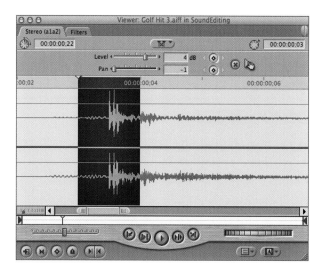

**NOTE** ▶ Sound is recorded in much finer gradations than video frames. There may be as many as 800 to 2,000 sound samples for each frame of video. Final Cut Pro allows you to make audio adjustments down to 1/100th of a frame.

**2**   Shift-drag the playhead until the beginning of the playhead lines up precisely with the initial impact of the sound.

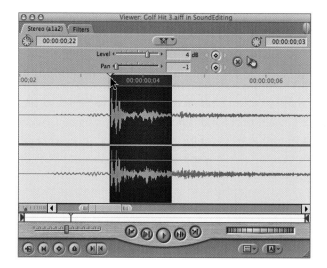

Now the sound begins precisely at the start of the frame.

Holding down Shift allows you to override the frame boundaries and establish a new beginning for your frames. However, in order to lock the playhead into this new position, you must mark a new In point.

**3**   Press I to mark a new In point.

After you set this In point, each surrounding frame will adjust itself to match, so each frame still has a constant duration. You can clear the In point now so that you can use the few frames of buildup sounds.

**4**   Press Option-I to clear the In point.

**5**   In the Timeline, position the playhead on the precise frame where the club appears to hit the ball (approximately 02:27).

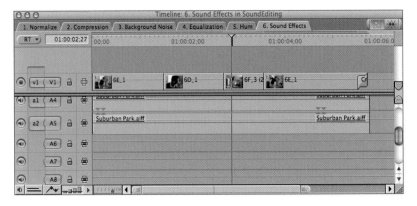

**6**   In the Viewer, click the Add Marker button to place a marker on the frame where the sound begins.

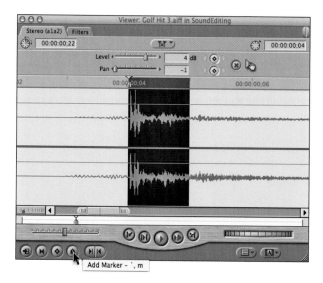

**7**   Drag the **Golf Hit 3** clip into the Timeline to tracks 6 and 7 (using the drag handle in the upper-right corner of the Viewer window). Align the marker with the playhead position.

> **NOTE** ▸ You may need to toggle off snapping by pressing N.

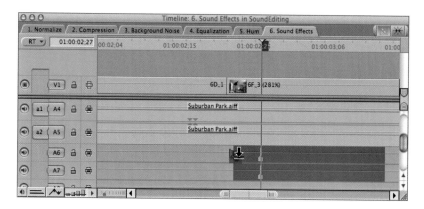

**8**   Press Backslash (\) to play around the edit.

**TIP** ▶ In the Timeline, you can use clip markers as snap points by directly clicking the marker when you select the clip. However, when you drag a clip from the Viewer into the Timeline, markers will not behave as snap points.

**NOTE** ▶ Sound effects such as the footsteps at the end of the sequence also can be dropped in using this technique. You will probably have to mark each footfall individually, and you should be thankful that there are only two. Because of the wide variance in footwear, ground surface, and gait, it's actually quite rare to use pre-recorded footsteps. It's much more common to record new footsteps timed precisely to the video playback. The process of recreating sound effects for onscreen action such as this is called *foley*.

## Enhancing the Scene

For "extra credit," take a few minutes to lay in the remainder of the sound effects. Be aware, however, that the hard part (and, some would say, the fun part) of the job has already been done for you. Choosing the sounds from your own library is where the creative aspect of sound design really occurs.

You may notice that the Sound Effects bin contains a breaking glass effect. If you're wondering why, think about the content of the scene. Here's a guy driving a golf ball inside his house. You have to ask yourself, where is that ball going to go? Sometimes the sound effects you add contribute story elements that are not otherwise apparent in the shot. Sound is nearly always just as vital to your story as the images.

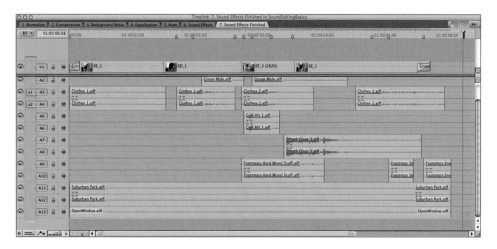

To examine one possible finished version of the scene, open and play the *7. Sound Effects Finished* sequence.

## Adding Music

Music has incredible power to add emotion to a scene. But it's not a cure-all. First of all, smothering a scene with music should never be done *instead* of the dialogue and sound effects work described previously. Music should always be added after the other stages are complete. You may be surprised that plenty of scenes need no music, or very little.

Second, music can wield a very broad brush. Although the right music can bring emotional aspects of a scene to the fore, the wrong music can alienate and confuse your audience. Using clichéd music to evoke suspense, or sadness, or triumph may offer an immediate sense of clarity about the dramatic tone of a scene, but the cliché quickly wears thin and your audience will disengage from the story. Good music, like a well-written character, is complex and subtle and unique.

Finally, it's imperative that your music support the story, and not the other way around. If a scene doesn't seem to work when you mute the music track, it probably needs to be recut (or removed entirely). If your story is taking a backseat to the music, then what you have is a music video, and the artistic credit should go to the musicians, not the filmmakers.

Having said that, music is amazingly powerful, and when used appropriately, it can be an incomparable element of the overall work.

1    Open and play the *8. Look Ma* sequence.

This scene desperately needs music to glue together the interviews and make it feel complete.

2    Expand the Look Ma music bin in the Browser, and then open and play the **Two Maidens Holding Pearls** clip.

The sequence already has In and Out points set.

3    Press F10 or drag the audio drag handle onto the Overwrite Edit Overlay in the Canvas.

The clip is laid in on the target tracks.

4    Play the sequence.

The music works for a while, but it does get a little repetitive. Plus, the scene changes tone midway through: The interviewees begin by talking about how overwhelming a pilot's first solo flight can be, but then they describe the moment of epiphany every pilot goes through. This is exactly the sort of emotional change in a story that music can subtly reinforce.

5    Mark an In point just after the man says, "It's up to you" (around 58:39).

6    From the Look Ma Music bin, open and play **Red Plane**.

7    In the Viewer, mark an In point just as the piano melody begins (around 26:10).

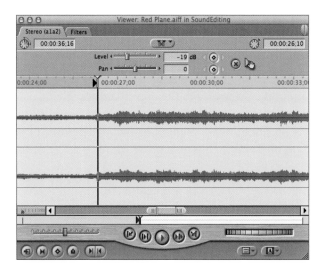

**8**   Press F10 to overwrite the clip into the sequence.

**9**   Press Backslash (\) to play around the edit.

Well, it sounds fairly ridiculous as a straight cut, but a crossfade will smooth it out nicely.

**10**   Control-click the edit between the two music clips and choose Add Transition 'Cross Fade (+3 dB)' from the shortcut menu.

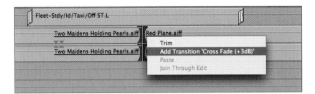

Unfortunately, the crossfade undermines the sense of transformation conveyed by the beginning of the piano. This is partly because the piano is still fading in at the cue point.

**11** Control-click the Transition and choose Transition Alignment > End On Edit from the shortcut menu.

This ensures that the transition is complete before the melody kicks in. However, the transition is still too blatant because it's too short.

**12** Drag the left edge of the transition by about 7 seconds until it lines up approximately with the beginning of the dialogue (visible on tracks 3 and 4).

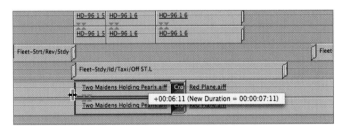

**13** Play across the transition.

This is a vast improvement, allowing the musical transition to support and reinforce the transition occurring in the narration. The melody kicks in right on cue, and the guitar fade-out doesn't draw undue attention to itself.

**14** Play the entire sequence.

Everything works except for a small problem at the end.

**15** Delete the piece of **Two Maidens Holding Pearls** at the end of the sequence.

Of course, your work isn't done. There's still the essential work of setting all the levels for all of the sound elements in your program. We'll begin to explore that process in Lesson 2, "Sound Mixing Basics."

## Lesson Review

1.  What is normalization?
2.  How can you remove the Normalize effect?
3.  What is dynamic range?
4.  What does compression do?
5.  Does compression make a clip sound louder or softer?
6.  What is a noise print?
7.  What does an equalizer do?
8.  Does a High Pass filter remove or preserve the high frequencies?
9.  How do you change an audio clip's frame boundaries?
10. Why would you want to change a clip's frame boundaries?

### *Answers*

1.  An automatic level adjustment designed to maximize volume without clipping.
2.  Delete the Gain filter from the clip.
3.  The difference between a clip's lowest level and its peak level.
4.  Attenuates the loudest portions to reduce dynamic range.
5.  Compression makes a clip louder only when the Preserve Volume setting is selected.
6.  In Soundtrack Pro, a noise print identifies and samples the area of your track considered "noise."
7.  An EQ allows different frequency bands to be boosted or attenuated independently.
8.  A High Pass filter preserves frequencies *above* a designated frequency threshold.
9.  Shift-drag the playhead in the Viewer's Audio tab.
10. To adjust audio timing at the subframe level.

# 2

| | |
|---|---|
| **Lesson Files** | Lesson Files > Lesson 02 > 02_SoundMixingBasics.fcp |
| **Media** | One Six Right |
| **Time** | This lesson takes approximately 100 minutes to complete. |
| **Goals** | Complete a full audio mix in Final Cut Pro |
| | Smooth edits using a variety of fade methods |
| | Adjust audio levels across multiple clips |
| | Record keyframes to automate a mix |
| | Create perspective effects using level and pan |
| | Export multitrack mixes to Soundtrack Pro |

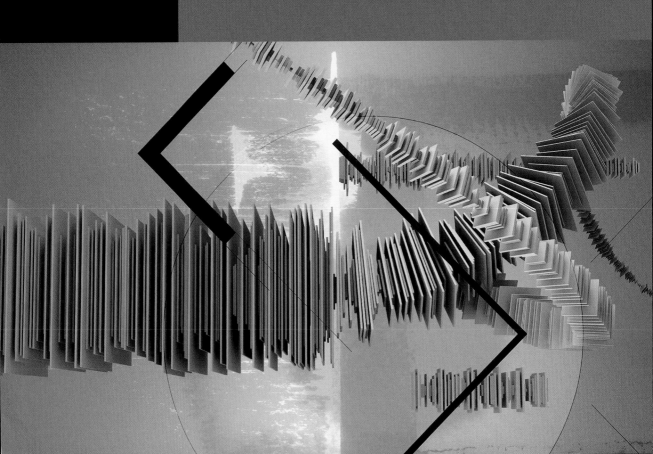

# Sound Mixing Basics

After sound is edited, the final task is creating the *mix* in which all the audio elements are combined and their volumes set to maximize the editor's control over the point of focus. Your choice of which sound elements are in the foreground and which are in the background is another essential storytelling tool that enables you to precisely guide an audience through the story.

Final Cut Pro contains a wide array of robust audio mixing tools— including an audio mix window, dynamic mute and solo controls, and full automation—that allow you to animate audio levels on the fly. In addition, it seamlessly integrates with the dedicated audio tool, Soundtrack Pro.

In Soundtrack Pro, you can complete your mix with even more control: *bussing* tracks to streamline filtering workflow, customizing audio fades, and creating mixes in surround sound. After your mix is complete, you can export it back to Final Cut Pro for final output.

## Mixing in Final Cut Pro

Although most productions will benefit from the advanced audio capability of Soundtrack Pro, some projects may be well served by the tools within Final Cut Pro. The sophisticated audio mixing tools in Final Cut Pro—both in the Timeline and in the Audio Mixer window—may be all you need to speed your workflow and execute every mixing decision.

## Fading In and Out

A critical aspect of mixing is that every single audio clip in your sequence should begin with a fade-in and end with a fade-out, even if the fades are only a few frames long.

Hard-cutting an audio clip—any audio clip—can create unwanted audio interference, such as a pop or click. Often you may not hear anything wrong as you're creating the final mix, but such hard cuts may still rear their ugly heads (and tails) when the audio is compressed for DVD, the web, or portable playback devices.

Fortunately, adding fades can be quick and easy, especially if done at just the right stage: after all editing is completed, but before you create your main mix.

1   Open Lesson Files > Lesson 02 > **02_SoundMixingBasics.fcp**.

   The *Audio Fades* sequence should already be open. This lesson uses footage from Brian J. Terwilliger's documentary, *One Six Right* (www.onesixright.com).

2   Play the sequence.

   Although there are no obvious errors, it's still advisable to smooth the head and tail of each clip, just in case. Begin working on the dialogue tracks.

3   On tracks A1 and A2, select the incoming edit of the first dialogue clip **HD-96 1 3**.

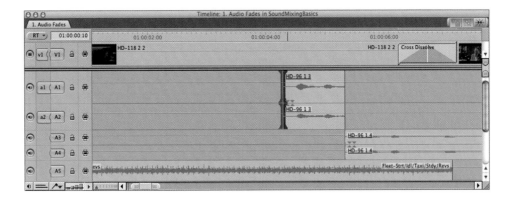

4   Press Command-Option-T to add the default audio transition (a +3 dB crossfade).

The crossfade transition is applied to the edit. In this case, the default duration is longer than the clip duration, so the transition covers the entire clip.

5   Double-click the transition.

The Duration dialog appears.

6   To change the length of the transition to 4 frames, type 4. Press Tab, and then click OK.

The default transition is the Cross Fade (+3dB), which is designed specifically for fading between two constant volume sources, such as music. This is sometimes referred to as a *constant power* crossfade because it slightly boosts the volume of both clips to prevent an audible dip in volume at the center point of the fade.

However, a constant power crossfade serves little benefit when fading to or from silence, and depending on the clip, can produce a more abrupt, less natural-sounding fade.

For fading to and from silence, Final Cut Pro offers an alternative: the Cross Fade (0dB), also known as a *constant gain* crossfade. This fades the two elements in a linear fashion.

**TIP** ▶ The enormous variety of sounds you'll encounter means that the 0 dB and +3 dB crossfades can both be used in a wide range of scenarios. If you're ever in doubt, try them both and listen to the results.

7   Control-click the transition and choose Cross Fade (0dB) from the shortcut menu.

The transition is updated.

This short, 0 dB transition is very handy, and you may use it quite a bit while mixing your projects. So why not save a copy of it for repeated use?

8   Drag the transition to the Browser, and place it in the Favorites bin of the Effects tab.

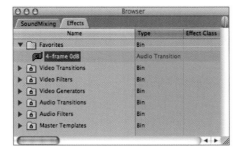

9   In the Browser, rename the transition *4-frame 0dB*.

You can make this new custom transition the default transition by Control-clicking it and choosing Make Default from the shortcut menu; but for this exercise, we'll leave the default transition as it is.

**10** In the Timeline, Option-drag the 4-frame transition to copy it from the head of the first clip to the end of the clip.

> **TIP** If you have difficulty copying the first transition, add a default transition to the second edit, change its duration to four frames, and then Option-drag it to each of the remaining edits.

**11** Option-drag the transition again to add it to the beginning and end of each of the other clips on tracks A1 and A2 and on tracks A3 and A4.

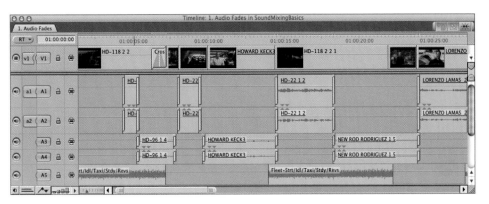

**12** Play the sequence and listen for errors.

In some cases, even the 4-frame fade might cut off the beginning or end of the audio.

**13** Navigate to around 8 seconds into the sequence and play around that edit.

The interview subject's line "You don't know when it's gonna happen" is cut off, so all you hear is "when it's gonna hap."

**14** Control-click the transition and choose Transition Alignment > Start on Edit from the shortcut menu.

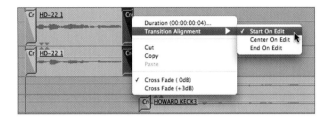

Beginning the transition on the end of an edit ensures that you'll retain all of the frames you were so careful to include during the trimming process. Similarly, if a sound is cut off at the head of a clip, you would set the transition alignment to End On Edit.

## Using Audio Keyframes to Fade

Another method for quickly applying a short fade-in and fade-out to each of your clips is to keyframe the audio level for a single clip, and then paste those attributes onto all the other clips. Many editors prefer this method because it allows more precise control over the shape of the fade than Final Cut Pro's fade transition.

NOTE ▶ Final Cut Pro provides only two types of fades, but Soundtrack Pro offers sixteen different fade shapes.

If you previously set specific audio levels on any of the clips, this method would obliterate those settings, so you should only paste attributes before independently finessing the levels.

NOTE ▶ Gain filter settings, such as those applied using the Normalize command, will not be affected.

1   Play the sequence.

The sound effect used for the plane has been properly placed to match all of the shots, but the way it cuts in and out draws unneeded attention to the edits.

**2**   Zoom in to fill the screen with the first sound effect as seen in the figure below.

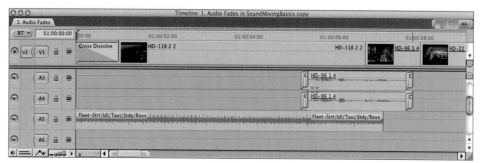

**3**   Press Option-W to turn on clip overlays.

**4**   Option-click the audio level overlay (the pink line) to add keyframes, and position the keyframes to create a short fade-in and fade-out for the clip.

Be careful not to modify the overall level of the clip.

**5**   Select the clip and press Command-C to copy it to the clipboard.

**6**   Press Shift-Z to zoom the window to fit, and then select all of the sound effects on tracks A5 and A6.

**7**    Press Option-V to Paste Attributes.

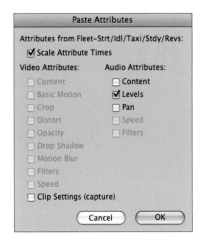

The Paste Attributes dialog appears.

**8**    Make sure Scale Attribute Times is selected, and then select the Audio Attributes Levels checkbox and click OK.

The fade-in and fade-out are applied to each of the remaining clips.

## Solo and Mute Controls

While playing this sequence, you've probably noticed that the music on tracks A7 and A8 was not audible. This might seem strange because the clips are enabled and the level settings are not turned all the way down.

It's very useful—often essential—to temporarily turn on and off individual components of the audio to focus on the rest of the mix. For this sequence, the music tracks were *muted* because adding the dialogue and effects fades would be much more difficult if the music were playing.

**1**    In the lower-left corner of the Timeline, click the Audio Controls button.

This adds two controls to the Timeline track header area. The first control is the mute button, which excludes that track from playback. When a track is muted, the speaker turns yellow. In this sequence, tracks A7 and A8 are muted.

The second control is the solo button, which effectively mutes all of the other tracks. You can *solo* multiple tracks to hear more than one track at a time. When a track is soloed, the headphone icon turns red, and all the other tracks display a mute icon with a yellow background.

Muting a track is fundamentally different from turning off the Track Visibility control. When a track is muted, it will still be included when you export a file or lay it off to tape. Clicking the Track Visibility control to disable the track essentially removes that track from the sequence entirely.

One of the most useful aspects of the mute and solo buttons is that they can be enabled while the sequence is playing—which reinforces their essential role in audio mixing. Often, you want to hear just the dialogue or just the effects tracks without the distraction of the other audio elements. Soloing those tracks is the perfect solution.

**2**   Play the sequence.

**3**   In the Timeline patch panel, click the solo button for tracks A1, A2, A3, and A4.

The music and sound effects are muted. The mute buttons for those tracks are inverted and turn yellow. Because tracks A7 and A8 are already manually muted, they appear a different color.

**4**   Click the solo buttons for tracks A5 and A6.

Now those tracks are added to the mix.

**5**   Click the solo buttons for tracks A7 and A8.

It's possible for a track to be muted and soloed at the same time. The mute overrides the solo, and the mute button appears in a slightly different color. This can be very helpful if you have a large number of tracks and, while a number of them are soloed, you want to temporarily mute one or two without changing the solo set you're working with.

When every track is soloed, the effect is the same as soloing no tracks at all.

**6**  Option-click any of the solo buttons.

All of the tracks are unsoloed. This works only when either all of the tracks or none of the tracks are soloed. If none of the tracks are soloed, Option-clicking will solo all of them.

**7**  Click the mute buttons for tracks A7 and A8 to unmute the tracks.

## Engaging the Button Bar

Final Cut Pro provides three preset collections of buttons designed for common work-flows. One of these is used specifically for audio editing.

**1**  Choose Tools > Button Bars > Audio Editing.

Audio editing buttons are added to the button bars in the Timeline, the Canvas, and the Browser. These buttons allow quick access to many common functions.

If you position your pointer over the different buttons, a tooltip appears that identifies the button and displays any keyboard shortcuts associated with that command.

A group of buttons is located at the right edge of the Timeline button bar. These buttons control how many tracks Final Cut Pro attempts to play in real time. By default, Final Cut Pro attempts to play eight tracks. Playing any additional tracks will require rendering.

**2**  Open the *2. Ready for Mix* sequence.

All of the fades are applied to this sequence.

At some places where crossfades occur, the audio render bar shows a red section. When playing across those sections, you'll hear a beeping sound.

Crossfades and some filters have an increased track processing "cost," so to play this sequence without rendering you must increase the number of available real-time tracks.

**3**　Click the Real-Time Audio Mixing: 12 Tracks button.

The red area in the sequence render bar disappears.

**NOTE** ▸ If you're wondering why you shouldn't always leave the number of real-time tracks set to the maximum (99 tracks), it's because the more processor power you allocate to audio mixing, the less you'll have for real-time video effects. By leaving this setting at the lowest required value, you'll preserve as much processing power as possible for picture.

## Setting Audio Levels

Momentarily, you'll dive into the Audio Mixer window, where you can animate all of your audio levels on the fly, dynamically adding fades and keyframes. But before you do, remember that there are several other ways to adjust audio levels that are sometimes more efficient than using the Mixer.

**1**　Play the *2. Ready For Mix* sequence.

It's probably apparent to you that the plane sound effect is a little too loud, and it competes with the dialogue tracks. You could individually adjust each of those sound effects clips, but because they're so similar to one another, you can adjust all of their levels simultaneously.

**2**    Select all of the clips on tracks A5 and A6.

**3**    Choose Modify > Levels, or press Command-Option-L.

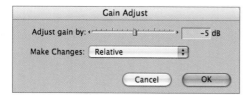

The Gain Adjust dialog appears.

In this dialog, you can modify the audio level of all the selected clips in one operation. You can choose to set an absolute level for all the clips, or to make a relative adjustment so that each clip's level is boosted or attenuated from its current setting.

**4**    Set the "Adjust gain by" slider to –5, leave Make Changes set to Relative, and click OK.

Each clip is attenuated by 5 dB. Notice that the fade-ins and fade-outs are not affected. If you set Make Changes to Absolute, any keyframes would be eliminated.

**NOTE ▶** Although this dialog uses the term *gain,* it's the clip level that's modified, not the gain filter as described in the "Normalizing Audio" section in Lesson 4.

**5**    Play the sequence.

If you're still not happy with the level of the sound effects, you can also make 1 dB or 3 dB adjustments using the keyboard.

**6**    While the sequence is playing, press Control-Plus (+) to boost the clip level by 1 dB. Press Control-Minus (-) to lower it by 1.

Or, you can press Control-Right Bracket (]) or Control-Left Bracket ([) to boost or attenuate the level by 3 dB.

These commands will affect all selected clips, or if no clips are selected, they'll apply to the clip currently under the playhead.

> ### ► What's a Good Level?
>
> Proper audio levels vary dramatically depending on your intended output format and exhibition location. A good sound mix for an iPhone video is very different from one intended for a movie theater. However, there are a few essential things to keep in mind:
>
> **Understand dynamic range:** Dynamic range is the difference between the minimum level and the peak level. If you want your music or sound effects to feel louder, rather than turning them up, turn down your dialogue track. The dialogue tracks should be set to your target "average level," which typically is −12 dB for television viewing, or −20 dB for theatrical exhibition. If your average level is too high, there's no room to get louder. On the other hand, if your dialogue is too quiet, a home viewer will turn up the volume to hear it, and when intense music or an explosion occurs at peak level it will wake the whole neighborhood, which makes for an unpleasant viewing experience.
>
> **Adjust for screening venue:** Certain exhibition environments have specific capabilities for handling dynamic range, so it may be necessary for you to engineer your product according to where your audience will eventually view it. For example, an airplane safety video will be watched in a noisy environment through cheap speakers, so don't mix a wide dynamic range program for that setting.
>
> *Continues on next page*

**Know your exhibition environment**: Before locking your sound mix, it's critical that you hear it in the same environment as your audience. If you create your entire mix in your bedroom using headphones and then show it to an audience at a film festival theater, you're going to be in for some big surprises, and so is your audience. If you mix your show on a professional soundstage and most viewers are going to watch it on their iPods, you'll run into similar problems. Different speakers are capable of playing back different frequency ranges. You may be monitoring on a system that can play those crystal high or room-shaking low tones, but if your exhibition equipment doesn't have the same capability, your audience won't hear all that you intended.

**Never exceed 0 dB**: Digital audio has no headroom. If an audio signal exceeds 0 dB, it will distort on playback. Because sound has such variance in loudness, it's always better to play it safe and set your absolute maximum ceiling for peaks (not average) of around –3 dB to –6 dB. That leaves a little headroom for unexpected spikes or for unforeseen peaks created by later transcoding or translations that may modify your program without your control (such as uploading a file to YouTube).

**Trust your ears (usually)**: Apparent volume can vary significantly from actual volume. Human ears are specially attuned to certain frequencies. In general, a higher-pitched sound "feels" louder than a lower-pitched one at the same measurable volume level. It's important to acknowledge this in your mix; don't turn up the siren sound effect so loud that it hurts just because you want to see it reach –12 on the audio meter. On the other hand, don't ever turn up a sound so that it risks peaking, even if it sounds relatively quiet to your ears. If any sound hits that 0 dB mark, you're likely to hear a click or buzz rather than the sound that you intended.

## The Audio Mixer Window

The Final Cut Pro Audio Mixer window offers another way to view the audio tracks in your sequence. But unlike the horizontal track arrangement seen in the Timeline, you view the tracks in vertical strips. The design of the Audio Mixer window emulates the layout of traditional mixing consoles such as the ones found in film dub stages.

One advantage to the Audio Mixer is that each track's level can be monitored independently, while you can simultaneously observe the overall audio level of the show. The other primary benefit of the Audio Mixer is that you can adjust audio levels while the sequence is playing, even adding keyframes on the fly for level changes and fades.

**1**   Choose Window > Arrange > Audio Mixing.

The windows rearrange, and the Audio Mixer window opens. Each vertical slider in the Mixer window represents a track in your sequence. There will always be one slider for each track in the sequence.

> **TIP**   You can open the Audio Mixer window without changing your window layout by choosing Tools > Audio Mixer or pressing Option-6.

**2**   Press the spacebar to play the sequence.

As the sequence plays, the meter beside each slider displays the audio level for its track. The sliders also move to reflect the level settings of each clip. On the right, the master slider displays the overall output level. The number of meters reflects the number of audio outputs in the sequence. By default, sequences are set to stereo output.

Above each slider are a pan control and mute and solo buttons identical to those in the Timeline.

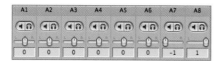

## Setting Up Views in the Audio Mixer

When using eight or more tracks, it may be difficult to monitor everything at once, so Final Cut Pro enables you to create four different views, each of which can display a custom selection of tracks in the Audio Mixer.

One common technique is to create one view just for dialogue tracks, one for effects, and one for music. The fourth view can be reserved for viewing all the tracks at the same time.

**1**   In the track list on the left, click the black circle to hide tracks A5, A6, A7 and A8.

The mixer view now shows only the dialogue tracks.

2    Click the View 2 button.

3    In the track list, hide tracks A1 through A4 and tracks A7 and A8.

This view now shows only the effects tracks.

4    Click the View 3 button.

5    Hide all but tracks A7 and A8.

View 3 now shows just the music.

6    Click each of the View buttons and observe the different collections of tracks.

NOTE ▶ Limiting the visible tracks in a view doesn't mute them; it only hides the sliders to allow you to better focus on a particular aspect of your mix.

TIP ▶ The view settings illustrate one reason for organizing your audio tracks efficiently. For example, if you put sound effects and dialogue on the same tracks, it makes the mixer far less effective.

## Mixing On the Fly

By now, you should understand the value of making editing decisions while watching your program, rather than while playback is paused. Audio mixing is another task that benefits immensely from that same ethic.

Be aware that anytime you adjust an Audio Mixer slider while a clip is playing, you change the level for that clip. There are two ways to employ this technique. By default, changes affect the level over the whole duration of the clip. Or, if you enable audio keyframe recording, every adjustment you make with the slider is recorded and applied to the clips in real time. This process is often called *automation*.

Automation is especially useful for adjusting the level of music as it plays under dialogue.

**1** In the button bar of the Audio Mixer window, click the Record Audio Keyframes button.

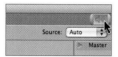

**2** Set the Audio Mixer to View 3.

**3** Play the sequence.

As it plays the first time, think about what you want to do with this sequence. In this case, the first piece of music has a good level, but the second piece seems to over-power some of the interviews.

**4** Play the sequence again, and position your pointer over the slider on track A7.

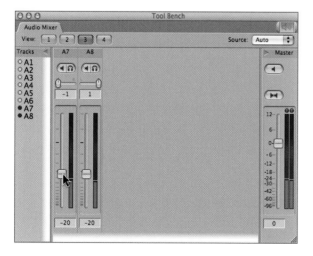

Because the clips on A7 and A8 are stereo pairs, changing one slider automatically changes the other.

5 As the sequence plays, listen to the mix. At the point where the music is too loud, pull the slider down slightly. After the last line of dialogue—"Look ma, no hands!"— quickly pull the slider all the way up to 0.

You've just added a few keyframes to the **Red Plane** clip, instantly mixing the sequence on the fly.

6 Play the sequence again and listen to your work.

The levels reflect the changes you just made. If you don't like what you did, don't fret. There are many ways to get rid of those keyframes.

First, you could use Undo, but an even simpler solution is just to play the sequence again and make different adjustments with the slider. Each time you move the slider, new keyframes replace any that occurred at the same points in time. If you don't move the slider for a while, any existing keyframes remain intact.

## Controlling Keyframe Frequency

There are times when you want every fine adjustment made with sliders to be recorded, and there are times when you want to record only the fewest number of keyframes. To accommodate both situations, Final Cut Pro provides a keyframe recording frequency with three settings.

In the previous example, you recorded keyframes with the default Reduced setting. When Record Audio Keyframes is set to Reduced, Final Cut Pro applies keyframes only as often as is necessary to smoothly reproduce your slider adjustments. In the real world, this setting works for nearly every situation.

1 Choose Final Cut Pro > User Preferences, and click the Editing tab.

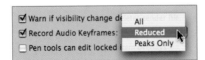

**2**  Set the Record Audio Keyframes pop-up menu to All, and click OK.

**3**  Play the sequence again, and make a series of adjustments to the audio sliders.

When Record Audio Keyframes is set to All, a new keyframe is added every time the slider is moved. Although this can be precise, the larger number of keyframes produced does make later adjustments more difficult.

You can also change the keyframe recording frequency using the buttons in the Timeline button bar.

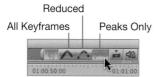

**4**  Click the Peaks Only button.

**5**  Play the sequence again and adjust the slider.

There's no need to delete or reset the old keyframes. Recording new keyframes will automatically overwrite any existing ones.

When Record Audio Keyframes is set to Peaks Only, the fewest possible keyframes are added to replicate the movements you made with the slider.

**6**  Click the Reduced keyframe setting in the Timeline button bar.

## Resetting All Keyframes

If you get in a situation where you just want to start fresh and eliminate all the keyframes you've recorded, you have two choices: You can play the sequence and use your mouse to hold the slider in place, thereby erasing any previously applied keyframes; or you can double-click the clip in question, and in the Audio Viewer click the Reset button.

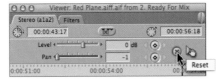

## Creating Perspective

One of the characteristics of successful sound design is the thoughtful implementation of perspective. If a visual event requiring a sound effect occurs on the right side of the frame or outside of the right side of the frame, use the pan controls to put the corresponding sound there. Similarly, if a noise-generating object is moving toward or away from the camera, be sure to change the level accordingly.

Perspective is just as important for dialogue as it is for effects. The audio level for a close-up should seem slightly louder than a shot of the same person talking in a *wide*. Be careful not to overdo it; your goal is not to replicate reality, but to subtly suggest the change in perspective that occurs when the camera moves or when an edit changes the viewer's point of view.

1   In the Audio Mixer, click the View 2 button to hear the sound effects.

2   Click the solo button for track A6.

**3**  Navigate the playhead to approximately 31 seconds and play.

This shot begins very close to the plane, and over time it moves farther away and toward screen right.

It may be helpful to mark the clip so you can play across just this section of the Timeline while you finesse this shot.

**4**  With your playhead positioned anywhere over the **HD118 2 4** clip, press X to mark it.

**5**  Press Shift-Backslash (\) to Play In to Out.

**6**  At beginning of the clip, raise the A6 slider to about the middle of its range. Then, as the plane moves farther away, slowly lower the slider to about the one-third point.

Remember that you don't want the sound to fade out completely, but rather to go from slightly louder to slightly quieter. It will likely take you a few tries to get it right.

**7**  Repeat steps 5 and 6 until you're happy with the fade.

When the fade is working correctly, you can tackle the pan settings. Just as with levels, adjusting the pan slider while the clip plays will automatically record the changes you make.

**8**  Play from In to Out, and while the clip plays, slowly move the pan slider away from the center point and slightly toward the right.

Because the plane doesn't actually move that far to the right, you only want to make a subtle adjustment, but even a tiny change has an impact that can bring your audience into the scene.

**9**  Play from In to Out again.

If you're not happy with your pan automation, do it again; remember that every time you move the slider, you erase any keyframes from the previous attempt.

**10** When you think you have it right, click the solo button to unsolo track A6, and listen to the effect in combination with the rest of the mix.

**11** For extra credit, go through the rest of the sound effects shots and apply similar perspective adjustments.

## Finishing Your Mix

The sound mix is typically completed in four stages. First, set the dialogue levels, ensuring that they're all at a uniform volume (usually –12 dB or –20 dB); then set the sound effects levels to make them feel natural and integrated into the scene; then set the music levels, fading them in and out so as not to overwhelm the rest of the mix; and finally, play all the tracks at the same time and hear how each element interacts with the others.

Remember to spread your sounds across the frequency spectrum. If you add music with a heavy bass track on top of a scene that already has a significant low-end ambience track, you risk getting a muddy sound from both tracks. You're much better off choosing a different song.

## Mixing in Soundtrack Pro

Although Final Cut Pro has all the tools necessary to successfully produce your mix, sound professionals crave controls, filters, and options that are more audio-specific than even the most full-featured video editor can contain. Fortunately, Final Cut Studio comes bundled with Soundtrack Pro, a professional application designed specifically for the audio post-production needs of film and video projects.

For example, Final Cut offers two types of audio fades, but Soundtrack Pro has 16—not to mention its 68 filters compared to 32 in Final Cut Pro. Soundtrack Pro offers *bussing*, which allows you to create submixes to simultaneously apply effects to groups of tracks and then automate them. It also offers graphical surround sound mixing, multi-take dialogue editing (ADR), a unique frequency spectrum editor, and automatic project conforming. Because Soundtrack Pro is dedicated to audio, it has an efficient workflow, advanced tools, and shortcuts that simplify and speed up your audio editing.

# Sending to a Soundtrack Pro Multitrack Project

It's often been said that any creative work—film included—is never finished; simply abandoned. (That paraphrased quote is variously attributed to artist Leonardo da Vinci and to poet Paul Valery, both of whom died long before the film medium was invented.) So it's a good idea to use the day you send out your audio for the final mix as the milestone for forbidding yourself from making additional edits. However, if you must make changes, there are ways to reconcile them that will be explored in the final lesson in this book.

Assuming that your picture is locked, and you've been diligent, your tracks have been organized into D, M & E (dialogue, music, and effects), and you're ready to move your workflow into Soundtrack Pro to perform a precision mix.

1    Open and play the *3. Ready For Soundtrack* sequence.

     This is another version of the *Look Ma No Hands* sequence. The fades haven't yet been added, and the levels of the sound effects and music are very rough.

2    Select the sequence in the Browser and choose File > Send To > Soundtrack Pro Multitrack Project.

A Save dialog appears. You're saving a Soundtrack Pro project file which, like a Final Cut Pro project file, contains no media but only pointers to the actual media, and is therefore very small. It's a good idea to save such files in the same location that you save your Final Cut Pro project files.

3   Navigate to the destination of your choice and click Save.

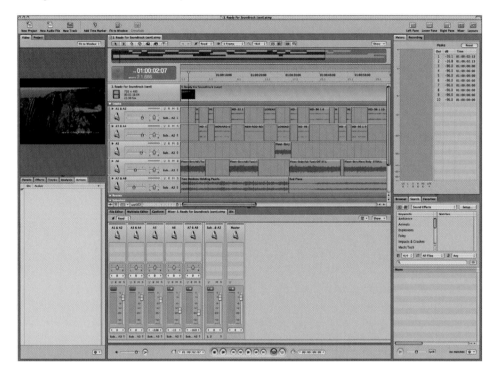

Soundtrack Pro opens and displays a Timeline nearly identical to the one in Final Cut Pro. Audio levels, pan settings, and crossfades are all present.

One notable difference is that Soundtrack Pro displays both channels of a stereo pair in a single track, compared to the two separate tracks in Final Cut Pro.

You can also rename tracks in Soundtrack Pro, which provides a huge organizational benefit, especially in complex projects that can quickly grow to include dozens of tracks.

4   Click the name area of track A1 & A2 and rename it *Dialogue 1*.

**5**   Click the name area for the next track and rename it *Dialogue 2.*

**6**   Rename tracks A5 and A6 *FX1* and *FX2* respectively, and rename tracks A7 & A8 *Music*, as shown below.

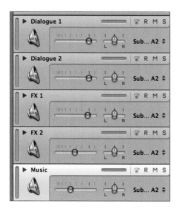

**7**   Press the spacebar to play the sequence.

> **TIP** ▶ You'll find that many of the familiar Final Cut Pro keyboard shortcuts also work in Soundtrack Pro, including J, K, and L for multispeed playback; I and O (as well as their Shift and Option key modifiers) to control In and Out points; Shift-Z to zoom the Timeline to fit in the window; N to toggle snapping; M for markers; and so on.

## Performing Basic Mixing Tasks

In Soundtrack Pro, you can do the same mixing tasks that you performed earlier in Final Cut Pro. Some of these are easier to do in Final Cut Pro, because there are fewer options; others are easier or faster in Soundtrack Pro.

## Muting and Soloing

The mute and solo controls are vital to effectively mix any multitrack project. On most projects, you'll frequently turn on and off groups of tracks to focus on one aspect at a time.

Soundtrack Pro tracks can be muted and soloed either in the Timeline track area or in the mixer window.

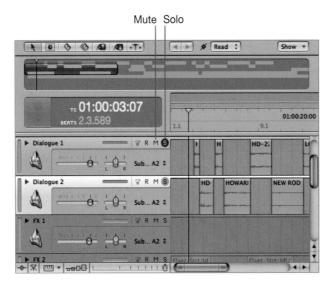

1   Click the solo button for the Dialogue 1 and Dialogue 2 tracks.

2   Play the sequence.

The tracks are successfully soloed.

3   Click the solo buttons again to unsolo those tracks.

**TIP** ▶ With a track selected, you can press the Y key to toggle Solo or the T key to toggle Mute for that track. You can press Control–Up Arrow to select the track above or Control–Down Arrow to select the track below the currently selected one.

## Adding Fades

Sound designers could talk for hours about fades. Fortunately, applying them in Soundtrack Pro takes almost no time at all.

**1**  Press Home to bring the playhead to the beginning of the sequence. Press Command-Plus (+) to zoom in, if necessary, until the first few dialogue clips fill the Timeline.

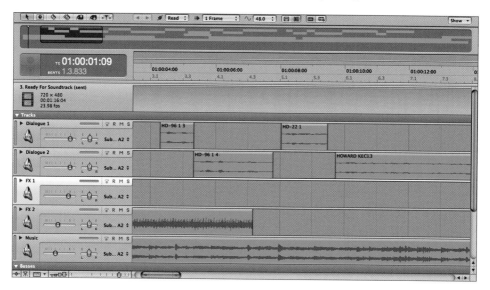

**2**  Position your pointer over the upper-left corner of the first clip (**HD-96 1 3**).

The pointer changes to the Add Fade pointer.

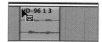

**3**  When the pointer appears, drag to the right, and extend the fade to the first bump in the waveform.

**4**  Double-click the fade.

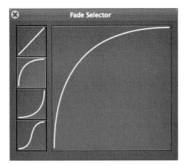

The Fade Selector Heads-Up Display (HUD) appears, allowing you to choose one of four fade patterns.

5    Click the various patterns to apply them to the fade on the clip, and then click the Close button to close the HUD.

Soundtrack Pro allows you to set either side of a crossfade to a different fade pattern.

6    Press Shift-Z to zoom the entire scene into view, and then scroll down until you can see the Music track.

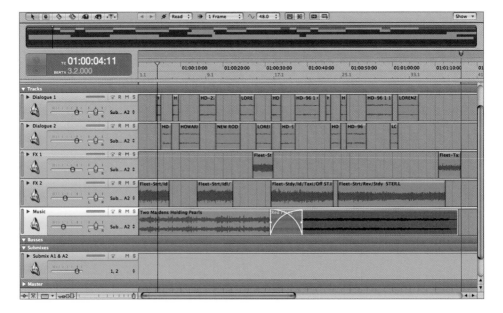

**7**  On the Music track, double-click the crossfade to open the HUD.

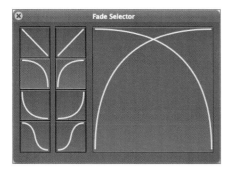

Now, the HUD shows both sides of the fade.

**8**  Experiment with different fade selections, and then close the HUD.

## Adjusting Levels

Just like Final Cut Pro, Soundtrack Pro has a mixer window in which you can set and monitor levels, and automate level changes by dragging sliders while a sequence plays.

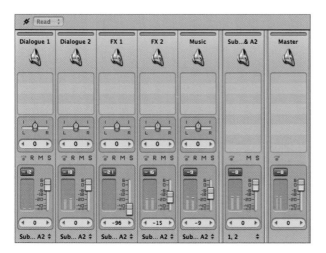

Moving a slider changes the values on the associated track. You can also change levels in the Timeline area. Volume and pan sliders are located under the track label for each track.

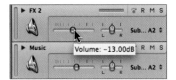

Positioning the pointer over either slider displays a tooltip that shows the current value.

The Timeline can also display graphs (known as *envelopes*) that show how levels change over time.

**1**   In the upper-left corner of the FX 2 track, click the disclosure triangle.

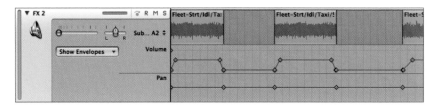

The envelopes for both volume and pan are displayed.

Adjusting the volume slider affects the clip currently under the playhead.

**2**   Position the playhead over the first clip. Drag down the volume slider to approximately –33 dB.

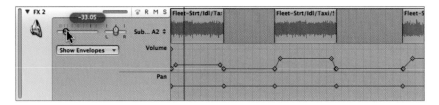

**3**   Play the sequence to hear the results.

You can continue dragging to finesse the level setting while the sequence plays.

NOTE ▶ When keyframes are added to the level envelope, adjusting the slider will affect only the segment under the playhead.

## Automating Level Changes

Of course, you can also add keyframes on the fly in Soundtrack Pro, and there are even multiple modes (*Latch* and *Touch*) that produce slightly different results. Latch mode adds keyframes as you adjust the slider and, after the last keyframe, the level remains constant. Touch mode does the same thing, except that after you release the slider, the level jumps back to wherever the level was before you first dragged the slider. Touch mode is helpful for doing quick *ducks* or boosts in a mix where you don't want to disturb the other levels.

1   In the upper-left corner of the mixer, set the Automation Mode pop-up to Latch.

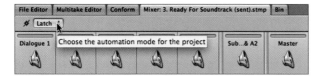

    This enables keyframe recording. It's not necessary to expand the tracks in the Timeline, but doing so allows you to see the keyframes as they appear.

2   Click the disclosure triangle to the left of the music track's label to display the level and pan envelopes.

3   Position your pointer over the mixer slider for the music track, and then play the sequence and drag the slider to adjust the levels of the music track as it plays.

    The keyframes are added while the sequence plays.

4   In the Timeline, drag a marquee around the keyframes, and press Delete.

    The keyframes are removed from the clip.

We've now touched upon the basic techniques of audio editing and mixing in both Final Cut Pro and Soundtrack Pro. However, Soundtrack Pro contains many more advanced tools and techniques for producing professional audio. In the upcoming lessons we'll go into an in-depth exploration of Soundtrack Pro's professional tools as they're applied in real-world post-production workflows.

## Returning to Final Cut Pro

When you're finished with your sound mix, it's time to move back to Final Cut Pro in preparation for final output.

**1** In Soundtrack Pro, choose File > Export.

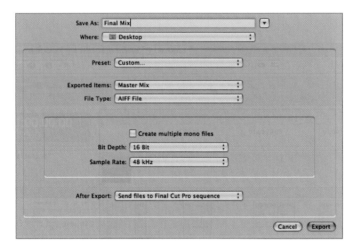

The Export dialog opens. In this example, you made only one stereo mix. As you get more comfortable in Soundtrack Pro, you'll learn how to create submixes and surround mixes, any of which can be exported in the same way.

**2** Name the file *Final Mix*. Leave all of the settings at their defaults, except After Export. Set it to "Send files to Final Cut Pro sequence." Click Export.

The mix is exported to an XML file, and Final Cut Pro is automatically brought forward with the Import XML dialog.

**3**    Leave all the settings at their default values, and click OK.

A Save dialog appears, asking you to save a project.

**4**    Navigate to the directory of your choice and click Save.

> **NOTE ▶** You may safely disregard any non-critical error warnings.

A new sequence named *Final Mix* is added to the Final Cut Pro project.

**5**    Double-click the sequence.

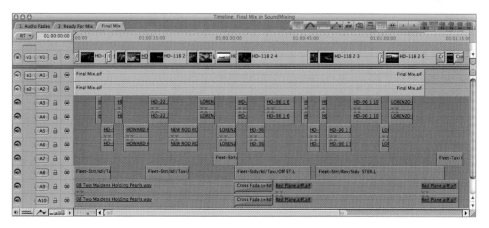

The sequence contains all of the clips from the original sequence you previously exported. Two new audio tracks have been added to tracks A1 and A2, and these contain the finished mix you exported from Soundtrack Pro. All the other audio tracks have been moved down and disabled.

## Lesson Review

1.  When should a clip be hard-cut (and no fade effect applied)?
2.  True or false: If a clip is soloed, all other clips must be muted.
3.  Are muted clips included in or excluded from an exported mix?
4.  How many tracks can be displayed in the Audio Mixer window?
5.  What is automation?
6.  What missing features prevent finishing your mix in Final Cut Pro?
7.  Name three editing and mixing features that are found in Soundtrack Pro but not in Final Cut Pro.
8.  Must "perspective" effects be performed in Soundtrack Pro?
9.  Can track labels be renamed in Soundtrack Pro?
10. How do you return your final Soundtrack Pro mix to Final Cut Pro?

### Answers

1.  Never.
2.  False. More than one clip can be soloed.
3.  Muted clips are included in an export operation.
4.  The Audio Mixer window will show up to 99 tracks—the same as can be displayed in a single sequence in the Timeline.
5.  The act of recording audio keyframes on the fly.
6.  None. Final Cut Pro has all the tools needed for completing a professional final mix.
7.  Here are five: more audio transition types; twice as many filters and effects; bussing and submixing; surround mixing; two automation modes.

8. No, perspective effects can be performed in Final Cut Pro using level and pan controls.

9. Yes.

10. Choose "Send files to Final Cut Pro sequence" from the After Export pop-up menu in the Export dialog.

# 3

| | |
|---|---|
| Lesson Files | Lesson Files> Lesson 03 > 03_STP Workspace.fcp |
| Media | One Six Right |
| Time | This lesson takes approximately 30 minutes to complete. |
| Goals | Open sequences from Final Cut Pro in Soundtrack Pro |
| | Explore the Soundtrack Pro workspace |
| | Configure the sampling rate |
| | Modify the starting timecode |
| | Explore playback techniques |
| | Work with volume and pan settings |
| | Complete the roundtrip process back to Final Cut Pro |

# Getting to Know Soundtrack Pro

In the previous two lessons we took an introductory look at the basics of editing and mixing audio in Final Cut Studio. In the coming lessons we're going to dive deep into advanced techniques of audio post-production by exploring Soundtrack Pro's professional toolset.

In this lesson we'll take a look at the Soundtrack Pro workspace and learn some important techniques for customizing the interface, playing audio clips, and navigating around your projects. One of Soundtrack Pro's most important features is its tight integration with Final Cut Pro through *roundtripping*. Because most audio editing projects begin with a Final Cut Pro project that needs audio sweetening, we'll start in Final Cut Pro and revisit the process of sending a sequence or clip to Soundtrack Pro where we'll work with the audio. At the end of the lesson, we'll review the simple process for returning the enhanced audio files to the Final Cut Pro Timeline.

## Opening Sequences from Final Cut Pro

To begin the roundtrip process, let's open a project in Final Cut Pro, look at the sequence we'll be working with, and then send the project to Soundtrack Pro.

**1**   Open the file **03_STP Workspace.fcp** in the Lesson 03 folder.

The sequence opens in Final Cut Pro.

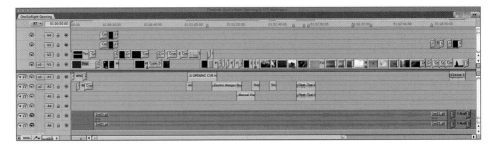

**2**   Play the sequence and watch the opening to Brian J. Terwilliger's *One Six Right* to get a good feel for the sounds in this sequence and what sounds might need to be added.

## Sending Sequences to Soundtrack Pro

Now that you're familiar with the media you're working with, let's send the Final Cut Pro sequence to Soundtrack Pro.

**1**   In Final Cut Pro's Browser, select the sequence titled *OneSixRight Opening*.

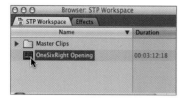

**NOTE** ▶ Selecting the sequence in the Browser is a good way to ensure that the entire sequence and all of its audio clips are sent to Soundtrack Pro. As you'll see in later lessons, you can also send individual clips to Soundtrack Pro for editing, but more on that later.

2   Choose File > Send To > Soundtrack Pro Multitrack Project.

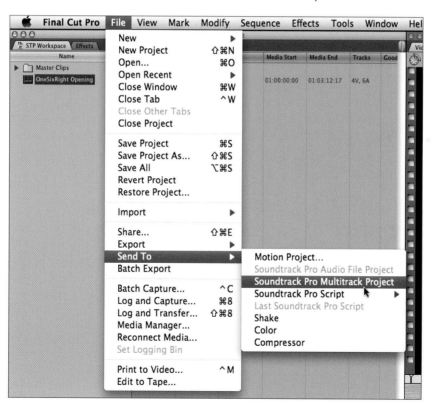

A Save dialog appears.

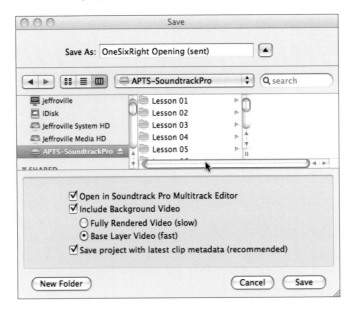

This dialog is used to save a project file that you'll edit in Soundtrack Pro. There are several settings available in this Save dialog. We'll make use of these in later lessons. For now, let's save the project with the current settings selected.

3   Navigate to a folder on your hard disk where you want to save the new Soundtrack Pro project.

4   Click the Save button.

Final Cut Pro exports the sequence to a Soundtrack Pro project file, and then opens the project in Soundtrack Pro.

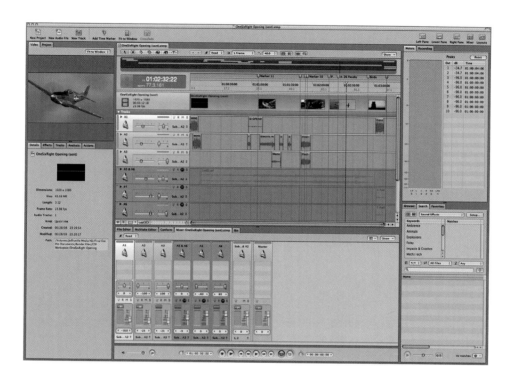

## Exploring the Soundtrack Pro Editing Workspace

Right now you're looking at Soundtrack Pro's editing workspace. It's divided into four *panes*: left, right, top, and bottom. The top pane is called the *Project Pane* and is where the Multitrack Editor lives. The Multitrack Editor contains Soundtrack Pro's Timeline. At the top of the Multitrack Editor you'll see buttons for the Timeline editing tools; below the buttons is the Global Timeline View; underneath that are the Time Display and Time ruler; and below them are the tracks.

You'll recognize that this project already contains several tracks. These tracks were imported from the Final Cut Pro sequence. The topmost track is the Video track and below that are the Audio tracks, each of which contains audio clips. Just as in Final Cut Pro, video clips are blue and audio clips are green. Below the tracks are the Timeline controls and the scroll bar. As we get our hands on each of these elements in the Multitrack Editor their functions will become clear. First let's continue to look at the Soundtrack Pro interface and the ways in which we can manipulate the panes.

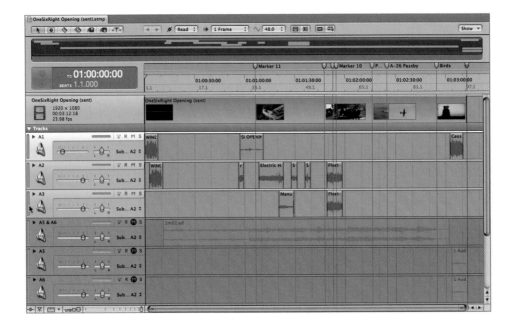

## Working with Panes

Like other Apple pro applications such as DVD Studio Pro and Motion, Soundtrack Pro's interface is a single-window workspace that is divided into panes. Within each pane is a set of tabs that contain editing functions. If you're using a large display, you may find it easiest to work with all of Soundtrack Pro's panes displayed at once. However, if screen real estate is tight, it may be more convenient to display only the pane(s) you're currently working in so you can see more of the Multitrack Editor. Let's look at hiding and displaying panes now.

1    In the upper-right corner of the workspace, click the Right Pane button in the Toolbar.

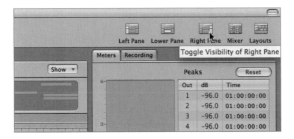

The right pane is hidden, and the Multitrack Editor becomes wider. This gives you more horizontal space in which to edit your tracks. If you're editing a long sound-track, increased horizontal space means you can see more of your project in detail, at a glance. As you work with Soundtrack Pro, you'll find yourself hiding and show-ing panes all the time as you balance the need to see your project in detail in the Multitrack Editor against the need to use the functions contained in the tabs located in the various panes.

NOTE ▶ You can't hide the middle pane that contains your tracks. Additionally, depending on the resolution of the monitor you're using, some parts of the GUI won't be visible with all the panes open (such as the timecode value sliders in the transport controls).

Let's toggle the visibility of the right pane to display it once again, using a slightly dif-ferent technique.

2   Choose Window > Toggle Right Pane (Control-D).

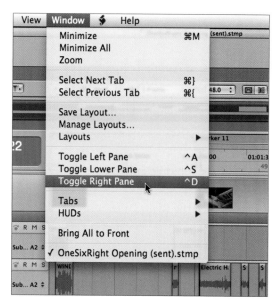

The right pane reappears.

NOTE ▸ The keyboard shortcuts for displaying the left, bottom, and right panes are adjacent to one another on the keyboard, with the left key (A) toggling the left pane, the right key (D) toggling the right pane, and the center key (S) toggling the lower pane.

## Working with Tabs

Each tab in the workspace contains a group of similar editing functions. You can rearrange these tabs at will, moving them from pane to pane or even dragging them out of their host pane to make them their own window. Soundtrack Pro's interface is built to be customized; using tabs, you can set up the workspace any way you like.

1    In the bottom portion of the left pane, drag the Effects tab out of the pane, and then release the mouse button.

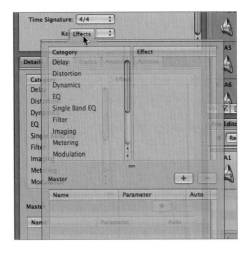

A floating pane is created, holding only the Effects tab.

NOTE ▸ If you have multiple displays attached to your computer, keep this trick in mind, as it's the best way to spread Soundtrack Pro's workspace across your displays.

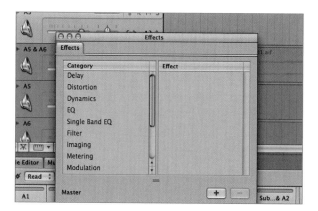

You can also move tabs to other panes, which allows you to customize the workspace to your individual workflow. This is perfect for when you need to see certain tabs at the same time while editing.

2  Drag the Effects tab until it's directly beside the Recording tab in the right pane.

**NOTE** ▶ A blue box will appear around the tabs to indicate when you're in the correct location to drop the tab.

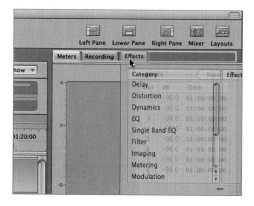

The Effects tab is added to the right pane, beside the Recording tab. You can also move tabs around inside their panes to reorganize the way they're displayed.

3  Drag the Effects tab to the left of the Meters tab.

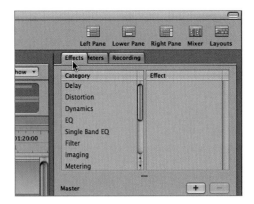

As you drag the tab, the Recording and Meters tabs slide out of the way.

## Using Window Layouts

Window layouts are preset window arrangements that you can jump between while editing in Soundtrack Pro. Out of the box, you get two window layouts, the default standard layout and a "Separate Mixer and Video" layout that's particularly suited to users with two displays. You can also create and save your own custom window layouts to tailor the workspace to your particular editing requirements.

The following steps show you how window layouts work. You'll start by creating a custom layout to save the changes you've made to the workspace, before resetting the workspace to the default layout.

1   To save your customized window layout, choose Window > Save Layout.

A Save dialog drops down from Soundtrack Pro's title bar.

**2**   Type *My Window Layout*, and click the Save button.

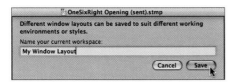

The window layout is saved.

**3**   Choose Window > Layouts.

Notice that your new custom window layout is at the top of the list of window layouts that appears. Below it are listed the two window layouts that come with Soundtrack Pro.

**TIP** ▶ To delete a window layout, go to the Window menu and choose the Manage Layouts option. Here you can rename or delete your custom window layouts.

**4** Choose Window > Layouts > Standard (F1).

Soundtrack Pro returns to the default window layout.

## Setting Project Properties

When you send a file from Final Cut Pro to Soundtrack Pro, the export process configures your Soundtrack Pro project to closely match the settings of your Final Cut Pro sequence. For example, the timecode format will be set to either drop frame or non-drop automatically to match the format of the source Final Cut Pro sequence. Similarly, the sample rate will be set to match the rate used in the Final Cut Pro sequence.

## Setting the Sample Rate

Sample rate is the number of times per second that the audio is measured—or *sampled*. It's analogous to a video's frame rate. In essence, a sample is a discrete recording of a sound at a precise moment in time, and the sample rate determines how many "moments in time" are measured and played back each second. Higher sample rates result in more accurate sound reproduction. However, the price to pay for that increased fidelity is a much larger strain on your computer's processing power.

The standard sample rate for video is 48kHz (48,000 samples per second) and almost all audio for digital video is recorded and mixed at this resolution. You may encounter an audio post-production workflow that requires you to work at a different sample rate (96kHz, for example) and Soundtrack Pro can easily accommodate this for you. Let's look at the sample rate setting in Soundtrack Pro.

1   At the top of the Multitrack Editor, position your pointer over the Sample Rate pop-up menu, which says 48.0.

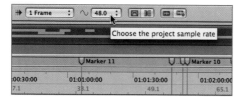

This menu controls the project's sampling rate.

2   Hold down the menu.

Sample rates from 32 to 192 kHz are displayed. As you can see, Soundtrack Pro is capable of working in every professionally recognized sample rate.

NOTE ▶ It's advisable to perform your audio editing at the same sample rate as your Final Cut Pro sequence unless you have a reason to transition the project to an alternative sample rate.

3   Leave the sampling rate set to 48 kHz.

## Working with Timecode

Timecode provides a method for identifying individual frames in a video sequence. The timecode standard is set by the Society of Motion Picture and Television Engineers (SMPTE), and it takes the form of *Hours : Minutes : Seconds : Frames.*

Soundtrack Pro is capable of reading all formats for timecode, including drop and non-drop frame. But even more importantly, Soundtrack Pro will let you change the initial timecode values of the sequences you're working on. This is a key feature if, for example, you're working on a small scene from a larger video sequence. Directors will often give you an edit decision list (EDL) with certain sound effects "spotted" to certain timecode values in the video. To ensure that the EDL lines up with the timecode values displayed in Soundtrack Pro, just change the initial timecode value in Soundtrack Pro to match the initial timecode value of the scene you're working on, and all of the information in your EDL will properly reflect the timecode values you see in Soundtrack Pro.

> **NOTE** ▶ In Final Cut Pro it's common to start timecode values at 1 hour (01:00:00:00). This standard has been accepted by the video community because color bars and a 1 kHz test tone are usually placed at the beginning of a video so the broadcast engineer can calibrate his or her equipment to properly play it. There should also be a countdown lead-in added before the first frame of video. All of this information takes time, and timecode values can't be negative numbers. Consequently, starting the show timecode at 01:00:00:00 provides space before the first frame to add this extra information.

The project you're working on uses timecode values that start at 1 hour. Let's change that now.

1   At the top of the left pane, click the Project tab.

**2**   Scroll down to the Properties area.

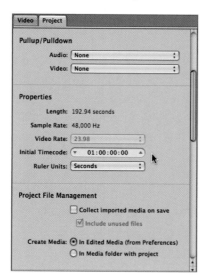

In the Properties area is an Initial Timecode setting that reads 01:00:00:00.

**3**   Drag down on the hours segment of the timecode value slider to set the Initial Timecode value to 00:00:00:00.

Now, the ruler along the top of the Multitrack Editor actually displays 3 seconds (00:00:03:00) into the song when you *are* 3 seconds into the song, instead of 1 hour and 3 seconds (01:00:03:00).

## Controlling Playback

Controlling playback of the Timeline in Soundtrack Pro is simple and straightforward, particularly for anyone already familiar with Final Cut Pro. For example, transport controls are located at the bottom of the workspace; they contain all the standard playback controls familiar to a Final Cut Pro editor (plus a few others we'll explore as the book progresses). You can also toggle playback by pressing the spacebar. To get a feel for how this works, let's play the song now.

> **TIP** ▶ Soundtrack Pro offers three different options for scrolling behavior: On, Off, and Centered. You may change the scrolling mode in the application Preferences.

**1** On your keyboard, press the Home key (if you're using a keyboard that does not have a dedicated Home key, such as a laptop, press Fn–Left Arrow).

The playhead jumps to the beginning of the song.

**2** In the transport controls at the bottom of the Multitrack Editor, click the Play button.

The project starts playing from the beginning and the Play button turns into a Pause button.

**3** To stop playback, click the Pause button.

Playback stops. Although the Play/Pause button provides a nice visual button for you to click, you'll probably prefer the next method for your everyday editing workflow.

**4** Press the spacebar.

Soundtrack Pro begins playing from the playhead's last position.

**5** Press the spacebar a second time.

Soundtrack Pro stops playback and the playhead holds its last position.

**6**  Press the spacebar to start playback again

**7**  Press the Return key.

Playback stops and the playhead returns to the position where playback began.

**NOTE** ▶ As you've seen, pressing the Return key causes the playhead to stop playback and jump to the position playback started from. Press Shift-Return to perform the same action but immediately initiate playback. You can use this key combination to quickly or repeatedly replay a point on the Timeline to evaluate an edit.

Pressing the Return key a second time will cause the playhead to jump to the beginning of the sequence regardless of whether the transport is currently in motion or how playback was initiated.

## J-K-L Playback

For years Final Cut Pro editors have been using the J, K, and L keys to play projects in forward and reverse. These keys also work in Soundtrack Pro, causing the playhead to play in reverse (J), to stop playback (K), and to play forward (L). Additionally, just as in Final Cut Pro, pressing the J or L keys multiple times causes the playhead to play backward or forward at two times the normal speed, four times the normal speed, and so forth.

**1**  Press the L key.

Soundtrack Pro plays the song at normal playback speed.

**2**  Press the L key a second time.

Soundtrack Pro plays at twice the normal playback speed.

**3**  Press the J key.

Soundtrack Pro decreases the playback speed once, and plays at normal speed again.

**4**  Press the J key a second time.

Soundtrack Pro plays at normal reverse speed.

**5**  Press the J key a third time.

Soundtrack Pro plays at twice the normal reverse speed.

**6**    Press the K key.

Soundtrack Pro stops playback.

**NOTE ▶** Other J, K, L playback control functions work in Soundtrack Pro just as they do in Final Cut Pro. Holding the K key while tapping the J or L key will cause the playhead to move one frame at a time; holding both the K key and either the J or L key will cause half-speed playback.

## Moving Around the Timeline

In the previous section you learned some quick methods for controlling playback. However, when you want to jump to a specific part of the project you need to know how to quickly reposition the playhead.

## Positioning the Playhead

The playhead indicates the current moment of time that's playing in your project. To jump around in your project, you move the playhead.

**1**    In the ruler at the top of the Multitrack Editor, click once.

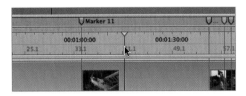

The playhead moves to the clicked position. You can also click within the tracks themselves to move the playhead, but this can be dangerous as it's possible to select and accidentally move a clip by clicking in that area.

If need be, you can also scrub the playhead. *Scrubbing* is the act of manually dragging the playhead across the Timeline. As you scrub the playhead, you'll hear Soundtrack Pro play back the audio under the playhead on all the enabled tracks. By controlling the speed of your scrubbing you can find and navigate to a specific section of the Timeline by ear.

**2**    Drag the playhead's triangular handle left or right.

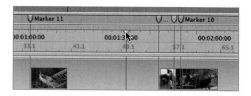

Soundtrack Pro plays the audio under the playhead at the speed at which you scrub.

> **NOTE** ▶ Take care to click directly on the playhead's triangular handle, or you may accidentally set a cycle region. We'll look at cycle regions in Lessons 7 and 8.

## Using the Scrub Tool

The Scrub tool provides a much more accurate reproduction of the sound directly under the scrubbed point, and it does so in a very intuitive way. When you scrub using the Scrub tool, only the clip under the pointer is played. This enables you to audition clips instantly to find particular sounds.

**1**    Select the Scrub tool at the top of the Multitrack Editor, or press H on your keyboard.

**2**    Position the Scrub tool over any audio clip, and then drag left and right.

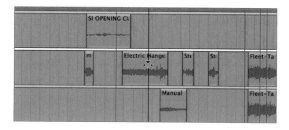

As you drag, the Scrub tool auditions the clip in a way that sounds similar to an audiotape scrubbing back and forth over the playhead. Depending on how you scrub, it might even sound like a DJ scratching a record. But the important thing to keep in mind is that only the clip you scrub will play, and all other clips will be temporarily muted.

NOTE ▶ If you scrub over a section of the Timeline that has no clips, the Scrub tool will make no sound because there's nothing directly under the pointer for it to play.

## Exploring the Track Header

In the Multitrack Editor, the track header is the area of the track directly to the left of where the audio waveform is displayed. The track header contains some important controls, including volume and pan sliders, as well as mute and solo buttons. Let's take a look at these controls now.

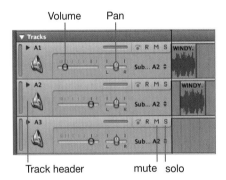

## Volume and Pan

The volume and pan settings affect the loudness and stereo positioning of each track in your project. These settings are your primary mix controls, used to position sounds in your audio soundscape.

1   Play the song.

2   On track A5 & A6, adjust the volume slider to hear the effect.

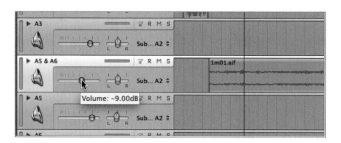

**3**   On the same track, adjust the pan slider to hear the effect.

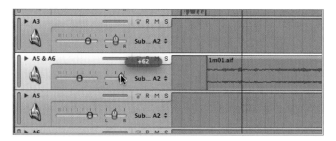

**4**   Once you're finished adjusting the volume and pan sliders, double-click each one.

The sliders return to their default positions. Remember this little trick, because it works to reset all sliders in Soundtrack Pro.

**TIP** ▶  If you need to fine-tune your volume and pan settings over time, use Soundtrack Pro envelopes. To show the envelopes, click the disclosure triangle to the left of the track name. As shown below, this reveals an automation row, and you can click the envelope (the line stretching across the length of the project) to add and move envelope points. We'll look at envelopes in more detail in Lesson 9.

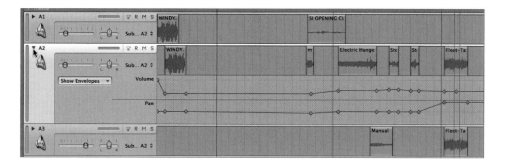

## Mute and Solo

The mute and solo functions are polar opposites of each other. Mute temporarily disables the playback of any muted track, whereas solo temporarily disables the playback of any track that isn't soloed.

**1** Play the project.

**2** On track A5 & A6, click the mute button.

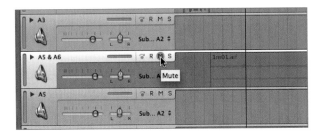

You can no longer hear the track, and the track itself is dimmed, which means that it's muted.

**3** Click the mute button again to enable playback of the track.

**4** On track A5 & A6, click the solo button.

You can now hear only the soloed track, and all the rest of the tracks are dimmed.

5   Click the solo button again to allow all tracks to play.

> **NOTE** ▸ You can press the T key to toggle mute for a selected track. You can press the Y key to toggle solo for a selected track.

## Returning to Final Cut Pro

After you've finished your edits in Soundtrack Pro, you need to get the finished audio back into Final Cut Pro. Whether your edits are light (such as the ones you've made in this lesson) or heavy (such as the ones you'll make in future lessons), the process is the same: Export the completed version of your Soundtrack Pro project, and add it to your Final Cut Pro sequence.

1   From the File menu, choose Export (Command-E).

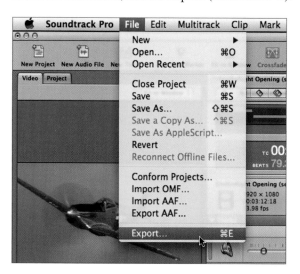

The Export dialog drops down from the title bar. There many options in this dialog and we'll discuss each one in sequence as these steps progress. To start, let's name the file and select a save folder.

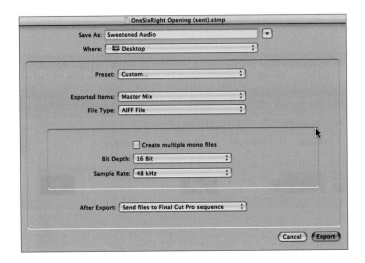

**NOTE** ▶ By default, Soundtrack Pro bounces from the beginning of the song to the red marker at the end of your project (End of Project markers are discussed in Lesson 9). However, there is one exception to this rule: If you've defined a cycle region in your project, Soundtrack Pro exports only the portion of the project between the In and Out points that define the cycle region (cycle regions are discussed in detail in Lessons 7 and 8).

2   Navigate to the folder where you'd like to save the file, and then name the file *Sweetened Audio* in the Save As field.

3   Leave the Presets menu set to Custom.

The other options in the menu can be used to store a collection of export settings as defined by the pop-up menus lower in the Export dialog. If you find yourself often exporting files using the exact same settings, it can pay in spades to take a moment and set up a preset. You'll save time down the road by not having to make selections from the menus every time you export.

4   From the Exported Items menu, choose Master Mix.

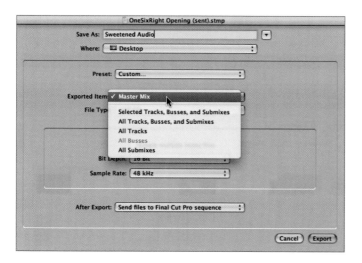

Pay attention to the other settings in this dialog. They can come in handy if, for example, you need to send a "tracked out" version of the project to an editor who isn't using Soundtrack Pro. For example, if you choose All Tracks, Busses, and Submixes in the Exported Items menu, Soundtrack Pro creates exported files for each individual track, bus, and submix that other editors can import into their digital audio workstations for further editing.

**5**   From the File Type menu, choose AIFF File.

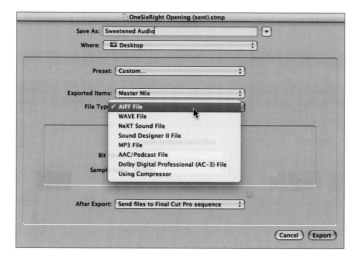

AIFF is the audio file type commonly used on Apple computers. Notice that there are also several compressed formats to choose from, including MP3, AAC, and Dolby Digital AC-3 files, which are used in DVD-Video and digital cable television.

**NOTE ▶** The export options contained in the area directly below the File Type menu will change depending on the type of file you export.

6 Leave the bit depth at 16 Bit and the sample rate at 48 kHz.

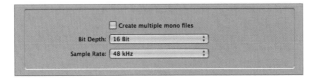

These are the same bit depth and sample rate as the original Final Cut Pro sequence, so there's no need to change them.

7 From the After Export menu, choose "Send files to Final Cut Pro sequence."

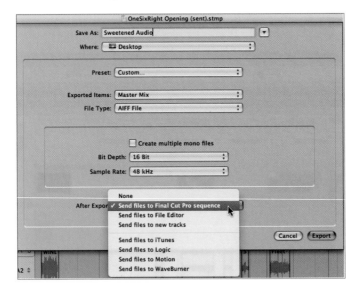

The mix will now be exported to an audio file and an XML file will be created, which Final Cut Pro will use to automatically import the audio back into your Final Cut Pro sequence where you can continue editing the video.

**8**    Click the Export button.

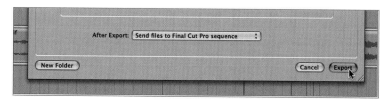

A window will appear indicating the progress of the export. When it's done, the original Final Cut Pro project will open and the Import XML dialog will appear in Final Cut Pro.

**NOTE ▶** If Final Cut Pro is closed when you initiate this action, it won't open the sequence for you. For the example above, the original sequence was left open during this lesson. But if the original project is not open, you'll need to open it in Final Cut Pro before initiating the step above.

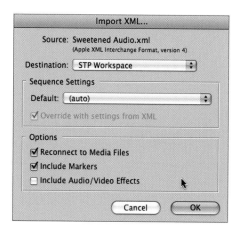

**9**   From the Destination menu in the Import XML dialog, choose STP Workspace, and
then click OK.

A new sequence is created in the Final Cut Pro Browser, and the sequence is automatically given the same name as your exported audio file. But it contains a whole
lot more than just your finished audio.

**10**  In the Browser, open the *Sweetened Audio* sequence.

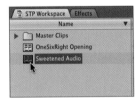

The *Sweetened Audio* sequence Timeline opens. The top two audio tracks are enabled
and contain the finished audio you exported from Soundtrack Pro. Below those
two tracks are all the audio tracks and audio clips from the original Final Cut Pro
sequence; however, they're disabled. If you need to redo your audio post-production
at any point, all the original elements are still available for yet another roundtrip.
This ensures a worry-free workflow.

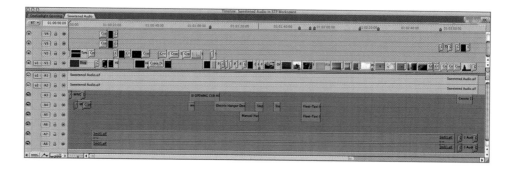

# Lesson Review

1. How do you send a sequence from Final Cut Pro to Soundtrack Pro?

2. True or false: All tabs must remain in their original panes and can't be moved.

3. What do the J, K, and L keys do?

4. What does the Scrub tool do?

5. When you export files and choose the "Send files to Final Cut Pro sequence" command, what happens?

### Answers

1. Select the sequence in Final Cut Pro's Browser, and then choose File > Send To > Soundtrack Pro Multitrack Project.

2. False. You can move tabs to different panes, or even drag them out of panes to create floating windows.

3. J plays the song in reverse, K stops playback, and L plays the song forward. Pressing J or L multiple times increases or decreases the playback rate, either in reverse or forward, depending on the circumstances.

4. The Scrub tool lets you audition the sound of individual clips in your project.

5. Soundtrack Pro exports the file, opens Final Cut Pro if it's not already running, and creates a sequence with the same name as the exported audio file. Better still, if the original Final Cut Pro project is already open in FCP, you can choose it from the Destination pop-up menu so that all of the video and audio clips from the original sequence you sent to Soundtrack Pro will be added to the new sequence. The original video clips will be added to the tracks above the exported Soundtrack Pro audio clips, and the original audio clips will be added to muted tracks beneath.

# 4

| | |
|---|---|
| Lesson Files | Lesson Files > Lesson 04 > 04_FixingAudioFiles.fcp |
| Media | Blind Date |
| Time | This lesson takes approximately 75 minutes to complete. |
| Goals | Send audio clips from Final Cut Pro to Soundtrack Pro |
| | Explore zoom techniques |
| | Edit audio files at the sample level |
| | Fix pops and clicks |
| | Reduce noise in an audio file |
| | Use Soundtrack Pro scripts |

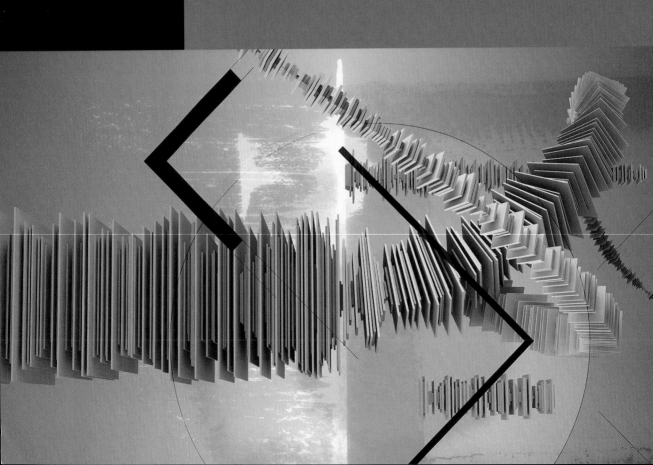

# Fixing Audio Files

Recent advances in camera technology have brought stunning HD video capture down to affordable levels. Nearly any modern camera, in the hands of a capable shooter, can produce the caliber of beautiful images once attainable only with prohibitively expensive camera systems and film.

Unfortunately, audio capture has not benefitted so greatly from technological advancement. Although you can achieve professional results with today's affordable equipment, quality audio recording remains highly susceptible to the ravages of improper technique or less-than-ideal environments.

Additionally, if you're like most people shooting digital video, it's likely that you're recording audio directly to your camera, possibly using only the camera's onboard microphone for the task. There are distinct advantages to this method. Recording your audio to the same tape or card that your video is recording to ensures that audio and video remain perfectly in sync, making them easier to edit once you bring the media into Final Cut Pro. The camera's onboard microphone is always ready to record and doesn't require an extra crew member or complicated setup to operate.

However, using the camera's built-in microphone has disadvantages. The microphone's proximity to the camera means that even the barely audible operating noise of the camera will be clearly picked up by the mic. Noise generated while handling the camera will similarly be captured. Compounding this effect, the camera mic is often far from the scene's action, resulting in a large amount of environmental sound being recorded along with the desired sound, such as the actors' voices.

There is no better method of achieving great-sounding audio than to record quality audio while on set. But even with good equipment and a sincere attempt to adhere to the best possible practices, there are still obstacles that can keep a recording from sounding as good as it should. Soundtrack Pro was made for taking problematic recordings and restoring them to the quality audio they were meant to be.

In this lesson, you'll begin exploring Soundtrack Pro's audio restoration and cleanup functions. Specifically, you'll learn how to remove pops and clicks, decrease background noise, and clean those audio files so that they're sonically pristine.

## Getting Ready to Perform Audio Restoration

As a professional digital audio tool, Soundtrack Pro is capable of working with audio files from any source. However, as part of Final Cut Studio, it was designed from the ground up to integrate seamlessly with Final Cut Pro. Through the course of this book you'll experience the effortless transition between Final Cut Pro and Soundtrack Pro. As a Final Cut Pro editor, it will be second nature for you to spot audio problems in your Final Cut Pro Timeline, send the clip or sequence to Soundtrack Pro to analyze and fix those problems, and then return to Final Cut Pro to find your Timeline automatically updated to reflect the improvements you made in Soundtrack Pro. This fluid collaboration between Final Cut Pro and Soundtrack Pro enables an extraordinarily powerful post-production workflow. To further our exploration of this workflow, let's open a Final Cut Pro sequence, examine it for audio issues, and perform the roundtrip to Soundtrack Pro to improve the quality of the production.

**1**   Open Lesson Files > Lesson 04 > **04_FixingAudioFiles.fcp** in Final Cut Pro.

The *Blind Date* sequence opens in Final Cut Pro.

2   Press the spacebar to play the sequence. Listen critically as you watch the picture. Identify any pops, hums, noise, or other audio artifacts that detract from the scene.

## Sending Audio Files to Soundtrack Pro

The shot-on-location, low-budget nature of this production has resulted in a number of distracting audio issues. Unpleasant background noise abounds, and room tone is inconsistent from scene to scene. There is a high-pitched whine, presumably from the camera's electronics, in certain shots. You can hear *clicks* in one clip as well.

> **NOTE** ▶ During the recording process, clicks and pops can appear as the result of improperly synced digital audio devices, buffer size set too low in the recording software, or interference between devices in the signal chain.

Left in the scene, these issues detract from the overall quality of the production. More importantly, they distract the viewer, which significantly diminishes the scene's intended impact. Fortunately, Soundtrack Pro provides the tools necessary to resolve each of these audio problems. Let's begin by addressing the clicks we heard in the clip **Thanks for the Paper**.

1   In the Final Cut Pro sequence, jump to the first marker by Control-clicking or right-clicking the ruler and choosing Clicks from the shortcut menu.

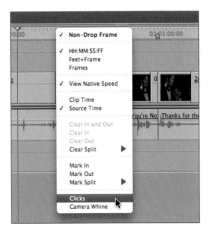

The playhead jumps to the first marker in the sequence, which sits at the beginning of the **Thanks for the Paper** clip.

**2**   In the Final Cut Pro Timeline, Control-click or right-click **Thanks for the Paper** and choose Send To > Soundtrack Pro Audio File Project from the shortcut menu.

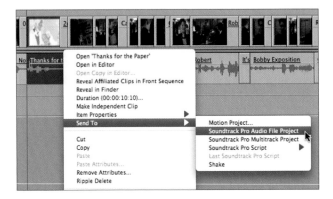

A Save dialog appears.

To send the file to Soundtrack Pro, you need to create a new Soundtrack Pro (.stap) project file. Both Soundtrack Pro and Final Cut Pro will need to reference this file, so it's a good practice to save this Soundtrack Pro project file with your Final Cut Pro project file.

**3**  In the Save dialog, navigate to the Lesson 04 folder on your hard disk.

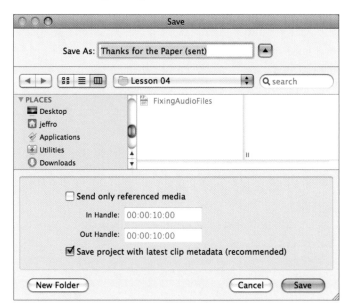

Notice that the Save As field has been filled in with a default name that's based on the name of the clip you're sending. You may keep this unchanged or you may enter a new name for the Soundtrack Pro project file in the Save As field. If you choose to rename the file, keep in mind that it's a good idea for the project file name to indicate which clip it references. In this instance, we're going to keep the default filename and save it in the Lesson 04 folder where it will live with the Final Cut Pro project file.

**4**  In the Save dialog, click the Save button.

The new project file is saved in the Lesson 04 folder and is automatically opened in Soundtrack Pro (which launches if it wasn't previously open).

**NOTE ▸** The .stap extension denotes a Soundtrack Pro Audio File Project file. This file is actually a package that contains several files such as the original audio file, render files, and a project file.

## Exploring the File Editor Project View

The preceding lesson introduced Soundtrack Pro's workspace, but focused specifically on the Multitrack Editor, which displays multiple audio tracks at the same time. In this lesson we're going to be working in Soundtrack Pro's Audio File Editor. For this type of project the workspace is bit different: There are no tracks visible. Instead you'll see only the single audio file that you're working on. Because the audio file you just opened is a mono file, you currently see only one audio channel. If it were a stereo audio file, you'd see two channels.

Soundtrack Pro is fully capable of surround mixing and editing as well. If, for example, you were to open a 5.1 surround audio file, you'd see six channels of audio in the File Editor.

**NOTE ▶** Soundtrack Pro can work with files that contain up to 24 channels of audio.

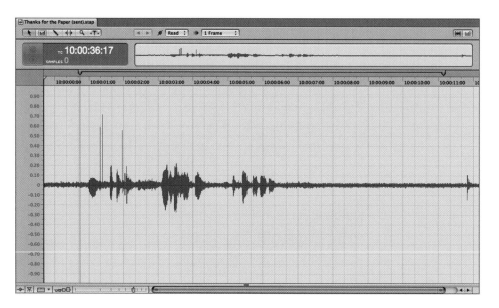

File Editor project view

**1** To play the file, click the Play button in the transport controls at the bottom of the File Editor project view, press the spacebar, or press the L key.

The Play button becomes a Pause button.

**2**   To stop playback, click the Pause button, press the spacebar a second time, or press the K key.

By default, the File Editor opens with the Waveform Display visible. This view shows you the amplitude, or volume, of the audio file at any given point in time. This is the most common way of displaying audio. At the top of the Waveform Display you see a timecode ruler, and to the left of the Waveform Display you see a scale representing amplitude.

Soundtrack Pro can display the amplitude scale in several different ways. It defaults to a *Normalized* scale that shows a linear range from -1 to +1 with 0 in the center. However, the *decibel* (dB) is a more common way for audio professionals to measure volume. So the first thing we'll do is change Soundtrack Pro's amplitude scale to the decibel measurement.

Amplitude scale ———

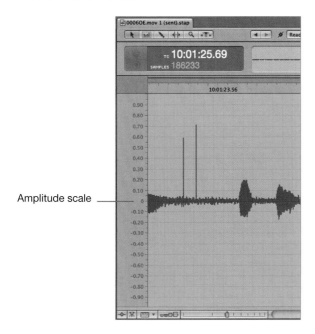

**NOTE ▶** Refer to the "Measuring Sound Intensity" section of Appendix B: Audio Fundamentals in the Soundtrack Pro Help for detailed information about the decibel measurement.

**3**   Control-click or right-click the amplitude scale.

   ▶   A shortcut menu appears.

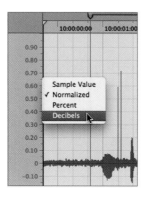

**4**   Choose Decibels.

The scale changes to decibels (dB). You can now see, for example, that the loudest sound in this file peaks at approximately –3 dB.

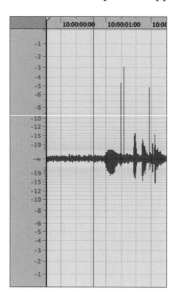

As the audio file plays, the playhead travels from left to right across the screen. You can reposition the playhead to any point in the audio file and then begin playback from that point.

5   Click the waveform close to the beginning of the file on the left side of the Timeline.

The playhead jumps to the point where you clicked.

As you play the file you should hear the three clicks we need to remove. These clicks are clearly visible in the File Editor—look for the three narrow spikes that reach a much higher amplitude than the rest of the waveform. To take a closer look we'll zoom in on the first click.

6   Position the playhead on the first pop in the wave by clicking directly on top of it.

7   Drag the Zoom slider, located at the bottom of the File Editor project view, all the way to the left to zoom in on the playhead.

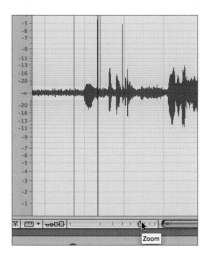

**NOTE ▶** Key commands make zooming fast and easy. To zoom in, press Command-Equal Sign (=) and to zoom out press Command-Hyphen (-).

Shift-Z resets the zoom to fit the project to the window, just as it does in Final Cut Pro.

**TIP ▶** In addition to changing the zoom level of the Timeline, you can also zoom the waveform height by pressing Command-Shift-Equal Sign (=) or Command-Shift-Hyphen (-). To return to the default waveform height, press Command-Shift-0.

## Using the Global Waveform View

Unless you were able to place the playhead precisely over the first click, you've probably found that in the process of zooming in to such an extreme level the click is no longer visible in the Waveform Display. We'll need to reposition the playhead to the precise place where the click occurs.

Located at the top of the File Editor is the Global Waveform view. The Global Waveform view displays a miniature version of the entire audio file. It also displays the current position of the playhead, indicated by a vertical line with a yellow triangle at the top. A rectangle in the Global Waveform view indicates the portion of the waveform that's currently visible in the Waveform Display. You can drag this visible area rectangle left and right to quickly navigate around in the audio file while you're zoomed in.

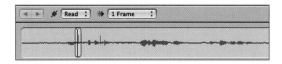

1   Grab the visible area rectangle and drag it so that it's centered on the first click in the audio file.

If you've gotten as close as you can by dragging the visible area rectangle over the click but still haven't managed to perfectly center the playhead on the click, there is an even more precise way of navigating the Timeline.

2   To the right of the scroll bar, click the left or right arrow buttons until you have the click centered on your screen.

**3**   In the Waveform Display, click directly on the click to center the playhead on it.

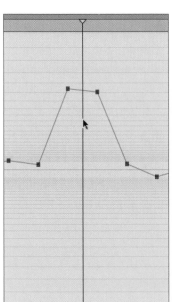

## Redrawing Waveforms

You're now zoomed in to the waveform as far as is possible. At this zoom level you'll notice that there are nodes spaced evenly along the waveform plot. Each of these nodes represents an individual audio sample. Viewing an audio file at this magnitude is referred to as viewing an audio file at the *sample level*. In Soundtrack Pro, these nodes can be manipulated by hand and doing so is one method for cleaning up problems such as clicks and pops.

Remember that there are 48,000 samples per second in an audio file such as this. When you change the amplitude of just a few samples, as we are about to do, you are performing micro-surgery on your audio file. You won't hear the effect of this manipulation as a change in volume; it's too quick of an alteration in amplitude to be heard that way. You will be able to eliminate the sound of that offensive click, however, by smoothing out its spike in the waveform. Let's do that now.

**1**   From the waveform editing tools, grab the Sample Edit tool (also called the Pencil tool), or press P.

**2**   With the Pencil tool, select the first node to the left of the click and drag a smooth, mostly horizontal line over the click's spike in the waveform. Alternatively, you can drag each of the nodes in the spike down to level out the waveform. Your result should look something like the image shown here.

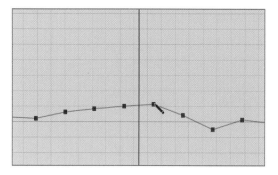

**3**   Zoom out so that you can see several seconds of the Timeline around the point at which this click occurred.

**4**   Move the playhead to a position before the point where the click used to be by clicking the Timeline ruler where you want to place the playhead.

**5**   Play the file.

The first click is gone.

NOTE ▶ Audio speakers reproduce sound by physically tracing the path plotted in the Waveform Display. The clicking sound occurred because the sudden spike in the waveform caused the speaker cone to snap in and out unnaturally. By smoothing the waveform with the Pencil tool you allowed your speakers to follow a more natural, gradual path. This results in the elimination of the clicking sound.

The first click in the file is gone, but two clicks remain. You could repeat the previous steps to redraw the waveforms around these clicks as well, but Soundtrack Pro has a faster way to find and eliminate common audio problems such as these. In the next exercise you'll use the Analysis tab to make Soundtrack Pro find and fix this same issue automatically. First we need to switch back to the Selection tool.

**6**   From the waveform editing tools, select the Selection tool, or press A.

## Analyzing an Audio File

Redrawing the waveform by hand was an effective way to fix the audio click, but it was also a tedious and time-consuming method. There is a faster way to address issues such as this. Soundtrack Pro can analyze an audio file for the presence of common audio problems, and then properly remove them with the press of a button. The six audio problems Soundtrack Pro can detect in an audio file are as follows:

► **Clicks and Pops:** Sudden, short peaks in the audio waveform mistakenly recorded due to problems in the recording process such as unsynchronized digital equipment or buffer under-runs.

► (**Power line**) **Hum:** Electrical current produces a steady hum that can leak into the audio signal either by a ground loop allowing the electrical current to flow back into the audio path, or by electrical wires running too closely alongside audio cables, which causes hum to be induced into the audio signal. Most of the Americas operate on a 60Hz electrical system, whereas most of Europe operates on a 50Hz electrical system. The frequency of the hum induced in the audio signal will likewise be either 50Hz or 60Hz; however, it may also contain low-order harmonics as well.

► **DC offset:** Audio waveforms are normally centered at 0 on the horizontal axis. If a DC offset is present, the center of the waveform will be shifted away from 0. Although this isn't typically noticeable by ear at first, it can decrease the potential dynamic range of the audio file and can also cause serious problems later when the audio is encoded for delivery in formats such as Dolby Digital (AC-3).

▶   **Phase problems:** Phase problems occur in multichannel audio files by inaccurate microphone placement or by delays in the recording signal chain resulting in a slight offset of one channel from another. This can cause audio in each channel to cancel the other out, resulting in partial or even complete loss of certain frequencies.

▶   **Clipped signal:** A clipped signal can result from recording at too high a level, a deficient power supply in analog equipment, or damaged analog components. The term *clipped* refers to the normally rounded shape of a waveform appearing squared-off as if someone had snipped off its peaks with scissors.

▶   **Silence:** The parts of the audio signal that fall to (or close to) 0 dB are silent. Soundtrack Pro can detect silent passages in the audio file. The threshold slider allows you to adjust the volume at which the audio is considered to be silent.

We're now going to use Soundtrack Pro's Analysis feature to detect and fix the remaining two clicks.

**1**   In the left pane of the workspace, click the Analysis tab.

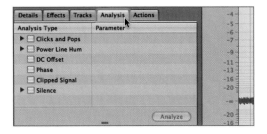

**2**   Select the Clicks and Pops checkbox.

   **NOTE** ▶ If desired, you can also select the checkboxes beside the other common audio problems, and Soundtrack Pro will analyze the file for these problems too.

**3**   Click the disclosure triangle next to the Clicks and Pops checkbox.

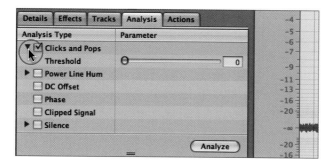

The Threshold slider appears. The Threshold slider is used to set the sensitivity of the Clicks and Pops analysis. Soundtrack Pro will look only for Clicks and Pops that are above the threshold that you set, so dragging the slider to the right results in only the more severe clicks and pops being detected.

The slider's scale covers a range from 0 to 100. Looking at the clicks in this file, you can see that they're all above the halfway mark on the amplitude scale, whereas all the other sounds are quite a bit lower than halfway up the amplitude scale, so let's designate a threshold setting of 50.

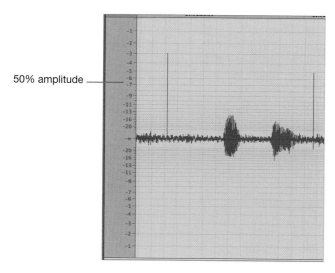

4   Move the Clicks and Pops Threshold slider to set a value of 50.

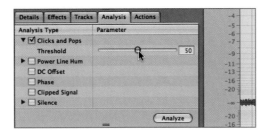

5   On the Analysis tab, click the Analyze button.

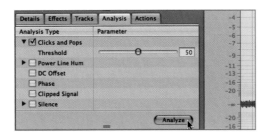

In the Waveform Display, Soundtrack Pro highlights potential problem areas in red.

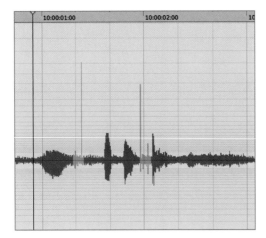

In the Analysis tab, Soundtrack Pro lists the problems it detected along with the status, location, and length for each instance.

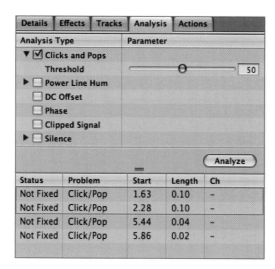

Although we were previously aware of two clicks in this audio file, Soundtrack Pro's analysis reports four such problems. Soundtrack Pro's advanced algorithms may often detect issues you haven't discerned by listening to the clip or studying the waveform. However, it may also report false positives. It's smart practice to review each item reported in the Analysis window to determine whether it's a legitimate issue before acting on it. It's extremely efficient to do this because Soundtrack Pro provides several means of quickly navigating to the detected problems and zooming in on them.

## Zooming In on Problems

Soundtrack Pro incorporates navigation tools specifically designed to enable zooming in on detected problems for closer investigation.

1   In the Analysis Results list, click the first problem to select it.

| Status | Problem | Start | Length | Ch |
|---|---|---|---|---|
| Not Fixed | Click/Pop | 1.63 | 0.10 | – |
| Not Fixed | Click/Pop | 2.28 | 0.10 | – |
| Not Fixed | Click/Pop | 5.44 | 0.04 | – |
| Not Fixed | Click/Pop | 5.86 | 0.02 | – |

In the Waveform Display, only the first problem area is now highlighted in red and a selection has been made around it.

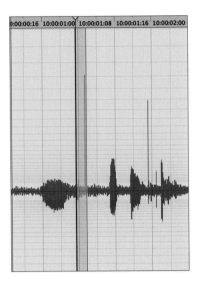

2   Press the spacebar to play the selection.

Because only the problem area is selected, it's hard to hear the problem in context.

3   In the Analysis Results list, click the first problem again.

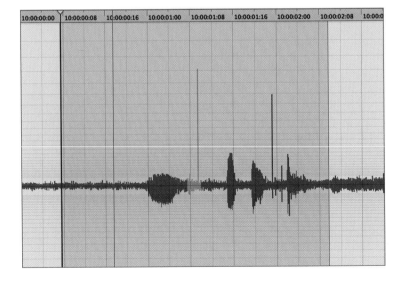

A wider selection has now been made around the first problem area.

**4**  Press the spacebar to play the selection.

It's now easy to hear the problem in context.

**5**  At the bottom of the Analysis tab, hold down the Magnify button.

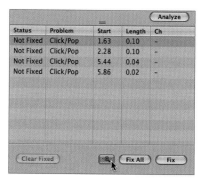

While the button is held, the File Editor temporarily zooms in to magnify the problem.

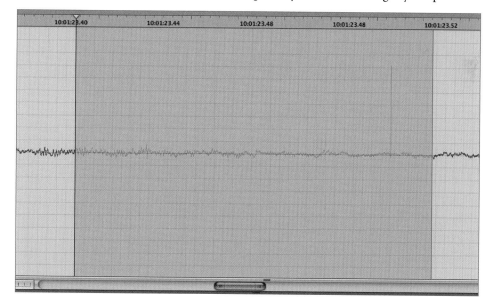

**6**    Release the Magnify button.

The Waveform Display returns to the previous zoom level.

**NOTE** ▶ To zoom in to the problem area and stay at the new zoom level, Option-click the Magnify button.

## Fixing the Problems Soundtrack Pro Detects

Analyzing the audio file to detect problems is the first step toward fixing them. The second step is telling Soundtrack Pro which problems you wish it to fix.

**1**    Make sure that the first problem is still selected in the Analysis Results list. Then, at the lower right of the Analysis tab, click the Fix button.

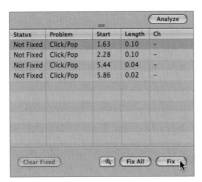

A progress indicator drops down from the Soundtrack Pro title bar to indicate the progress of the operation. This task may process so quickly that you don't even notice it happening.

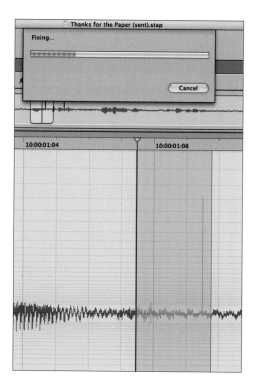

The red indication of a problem in the waveform view is now gone, the sharp spike where the click occurred has also disappeared, and in the Anaylsis tab the first problem's status now reads Fixed.

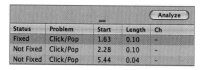

2   To fix the remaining clicks and pops you could repeat this procedure for each problem in the list. Instead, click the Fix All button to have Soundtrack Pro repair all the problems at once.

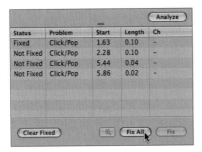

Soundtrack Pro fixes all of the remaining pops.

NOTE ▶ The third and fourth problems in the list may not be true clicks or pops. Instead they may be sounds that occurred on-set that sound similar to pops. You can make your own decision whether these two problems should be fixed or not. One option is to have Soundtrack Pro fix them, and then decide if you like the results better than the original sound. If you wish to undo the Fix operation, you can do so by pressing Command-Z.

## Working with Actions

The Analysis tab is a powerful tool for automatically detecting and fixing common digital audio issues. To go beyond fixing these specific problems and utilize Soundtrack Pro's advanced processes for editing audio files we need to use *actions*.

Actions are a core part of Soundtrack Pro's editing arsenal and an extraordinary feature that's unique to this application. An action is an audio process that is applied to an audio file or a selected part of the file. What makes actions in Soundtrack Pro such a uniquely powerful feature is that at any time an action can be modified, turned on or off, or reordered in the Action list, and the audio file will be instantly updated to reflect the result. All actions are nondestructive. At any time you may reopen the Soundtrack Pro Audio File Project, change the parameters or order of the actions, resave the project, and see your new edits instantly updated in your Final Cut Pro project. In the next exercise you'll use actions to perform powerful editing operations.

1   In the left pane of the workspace, click the Actions tab.

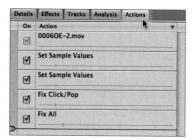

The Actions tab displays a chronological list of all the actions that have been applied to the audio file so far. Redrawing the waveform (referenced by the Set Sample Values Actions) and using the Analysis tab to fix problems are two types of actions, so they're listed here in the Actions tab.

**NOTE ▶** If you weren't precise while using the Pencil tool earlier in this lesson, or if you did a bit of experimenting outside the exercises, you may see more actions than are shown in this screenshot.

**2**   Deselect the checkbox to the left of the Fix All action.

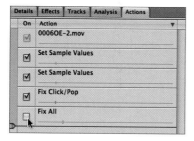

In the Waveform Display, the third click has reappeared.

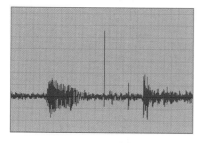

**3**   Toggle the Fix Click/Pop action on again to remove the click from the file.

## Locating an Action

An action can be applied to a whole audio file or just to a portion of it. After heavy editing in an audio file, the Action list can become quite long. The same type of action may have been applied to various sections of the audio file. Later on, this can make it tricky to find the exact item in the Actions tab that corresponds to an action that you applied to a specific section of the audio file. Soundtrack Pro provides visual indicators to help you quickly identify which item in the Action list is the one you're looking for.

Look closely at the Actions tab and you'll see that below the name of each action in the list is a horizontal green bar. This green bar represents the entire audio file. Somewhere on the green bar you'll notice a small rectangle. This rectangle represents the section of the audio file on which the action was applied.

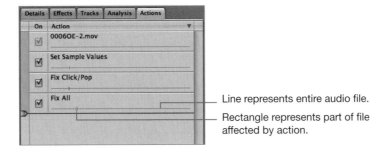

Line represents entire audio file.

Rectangle represents part of file affected by action.

Let's apply a new action, this time to the entire audio file, to see how that's represented in the Action list.

1   In the File Editor, click anywhere on the waveform to ensure that the File Editor is the active window and can thus accept keyboard input.

2   Press Command-A to select the entire audio file.

3   On the main menu bar, click Process.

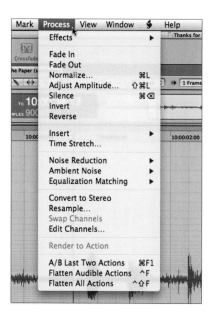

Each item in the Process menu is an action you can apply to your audio.

**4**   Choose the Normalize option.

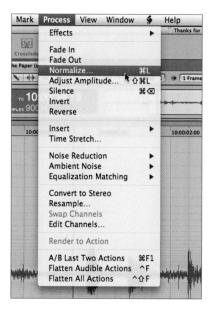

The Normalize dialog drops down from Soundtrack Pro's title bar. This dialog contains the normalization level controls.

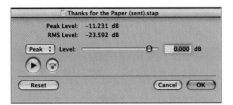

You may recall from Lesson 1 that Normalization is a process that raises the level of the audio file (or a selection) to a specific decibel level that you set. New in Soundtrack Pro 3 is the ability to normalize the RMS level (the average level) in addition to the Peak Normalization process. For this exercise we're going to use the Peak method of normalization to raise the highest level in this audio file to –6 dB, the television industry standard.

**5**   Set the Normalization Level value to –6 dB and click OK.

In the File Editor project view, the waveform grows, indicating that the volume has become louder.

**6**   Play the file to hear how normalization has affected its volume.

**7**   In the Actions tab, look at the Action list.

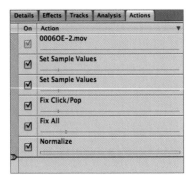

The Normalize action has been added at the bottom of the list. Notice that the box under the Normalize action covers the entire green line, indicating that the entire file was normalized.

## Reordering Actions

Actions are a nondestructive process in Soundtrack Pro; the source audio files are not permanently altered by an action. Because of this, actions can be modified after they've been applied or even reordered in the Action list.

Actions are applied to the audio in order from the top of the list to the bottom. Keep in mind that the order in which actions are applied can greatly affect the end result. Even the result of a simple Normalize action will be quite different if applied at a different point in the Action list.

**1**   Drag the Normalize action to the top of the Action list.

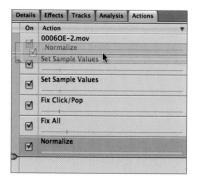

In the Waveform Display, the waveform updates and grows smaller, not larger, as it did when the Normalize action appeared at the end of the list. This is because Soundtrack Pro is now normalizing to the peak level of the clicks and pops, which peaked considerably higher than the peaks in the normal audio in the file.

## Removing Actions

In later lessons we're going to be adjusting volume in other ways, so the Normalization action isn't necessary after all. Let's delete it from the Action list.

**1**   In the Action list, Control-click or right-click the Normalize action.

**2**   From the shortcut menu that appears, choose Delete "Normalize."

The Normalize action is deleted from the Action list.

**NOTE** ▶ You can also select the action and press the Delete key to remove it from the Action list.

## Reducing Noise

*Noise* is a problem that plagues many video productions and can make an otherwise good production appear amateurish. There's no substitute for capturing good, clean audio at the beginning of a production. However, there are situations in which even the best practices can't entirely eliminate noise from being captured in the recording. Soundtrack Pro includes excellent noise reduction tools that can save your production from being ruined by noise in its audio tracks. Before we explore these tools, let's take a moment to examine what noise is and why it's such a serious issue.

## Exploring Noise

Simply put, *noise* is an unwanted sound that obscures a desired sound. Humans have a remarkable ability to tune out unwanted sounds and focus only on the specific sounds that are useful. If you take a moment to really listen to the room you're in, you'll hear countless noises and miscellaneous sounds such as hums or hisses from equipment in the room, the whirring of a refrigerator, air flowing out of air conditioning vents, the subtle rustle of clothing as you move, or the breathing of the person next to you. Most of the time your brain selectively ignores these sounds, allowing you to focus your attention on the sounds you consider most important, such as the voice of a person who is talking to you.

Effective video focuses the viewer's attention on the story. Consequently, it's important to minimize any elements that may distract the viewer from important sounds, such as the actors' voices. It's the audio engineer's job to ensure that only sounds that contribute to the immersion of the viewer in the story are allowed to air, while any distracting sounds are filtered out.

Let's examine some of the noise in *Blind Date* to get a feel for this.

**1**   In the File Editor project view, scroll so that the beginning of the audio file can be seen.

**2**   Make a selection in the "silent" part at the beginning of the audio file.

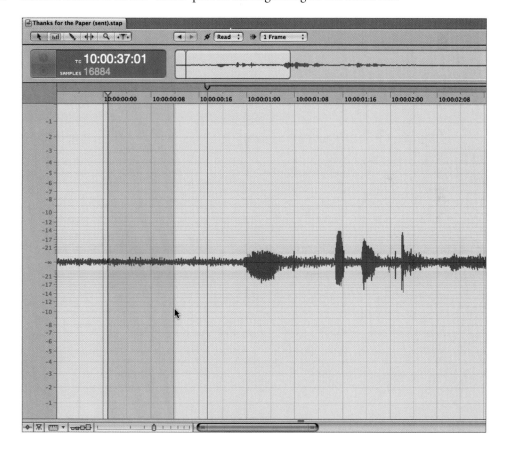

This part isn't true silence, but it is a section where none of the characters are speaking.

3    At the bottom of the File Editor project view, make sure that the Cycle button is turned on.

The Cycle button causes the selected portion of the audio file to repeat continuously, which makes it easier to listen to the sound you've selected.

4    Click the Play button and listen carefully.

Depending on the exact selection you made, there may be a very small amount of ambient sound heard here, but most of what you're hearing is noise. There seems to be a whirring sound that may be coming from something in the room or even from the camera itself (the motors that drive the tape transport in some cameras can be picked up by the onboard microphone). Whatever the source of the noise, it's important that you make it as quiet as possible in relation to the spoken dialogue, which naturally should be the focus in this scene.

NOTE ▶ A distinction must be made between noise and ambient noise. Ambient noise is the natural sound of an environment, such as the sound of people talking in the café or the sound of cars and buses passing by on the street outside. Although a sound editor must take care to ensure that it doesn't distract from the most important sounds in the scene—typically, dialogue—ambient noise does serve a purpose in setting a scene, and therefore isn't entirely bad. Noise, on the other hand, refers to the hisses, hums, and mechanical sounds that are not natural elements of the scene. These extraneous sounds only distract from the important sounds, and serve no beneficial purpose. It's this type of noise that we're addressing in this exercise.

## Setting a Noise Print

The first step in using Soundtrack Pro's noise reduction feature is to tell it what, in fact, the noise in the file sounds like. To do this, you set a *noise print*. A noise print is much like the fingerprint of the noise in a file: It's the unique frequency spectrum of the background noise that you wish to reduce. To use a video analogy, the noise print functions much the same as the key color selected when you're pulling a blue or green screen—the color you select is the base for the colors removed. Similarly, the noise print is the base for the frequencies that are removed.

If the selection you've made doesn't contain any of the actors' dialogue, you can be reasonably certain that your selection consists exclusively of background noise. This makes it a good choice for use as your noise print.

1   From the Process menu, choose Noise Reduction > Set Noise Print.

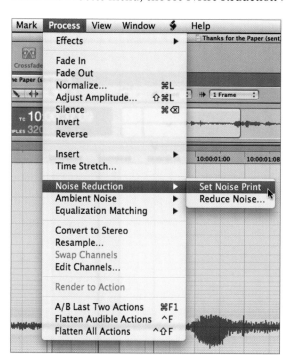

Soundtrack Pro sets the selected audio as the noise print.

## Using the Reduce Noise Dialog

Noise reduction is both an art and a science and it can take some experimentation to achieve the best results. If you're too aggressive in your noise reduction settings, you risk making your audio sound tinny or robotic. If you're not aggressive enough, the noise will remain an issue. The secret is to balance your settings to remove as much noise as possible without unacceptably altering desirable elements in the audio.

Although trial and error plays a big part in optimizing noise reduction settings, there are a few techniques you can use to achieve great results quickly. Your noise print is already set; now let's work on the noise reduction settings.

**1**  From the Process menu, choose Noise Reduction > Reduce Noise.

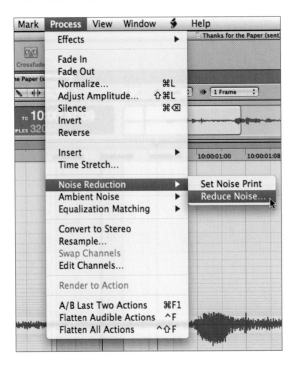

The Reduce Noise window appears onscreen. It contains Noise Threshold, Reduction, and Tone Control settings, each of which plays a part in the noise reduction process. We'll now work with each of these parameters to remove the noise from this audio file.

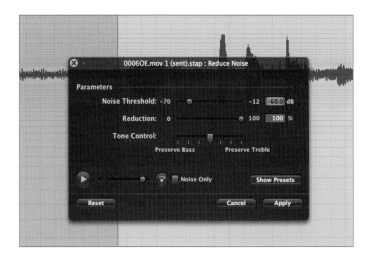

The Noise Threshold setting is at the top of the Reduce Noise window. It was placed there for a reason: Setting the correct threshold is the first task in the noise reduction process. Let's play the file, and then set the threshold.

**2**    Click the Play button.

Soundtrack Pro begins cycle playback of the selected area at the beginning of the file. Because the Reduce Noise window is open, you're hearing a preview of the effect of the noise reduction process. This is referred to as *auditioning* the effect.

**3**    As the selection plays, refer to the audio level meters on the Meters tab in the right pane.

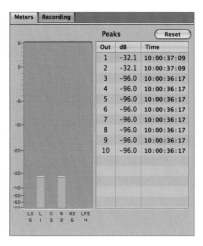

**NOTE ▶** Although the meters themselves are not affected by the number of channels in the clip, what you see may differ from the previous figure depending on the number of outputs that your hardware interface has.

Notice that the volume of the noise peaks at around –32 dB. This value can be considered the *noise floor* of the audio file: In other words, this is the threshold below which there is noise and above which there is clean audio. This value gives you a pretty good indication of where to start experimenting with the Noise Threshold setting.

4   In the Reduce Noise dialog, set the Noise Threshold value to approximately –32 dB.

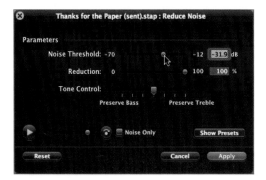

As you reduce the Noise Threshold value, notice that the noise is dramatically reduced.

## Bypassing Noise Reduction to Hear Your Original Sound

As you continue to experiment with noise reduction, it's important to occasionally toggle back to the original sound to get a clear perspective on how your noise reduction settings are affecting the audio. The Reduce Noise window has a button that lets you do just that: the Preview Effect Bypass button, commonly referred to as the Bypass button.

1   As the selection plays, click the Bypass button located to the right of the volume slider in the Reduce Noise window.

The Noise Reduction plug-in is bypassed and the original sound of the selection is heard.

2   Click the Bypass button again to disable its function.

You once again hear the effect of the Noise Threshold setting.

## Adjusting the Noise Reduction Level

We've set the noise threshold; now it's time to experiment with the Reduction setting. At the moment, however, we have only noise selected in the audio file. This was useful for determining the noise floor and adjusting the threshold setting; however, it's not appropriate for making the Reduction setting. We need to listen to the elements we wish to keep, the actors' voices, to be sure that we're not adversely affecting them as we attempt to reduce the background noise. We'll want to apply our noise reduction to the entire audio file, so let's select the whole file now.

1   Click the file to ensure that it's selected, instead of the Reduce Noise window.

2   As the file plays, press Command-A to select the entire file.

Listen as the character speaks. Unfortunately, the actor's voice is now noticeably and unpleasantly tinny.

3   In the Reduce Noise dialog, adjust the Reduction slider until the character's voice begins to sound normal.

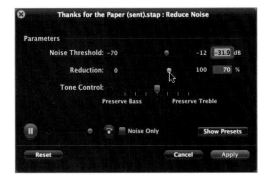

At a setting of around 70, the tone of the character's voice begins to sound natural while the noise remains reduced enough in the background. Take a minute to experiment with this parameter to find the sweet spot where the most noise is reduced with the least detrimental effect to the sound of the dialogue. As you do this, toggle the Bypass button to check your progress against the sound of the original audio.

**NOTE** ▶ The Tone Control setting is used to favor certain frequency ranges in the audio, allowing them to more easily pass through the noise reduction filter unattenuated. For example, removing a hiss from the sound of a foghorn would probably benefit from a Preserve Bass setting, whereas removing a low-pitched hum from the sound of birds chirping in a forest might require a setting more biased toward preserving the treble. For human voices, a setting right in the middle is typically the most effective.

## Applying Noise Reduction

In your experimentation you should have found acceptable settings for reducing the noise in this scene, so let's apply this action to the audio file. Remember that every action in Soundtrack Pro is nondestructive, so if you wish to modify your settings later, it's always possible to do so.

1   Click the Pause button to stop playback.

2   In the lower-right corner of the Reduce Noise dialog, click the Apply button.

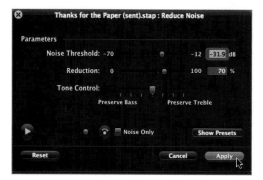

Soundtrack Pro applies your settings to the file and redraws the waveform to reflect the changes made to the audio. You'll immediately notice that the sections of audio between the actor's dialogue now have a much lower amplitude than they did before, showing that the volume of the noise has been reduced. Visually, it appears to be a dramatic reduction in background noise but, as always, the only thing that matters is how it sounds to your ears.

## Refining Noise Reduction Settings

If you listen to your file a few times and decide that the noise reduction settings could be improved, it's easy to reopen the Reduce Noise window and refine your settings.

**1**   In the Actions tab in the left pane of the workspace, double-click the Reduce Noise action.

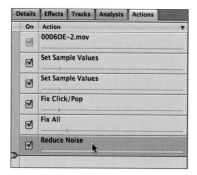

The Reduce Noise window reopens.

**2**   Adjust the noise reduction settings until you've achieved the desired effect. Then click the Apply button.

The new noise reduction settings replace the previous settings.

## Rippling Your Changes to Final Cut Pro

In this lesson you've dramatically improved the sound of this audio file by eliminating clicks and pops and reducing the terrible background noise. Now it's time to return the file to Final Cut Pro to see how the improvements you made sound when the clip is played in the Final Cut Pro Timeline.

**1**   From the File menu, choose Save, or press Command-S.

A dialog pops up to ask you whether you'd like to include the source audio in your new file, or simply reference the source audio.

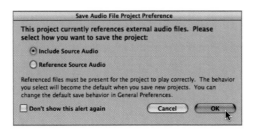

**2**   Choose Reference Source Audio, and click OK.

Selecting this option creates smaller files that take up less of your hard disk because Soundtrack Pro will reference the original audio files instead of copying the original audio files into your new project file. However, if you plan to move the audio file to a new computer, you should be certain to include the source audio files to ensure that all the media you need to play the file will be present on the new system.

Soundtrack Pro saves the project file.

**3**   Switch back to Final Cut Pro (either from the Dock, or by pressing Command-Tab until Final Cut Pro is highlighted).

Notice that the **Thanks for the Paper** clip now has a green line across the top. This green line indicates that the clip has had a process applied to it. Additionally, if you look closely you'll see that the name of this clip's audio is now **Thanks for the Paper (sent)**, indicating that the clip is now referencing the Soundtrack Pro Audio File Project instead of the original source audio.

**4**   Play the sequence, paying particular attention to the sound of the **Thanks for the Paper** clip.

As you can hear, the changes you made to this clip in Soundtrack Pro have automatically appeared in Final Cut Pro. Any subsequent changes you make to the Soundtrack Pro Audio File Project will also automatically ripple to the Final Cut Pro clip that references it.

## Using Soundtrack Pro Scripts to Speed Up Your Work

At this point, you have one vastly improved clip in this Final Cut Pro sequence, but there are several more clips that suffer from the same problems. You could open the clips one at a time in Soundtrack Pro to repair them, but that would be time-consuming and tedious work. Fortunately, there's a quicker way.

Most videos contain audio from only one or two cameras, and because of this, the recording environment is fairly consistent. The noise or other problems in the clips will similarly be fairly uniform. In the present sequence, for example, the **Thanks for the Paper** clip is from the same camera as the **Caroline w Bob** clip. Thus, you should be able to apply the same noise reduction settings to both clips. You can use a Script to have Soundtrack Pro perform this action—without ever leaving Final Cut Pro.

**1**   In the Final Cut Pro sequence, play and compare the clips **Caroline w Bob** and **Thanks for the Paper.**

These clips use the same camera angle, and they sound as though they have the same type of noise in them. That makes them a great candidate for the use of a script. First we need to define the actions our script will use.

**2**   Return to Soundtrack Pro (click the application icon in the Dock).

**3**   On the Actions tab in the left pane of the workspace, deselect the Set Sample Values action and the Fix Click/Pop actions.

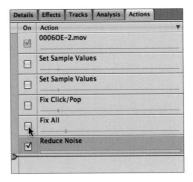

These actions are applicable only to the **Thanks for the Paper** clip, so you don't want to apply them to any other clips. At the moment, only the Reduce Noise action should be selected.

**4**   From Soundtrack Pro's File menu, choose Save As AppleScript.

A Save dialog drops down from the title bar.

**5**   In the Save As field, type *myNoiseReducer*.

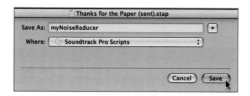

**6**   Click the Save button.

Soundtrack Pro saves the actions as an AppleScript script.

**7**   Return to Final Cut Pro.

**8**   Control-click or right-click the **Caroline w Bob** clip.

**9**   In the shortcut menu that appears, choose Send To > Soundtrack Pro Script > myNoiseReducer.

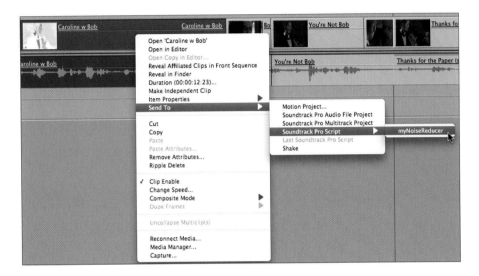

A warning appears asking if you want to convert the selected clip to a Soundtrack Pro project before applying the script. If you don't convert the clip to a Soundtrack Pro project, the actions will be applied *destructively* and the clip will be permanently altered. You don't want that to happen. Choose Yes to have the clip converted to a Soundtrack Pro Audio File Project so the script's actions will be applied nondestructively just as they were throughout this lesson.

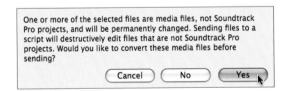

**10**  Click the Yes button.

A dialog appears asking you to choose a project destination. By default, the last folder you used is selected, which should be the project folder you saved the previous Soundtrack Pro Audio File Project in. Let's save this new project file in the same folder.

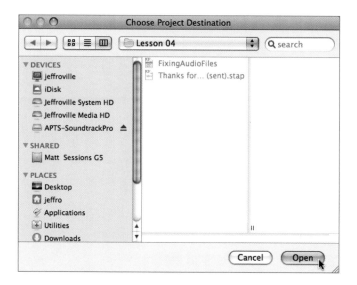

**11** Click the Open button.

Now the script runs and several things happen very quickly. The clip opens in Soundtrack Pro, the Reduce Noise action is applied, and then Soundtrack Pro saves the clip, which causes the changes made to the audio file to be rippled back to the Final Cut Pro sequence.

**12** Return to Final Cut Pro.

Notice that the clip you just applied the script to is now named **Caroline w Bob (sent). stap**, indicating that it now references a Soundtrack Pro Audio File Project, and the green render bar appears at the top of the clip.

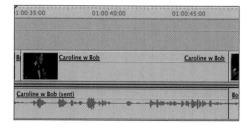

**13** Play the clip **Caroline w Bob** in Final Cut Pro.

Notice that the noise is reduced.

## Lesson Review

1.   Does the Waveform Display show an audio file's amplitude, or its frequency spectrum?

2.   What is the function of the Sample Edit (Pencil) tool?

3.   Is Soundtrack Pro a destructive or a nondestructive audio editor?

4.   What common audio problems will Soundtrack Pro analyze in an audio file?

5.   Which menu contains options that can be applied to clips as actions?

6.   When setting a noise print, which part of the file should you select?

7.   What is the best level to use as the Noise Reduce dialog's noise threshold when you begin the process of reducing noise from a file?

8.   True or false: Once you apply noise reduction to a file, you can't undo it.

9.   What happens when you save an audio file with actions applied and then return to a Final Cut Pro sequence that contains that audio file?

10.  What is the fastest way to apply noise reduction to a set of clips in Final Cut Pro?

### Answers

1.   Amplitude.

2.   The Sample Edit tool lets you change the amplitude of individual samples in an audio file.

3.   Soundtrack Pro is a nondestructive audio editor.

4.   Soundtrack Pro can analyze an audio file to detect and remove pops and clicks, power-line hum, DC offset, phase problems, clipped signals, and silence.

5.   The Process menu.

6.   Select a part of the file that contains *only* noise, and not important parts of the file you want listeners to hear.

7.  Set the Noise Threshold slider to the peak level (in dB) of the noise in the file.

8.  False.

9.  The actions you applied to the file ripple onto your Final Cut Pro sequence, and you now hear the file with the actions applied.

10. Save the actions as an AppleScript script in Soundtrack Pro; then send the Final Cut Pro audio clips to this new Soundtrack Pro AppleScript script to apply the actions.

# 5

**Lesson Files**

**Media**

Blind Date

**Time**

This lesson takes approximately 30 minutes to complete.

**Goals**

Open the Frequency Spectrum view

Explore linear and logarithmic frequency scales

Adjust the look of the Frequency Spectrum view

Edit frequencies in an audio file

Lesson **5**

# Editing in Frequency Spectrum View

In the last lesson you used the File Editor to edit an audio file. You used the Sample Edit (Pencil) tool to redraw the amplitude of individual samples. You applied a Normalize action to adjust the level of the audio. You also used the Analysis tab functions to automatically perform the same tasks. You did all this while using the Waveform view. The Waveform view graphically displays the audio file's amplitude over time. It's the most commonly used view in Soundtrack Pro. In fact, if you open any other digital audio editing application you'll find that this type of view is virtually the only one available. Soundtrack Pro, on the other hand, offers an alternative view that provides an entirely different way of way of looking at audio.

Sound consists of two components: amplitude, which equates to volume; and frequency, which equates to pitch. The Waveform view gives an accurate view of a sound clip's amplitude, but it can't tell you very much about its frequency content. Soundtrack Pro's Frequency Spectrum view is designed to show you in detail the frequency makeup of an audio file. Furthermore, in Frequency Spectrum view you can use most of the same editing techniques that you're already accustomed to using in Waveform view. This is a powerful way of working with audio that is exclusive to Soundtrack Pro. In this lesson we'll focus on the unique capabilities of Frequency Spectrum view.

## Using Frequency Spectrum View

Soundtrack Pro's Frequency Spectrum view is a powerful editing tool because it shows you a visual representation of the frequency content of your audio file. This allows you to focus your work on specific frequency ranges in a selected portion of the clip. The editing tools in Frequency Spectrum view allow you to remove, attenuate, and even copy and paste frequency ranges in the audio file.

1   In Soundtrack Pro, open the audio file titled **05_FreqSpectrum.stap**, or continue working on the audio file you had open at the end of Lesson 4. We're about to pick up right where we left off at the end of the last lesson.

2   In the upper-right corner of the File Editor project view, click the Frequency Spectrum View button.

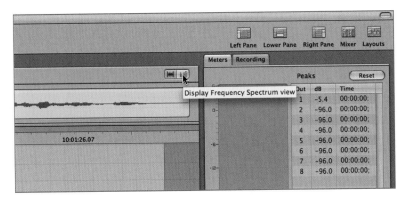

The Waveform view changes to the Frequency Spectrum view. If you've never seen a spectrum analyzer like this before it may appear strange, but it's actually a very simple way of looking at audio.

## Exploring the Frequency Spectrum View

The Frequency Spectrum view is a three-dimensional graph that displays time along the X-axis and frequency along the Y-axis. In the graph, points are plotted for each frequency at each point in time.

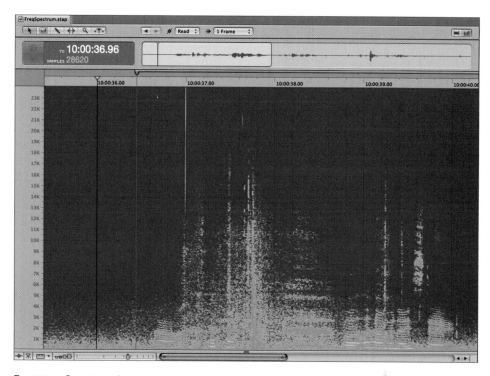

Frequency Spectrum view

The points are displayed in a range of colors and it's these colors that make up the Z-axis of the three-dimensional graph. The colors represent the amplitude of the frequency at that time. In Soundtrack Pro's default color configuration, a deep blue point means the plotted frequency is absent at that time, and a bright red point means the frequency is at full amplitude at that time. Between deep blue and bright red are shades of yellow and green that represent the varying levels of amplitude for each of the frequencies shown on the graph.

As you can imagine, this view is incredibly powerful, and it allows you to visualize audio in a very detailed manner. For example, in the previous lesson we discussed the nature of background noise and the term *noise floor*. In Frequency Spectrum view we can actually see this noise. We'll do so in the next exercise.

1    In the Actions tab in the left pane of the workspace, deselect the Reduce Noise action's checkbox.

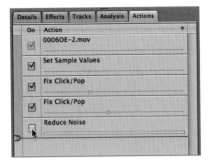

With the Reduce Noise action deselected, Frequency Spectrum view updates to display the noise you removed from this file in the preceding lesson. The difference is dramatic. You can see that relatively distinguishable plots of the actor's voice and other foreground sounds are now being visually obscured by the background noise. Play the clip and you'll see that it sounds just as it looks.

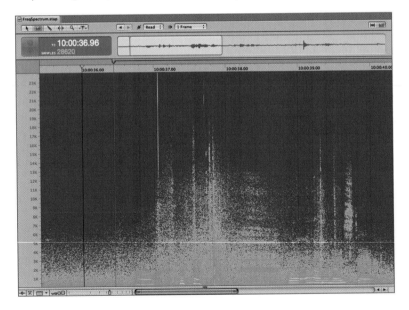

Let's get rid of that noise again by turning the Reduce Noise action back on.

2   In the Actions tab, select the Reduce Noise action's checkbox.

The noise is once again removed from the audio file.

# Linear Versus Logarithmic Scales

The way humans perceive sound is quite interesting. We hear both volume and frequency in a logarithmic manner, not a linear one. This is easy to understand when using the frequency of musical notes as an example. In terms of the pitch of a musical note, doubling the frequency is perceived as going up exactly one octave musically. The lowest A note on a piano has a fundamental frequency of 55Hz. Playing the A note one octave up produces a 110Hz tone. Moving one octave up to the next A note produces a 220Hz tone, and the next octave up is at 440Hz (also referred to as middle A). It's important to keep in mind that we perceive sound this way. Although there are only 20 frequencies between 20Hz and 40Hz, we perceive that range as one octave. Meanwhile, there are 10,000 frequencies between 10,000Hz and 20,000Hz, but this range is also perceived as exactly one octave.

For this reason, frequency is most commonly graphed on a logarithmic scale. The logarithmic scale more naturally represents the way we hear and think about sound. A person with great hearing can hear frequencies between 20Hz and 20,000Hz (20kHz), or just over 10 octaves. Most people have a slightly narrower range that tops out around 15kHz. This commonly happens as a person gets older.

As you explore Soundtrack Pro in more depth, you'll notice that in nearly all the tools in which a frequency graph appears, it's displayed in a logarithmic scale. By default, Soundtrack Pro's Frequency Spectrum view displays a linear scale. There are situations that favor a linear scale view, but in general, a logarithmic scale will prove to be more useful to you. Frequency Spectrum view lets you toggle between the two scales, so let's explore the difference between linear and logarithmic views.

1 At the left edge of the File Editor project view, Control-click or right-click the scale.

A shortcut menu appears and indicates that the Linear scale is currently selected.

**2**   From the shortcut menu, choose Logarithmic.

The File Editor updates to display the frequency spectrum logarithmically.

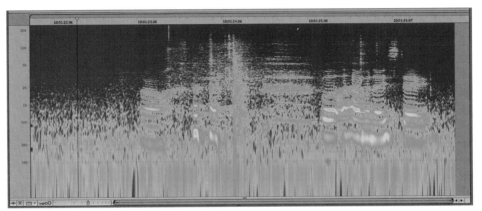

The logarithmic view effectively spreads the lower frequencies out across a larger area, as you can see by looking at the scale on the left side of the File Editor. This scale is particularly useful when the bass and mid-range frequencies are primarily what you need to focus your editing on. Each horizontal line denotes a doubling in frequency relative to the line below it. As you now know, this also indicates an increase in pitch of one octave.

At this point the graph probably still looks cluttered to you. A broad spectrum is being displayed here, making it hard to distinguish individual sounds. By fine-tuning the display you can eliminate the clutter and focus Frequency Spectrum view on precisely what you need to see. We'll look at the tools Soundtrack Pro provides for doing that now.

## Controlling the Spectrum

Frequency Spectrum view's power comes from its ability to let you literally *see* the sound you're working with so you can accurately analyze and manipulate frequencies in the file that need attention. It's hard to do this when the graph is displaying too much information. This view's greatest asset is that it allows you to visually understand how the frequencies in the file work together to make the sound you hear. You may find it easier to see the sound by adjusting the spectrum controls, so let's try that now.

**1** In the spectrum display, Control-click or right-click the background.

**2** In the shortcut menu that appears, choose Show Spectrum Controls.

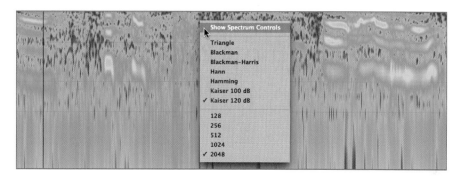

The Spectrum View HUD (heads-up display) opens. This window allows you to tailor Frequency Spectrum view precisely to your needs. By adjusting these view parameters you quickly unlock the potential of this view.

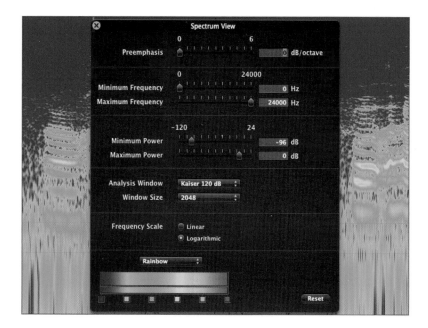

## Setting the Frequency Range

The Spectrum View HUD's frequency controls let you zoom in on certain frequencies to make them fill the spectrum display. For example, before editing the dialogue in this clip it may help to narrow the spectrum to display only frequencies that the human voice typically produces, a range that includes roughly 500 Hz to 3000 Hz.

1   In the Spectrum View HUD, set the Minimum Frequency slider to approximately 500 Hz.

> **NOTE** ▸ You don't need to set this to *precisely* 500Hz; a value close to it will be fine. If, however, you wish to enter a range precisely, you can click the value box to the right of the slider and type in the exact number you desire.

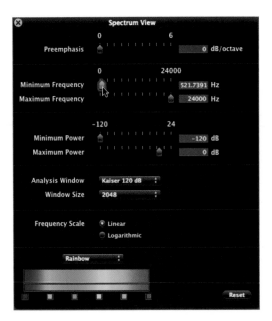

2   In the Spectrum View HUD, set the Maximum Frequency slider to approximately 3000 Hz.

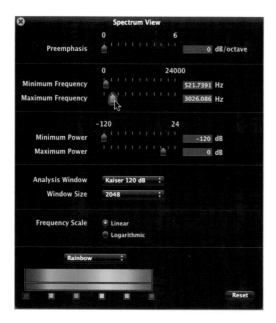

A quick check of the scale along the left of the File Editor project view shows that the spectrum display now shows only frequencies between 500 Hz and 3000 Hz.

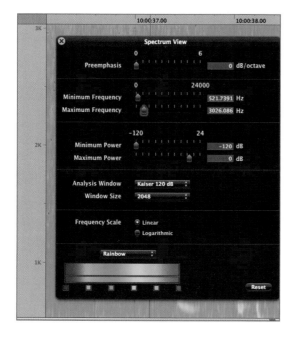

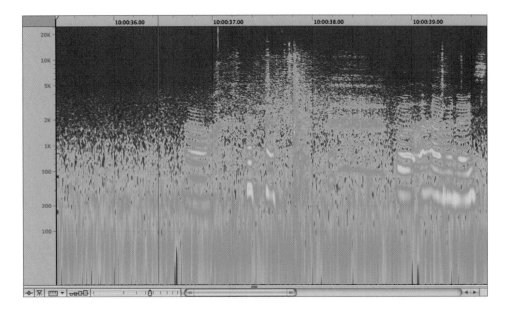

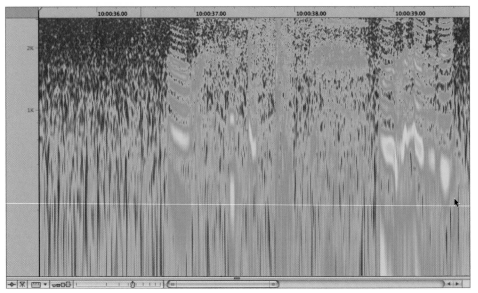

The Frequency Spectrum view displaying full-range (top) and 500Hz to 3000Hz (bottom)

The Frequency Spectrum view is now focused on the frequency range the actor's voice occupies; however, there is a considerable amount of extraneous noise present in this same frequency range. Because the dialogue is louder than the noise it's visible as the yellow plots in Spectrum view, while the background noise is green. The amount of green does make it difficult to accurately distinguish the dialogue from the noise, however, so our next step should be to clean up this view in that regard.

## Adjusting the Spectrum Power Controls

Just as the Spectrum View HUD's frequency sliders were used to narrow the frequency range shown in the display, the power sliders in Frequency Spectrum view are used to narrow the range of volume that will be shown. By adjusting the power sliders you limit the display to a certain decibel range and spread the color spectrum out between the minimum and maximum dB values that you set. For example, all the dialogue in this audio file is above –60 dB, whereas most of the background noise is not. You can adjust the Minimum Power setting to exclude the background noise from view.

**1**    In the Spectrum View HUD, set the Minimum Power slider to approximately –60 dB.

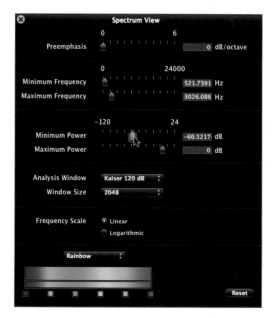

Any frequency below –60 dB has dropped out of view leaving only the dialogue visible. However, in the frequencies that remain, it's hard to distinguish which have more power than others because nearly all of the frequencies displayed fall into the green range. By lowering the Maximum Power setting you can make the difference in power much easier to see.

2   In the Spectrum View HUD, set the Maximum Power slider until some portions of the graph turn red to indicate maximum power. This should occur when you lower the slider to approximately –25 dB.

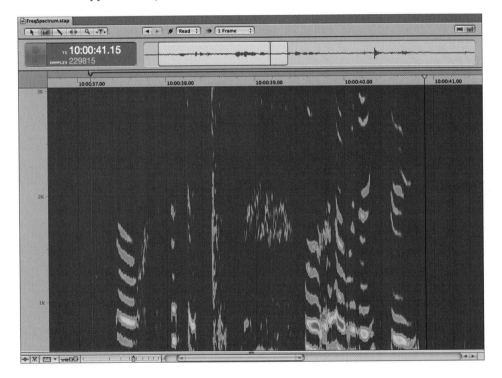

You've set the Frequency Spectrum view to display only frequencies between 500 Hz and 3000 Hz and sounds that are louder than –60 dB but quieter than –25 dB. This has configured the display to show only the frequency range that the dialogue occupies and eliminated the background noise because it's quieter than the dialogue.

The display now gives you a very clear and accurate view of the dialogue in this audio file.

3   Play the file.

The dialogue you hear matches the visual representation in the display.

## Adjusting View Color Scheme

At the bottom of the Spectrum View HUD is a pop-up menu that allows you to select the color scheme of the graph. Right now you're looking at the Rainbow setting in which loud frequencies are red, quiet frequencies are blue, and the remaining frequencies span a rainbow of colors in between. If this doesn't appeal to you, you can change the palette to one of the five other presets and then customize it further, if you choose. Sometimes viewing the display in a different color scheme can help you see frequency information that you may have missed.

1   From the Color pop-up menu at the bottom of the Spectrum View HUD, choose Red Hot.

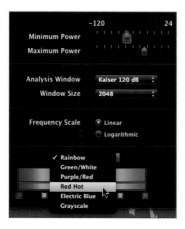

Frequency Spectrum view now displays the same information, but in a color scheme that shows quiet frequencies in black, medium frequencies in red, and the loudest frequencies in yellow.

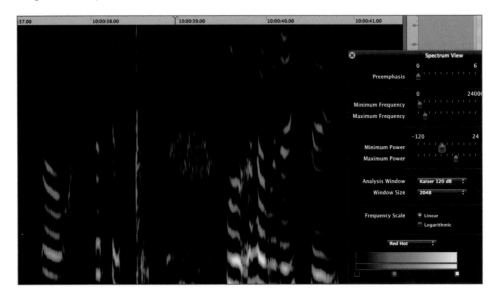

## Resetting the Frequency Spectrum View

You've just customized the Frequency Spectrum view's display to best suit your needs for this editing task. You'll find that for each task, and for each audio file, you'll want to quickly customize the display to give you the information you need for the job at hand. Once you've accomplished that particular editing task, it's beneficial to reset the Frequency Spectrum view back to its defaults so you can move on to the next item you need to address.

**1** At the bottom right of the Spectrum View HUD, click the Reset button.

The Frequency Spectrum view is reset to its default settings.

2    At the top left of the Spectrum View HUD, click the close button.

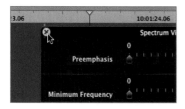

The Spectrum View HUD closes.

## Working with Frequency

Now that you know how to optimize Frequency Spectrum view to give you a clear visual of your audio file, you'll use this view to restore more problematic audio from the **Blind Date** sequence.

Listen closely to the audio in the **Blind Date** sequence and you can tell that the cameras' onboard microphones were used to record the audio for most shots in this scene. Several of the shots contain background noise that should be removed. For example, there's a high-pitched whine in the **I Guess I Am** clip that is unpleasant and particularly noticeable because there's no similar noise in the clips before and after it. We need to eliminate this noise.

1    Switch back to the Final Cut Pro sequence you had open in the preceding lesson, or open Lesson 05 > **05_FreqSpectrum.fcp**.

    **NOTE** ▶ Since this Final Cut Pro project uses a reference file, you may receive a dialog indicating that the application is "Searching for movie data." This may take several seconds to resolve.

**2**  In the Current Timecode field at the upper left of the Final Cut Pro Timeline, type *01:01:11:11* and press Return.

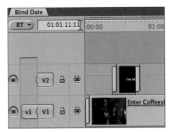

The playhead jumps to the beginning of the **I Guess I Am** clip.

**3**  Play **I Guess I Am** and listen closely.

Notice the high-pitched whine present in the clip.

**4**  Send the clip to Soundtrack Pro as an audio file project (for more information, see the section "Opening Audio Files from Final Cut Pro" in Lesson 4).

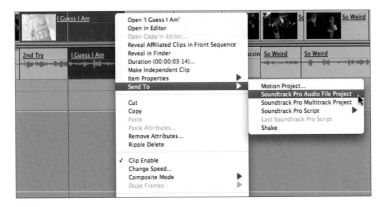

The clip opens in Soundtrack Pro's Waveform view. You want to look at this clip in Frequency Spectrum view, so you need to switch views.

**5**   At the upper right of the File Editor project view, click the Display Frequency Spectrum View button.

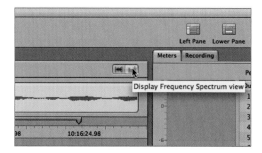

The audio file is now displayed in Frequency Spectrum view.

Frequency Spectrum view can show you the frequency of the high-pitched whine you want to remove. Look carefully and you'll see three frequencies with horizontal green lines extending throughout the entire audio file. This indicates a constant, unchanging sound, which is exactly what the high-pitched whine is.

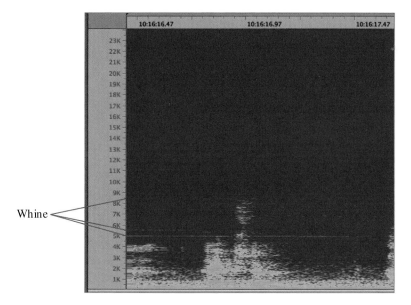

Are those three frequencies the only elements in the whine, or are more harmonics hidden in the view? We need to use the Spectrum View HUD to take a more detailed look at this audio file.

**6** In the spectrum display, Control-click or right-click the background.

The Spectrum View HUD appears.

**7** Lower the Minimum Power slider until the previously hidden horizontal green lines are easy to see. Don't lower the slider so far that background noise makes the display hard to read.

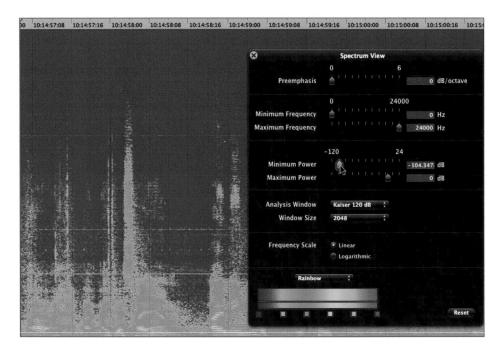

Several additional noise frequencies are now visible between 16kHz and 18kHz.

You may also find it helpful to adjust the Preemphasis slider. *Preemphasis* adds a bias to the display of higher frequencies. It effectively adds an increasing amount of gain to each higher octave.

**NOTE** ▶ As with all adjustments made in the Spectrum View HUD, the Preemphasis control affects only the way the audio is displayed. It does not affect the sound or modify the audio file in any way.

**8**   Raise the preemphasis to approximately .75 dB/octave and close the Spectrum View HUD.

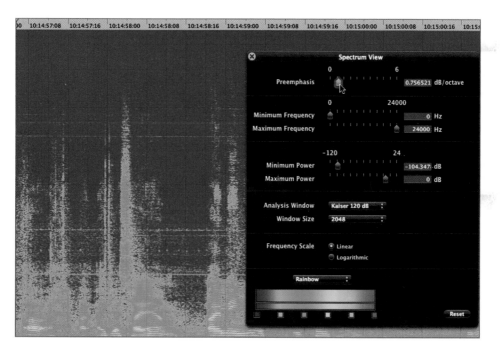

The upper frequency aspect of the whine should now be fairly easy to distinguish. The next step is to remove it.

## Removing Frequencies

The ability to hand-edit frequency is a powerful post-production tool in Soundtrack Pro. Using the Frequency Selection tool, you can surgically select and delete frequencies you wish to remove.

1   Press Shift-Z to zoom to see the entire duration of the clip. From the waveform editing tools, choose the Frequency Selection tool (or press W).

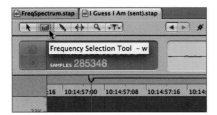

The Frequency Selection tool behaves like any other selection tool you've used: Just drag to select the frequencies you want.

2   In the spectrum display, drag a selection rectangle around the horizontal line at 16 kHz from the beginning of the file until the end.

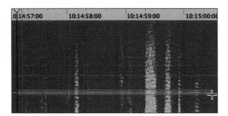

**NOTE ▶** To easily and precisely select frequencies, you may wish to zoom in on the frequency range you're working in. Remember: You can Control-click or right-click the background in the spectrum display, and then choose Show Spectrum Controls in the shortcut menu to open the Spectrum View HUD. Use the Spectrum View HUD's Minimum Frequency and Maximum Frequency sliders to zoom in, and then select the frequency you intend to remove.

**3**   Press Delete.

The selected frequency is deleted.

**4**   Select and delete the remaining horizontal lines that are indicative of noise.

When you're finished editing the file, it should look similar to the following figure. You should be careful when cutting frequencies out of an audio file; this approach can cause problems such as comb filtering or simply removing frequencies that are a part of desirable audio like the dialogue. In this instance, however, the results are quite good. You removed only thin frequency bands, none of which occupied the same frequency range as the human voice.

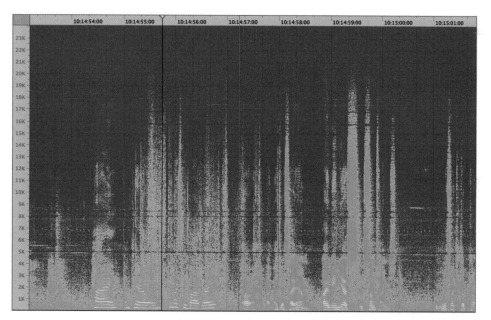

**5**   Play the file.

The whine is gone and no adverse effects of the editing can be heard. However, there is still quite a bit of background noise in this file. To practice your new skills, try creating a noise print (see Lesson 4, "Setting a Noise Print") and reducing the remaining noise (a good place to pull a noise print is immediately after the director says "Action!").

**NOTE ▶** It's a good workflow practice to manually remove any simple noises, such as the whine in the previous example, before using the Noise Print and Reduce Noise processes to reduce the remaining noise.

**TIP ▶** In addition to removing frequencies by selecting and deleting them, you can also use the Frequency Selection tool to adjust the amplitude of a frequency selection by choosing Process > Adjust Amplitude.

## Finishing Up

Once you've satisfactorily cleaned the noise from this audio file, you can return to the Final Cut Pro sequence to hear it in context and to continue your editing process.

1   Save your audio file (for more information on saving audio files that have actions attached, see the section "Rippling Your Changes to Final Cut Pro" in Lesson 4).

**NOTE ▶** It's very likely that the other clips in the **Blind Date** sequence that were shot on the same camera as this clip will contain the same whine. To quickly fix all of these clips, you can save a script based on the action set in this audio file project and then apply it to the clips in Final Cut Pro. For more information, see the section "Using Soundtrack Pro Scripts to Speed Up Your Work" in Lesson 4.

## Lesson Review

1.   Which frequency scale most closely matches the way humans perceive sound: the linear or logarithmic scale?

2.   What does the Spectrum View HUD do?

3.   True or false: You can't zoom in on frequencies in Frequency Spectrum view.

4.   How do you delete specific frequencies from a file?

*Answers*

1.  The logarithmic scale.

2.  The Spectrum View HUD lets you control the way Frequency Spectrum view displays frequencies.

3.  False. You can use the Spectrum View HUD's Minimum Frequency and Maximum Frequency settings to zoom in on specific frequencies.

4.  Use the Frequency Selection tool to select the frequencies and then press Delete.

# 6

**Lesson Files**    Lesson Files > Lesson 06 > 06_RecordingDialogue.fcp

**Time**    This lesson takes approximately 45 minutes to complete.

**Goals**    Send a multitrack project to Soundtrack Pro from Final Cut Pro

Work with audio in tracks

Choose audio interface inputs for recording

Set recording levels

Record a track

Collect a project

Use punch recording

## Lesson 6

# Recording in Soundtrack Pro

It's often necessary to record new audio during the post-production phase of a project. Some projects require the recording of foley sound, whereas others need voiceover or narration tracks added. And all too frequently, some of the dialogue that was recorded on set is simply inadequate and the project is best served by rerecording actors' lines in the studio. Soundtrack Pro is a full-featured digital audio recorder that's more than capable of handling all these scenarios.

In this lesson you'll identify dialogue in a Final Cut Pro sequence that needs to be rerecorded. You'll send the sequence to a Soundtrack Pro multitrack project so that new dialogue can be recorded. Then you'll learn how to set up Soundtrack Pro for recording and use it to record new audio files to replace the sections of the project in which the dialogue is badly recorded.

This lesson focuses on the recording of a simple dialogue part, but the skills you learn here in setting up Soundtrack Pro for recording in a multitrack project can be used to record anything you may need. Soundtrack Pro is an extremely flexible application capable of recording as many inputs as your audio interface provides, with professional routing and monitoring options.

## Opening a Multitrack Project

In this lesson you'll be working in a multitrack project. You should recall these steps for sending a Final Cut Pro sequence to a Soundtrack Pro multitrack project from Lesson 2, "Sound Mixing Basics."

**1**   In Final Cut Pro, open the project **06_RecordingDialogue.fcp**, or continue working on the Final Cut Pro project you had open at the end of Lesson 5.

**2**   In Final Cut Pro's bin, select the **Recording Dialogue** sequence if it's not selected already.

**3**   Choose File > Send To > Soundtrack Pro Multitrack Project.

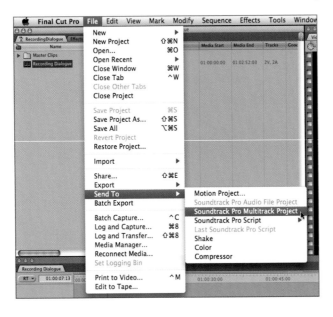

**4**   In the Save dialog that appears, type *myMultitrackProject.stmp* and then click Save.

The project opens as a multitrack project in Soundtrack Pro.

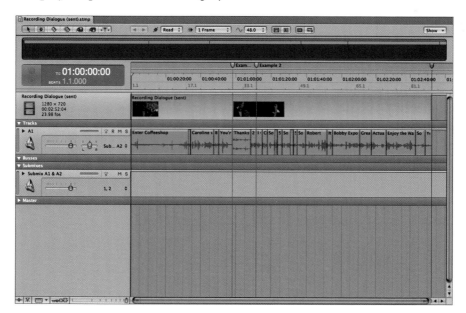

The Recording Dialogue sequence in the Final Cut Pro project has just one track of audio, so this multitrack project in Soundtrack Pro also opens with one track of audio. In the next few exercises you're going to add more tracks to this project and record new audio onto them. First you'll take some steps to prepare the workspace for recording.

## Using the Timecode HUD

The Timecode heads-up display, or HUD, shows you the playhead's current position in the sequence. It's also used to quickly place the playhead at a specific place in the Timeline.

It's useful to have the Timecode HUD open during recording sessions.

1   In Soundtrack Pro, choose Window > HUDs > Timecode.

The Timecode HUD opens and floats over the project.

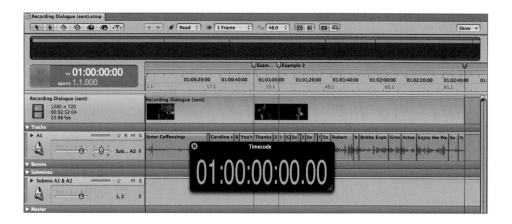

**NOTE ▶** Drag the lower-right corner of the Timecode HUD to make the HUD bigger or smaller. Changing the size of the HUD can be handy when you need to make it big enough to see the timecode value from across the room (for example, when recording foley sounds), or when you need to make it small enough to sit in a particular section of the screen.

**2**   Position the pointer over the seconds value.

Two white arrows appear directly over the seconds value: one at the top and one at the bottom of the Timecode HUD.

**3**   Drag up until the seconds display reads 30.

As you drag, notice that the playhead moves across the Timeline. The playhead's position always reflects the timecode value displayed in the Timecode HUD.

4   Play the project (and watch the scene) to approximately timecode value 01:01:00:00.

In the section of the scene that you just watched, the male character says "yes" several times. This is the dialogue that you're going to replace. It will be helpful for you to watch this section several times to get a feel for the timing of the dialogue.

**NOTE ▶** While the scene is playing, you can return the playhead to the start of the section and resume playback by pressing Shift-Return.

Once you're familiar with the interaction of the characters, return the playhead to the start of the section by doing the following:

5   In the Timecode HUD, double-click the display.

The Timecode HUD updates to display a text field.

6   Type *01:00:30:00* and press Return.

**NOTE ▶** You don't need to type the colons.

The playhead jumps to exactly 30 seconds and 0 frames from the start of the sequence.

**NOTE ▶** To position the playhead, you can also double-click the timecode area in the upper-left corner of the Timeline to open a text field and type a timecode value.

## Working with Tracks

In a Soundtrack Pro multitrack project, all audio clips live on a track, just as they do in Final Cut Pro. In the next exercise you'll create, rearrange, and delete tracks to prepare the workspace for the recording you're about to do.

## Creating Tracks

The project currently has one track that contains the audio clips from the Final Cut Pro sequence. You don't want to record over, or delete, this audio, so you need to create a new track.

**1**   Choose Multitrack > Add Track (Command-T).

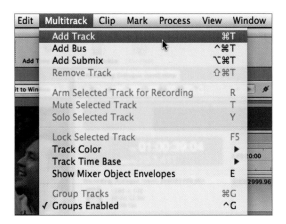

A new track (titled Track 2) is created. You can also create new tracks using a shortcut menu.

**2** Control-click or right-click the header of Track 2.

A shortcut menu appears. At the top of this menu are two options: Insert Track Before and Insert Track After. This shortcut menu provides a quick way of simultaneously creating a new track and placing it in the track list.

**3** Choose Insert Track Before.

Track 3 is created and placed before Track 2.

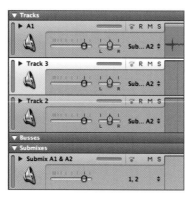

## Reordering Tracks

You can reorder tracks at any time by clicking any track's header and dragging it to the desired position in the track list.

**1**  Drag Track 2 to the position above Track 3.

When you've dragged Track 3's header far enough over Track 2's header you'll see a bar appear above Track 2.

**2**  Release the mouse button to drop Track 2 into that position.

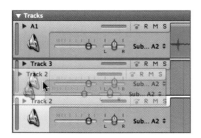

## Deleting Tracks

You have two empty tracks in the project. You need only one, so you can delete the extra one now.

**1**  Control-click or right-click Track 3.

**2**  From the shortcut menu that appears, choose Remove Track (Shift-Command-T).

Track 3 is deleted.

## Naming Tracks

An elaborate project may contain dozens of audio tracks. It's important to keep your projects organized so that you can quickly find and manage audio elements. Soundtrack Pro allows you to name audio tracks. It's highly recommended that you do so in all your projects, big or small.

1  In Track 2's header, click the text "Track 2."

A text field appears.

2  Type *myVoiceOver* and press Return.

The track is renamed "myVoiceOver."

## Locking Tracks

When there are tracks in your project that you know you won't be editing, it's a smart idea to lock them. Locking a track prevents any changes from being made to the clips on that track. You'll lock the first track in the project to ensure that it's not accidentally changed while you record and edit in the myVoiceOver track.

1  Control-click or right-click track A1.

2  From the shortcut menu that appears, choose Lock Selected Track.

The track is locked. Textured diagonal lines appear over the clips on the track, indicating that they can't be edited, and the track header is dimmed.

**NOTE ▶** To unlock the track, choose Unlock Track from the same shortcut menu.

## Setting Up for Recording

You now have the playhead positioned at the section where you need to record new audio, and you've prepared a track for the new recording. The final step before recording audio is to configure the audio interface and recording parameters.

The Recording tab contains many of the parameters you need to configure the recording system. The Recording tab lives in the right pane. If the right pane isn't currently visible, follow these steps to add it to the workspace:

1  In the upper-right corner of the Toolbar, click the Right Pane button, or choose Window > Toggle Right Pane (Control-D).

The right pane appears.

**2** Click the Recording tab.

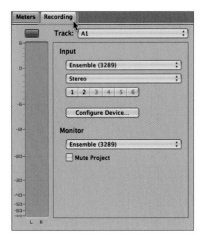

## Choosing a Track to Record

Soundtrack Pro is an extremely versatile multitrack recorder with the capability to record multiple tracks at once and assign different input, channel, and monitor settings for each track (we'll explore these features in a moment). The first step is to choose a track for recording.

**1** From the Track menu at the top of the Recording tab, choose the myVoiceOver track.

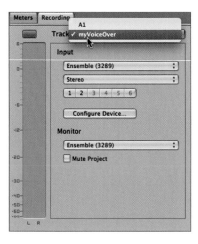

## Choosing a Recording Input

Soundtrack Pro works with any Core Audio–compatible interface. Each input on your audio interface can record to its own track in Soundtrack Pro, or several inputs can be assigned to a multichannel track (up to 6 channels can be recorded to one track in Soundtrack Pro, a feature that enables recording surround sound). This is a standard way of recording multiple performers simultaneously (each performer on his or her own mic, recorded to a separate track). The recording you're about to do isn't that complex—you're just one performer using one microphone—but you still need to tell Soundtrack Pro which audio interface you intend to use and with which input you'll be recording.

If you don't have an audio interface attached to your computer, the built-in microphone or the default inputs are all that will be available. If you have an Apple laptop or iMac, you can complete this lesson using the built-in microphone. Mac Pro users, however, will need to have an audio interface and a microphone to continue, because there is no microphone included with those systems directly out of the box.

1   From the Recording tab's Input menu, choose your audio interface, if you have one, or select Built-in Microphone to use the mic built into your iMac or MacBook.

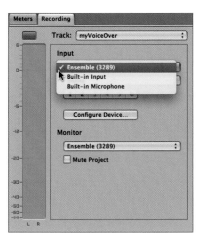

## Choosing a Channel Configuration

The channel configuration determines how many channels of audio you'll record to the track. You can choose one channel (mono), two channels (stereo), or up to six channels (for 5.1 surround). Soundtrack Pro records all channels on the assigned track into a single multichannel clip. This makes editing multichannel clips extremely easy. The recording you're currently setting up is one microphone recording a mono clip.

**1** In the Recording tab, click the Input Channel pop-up menu.

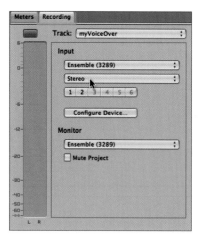

**2** Choose Mono.

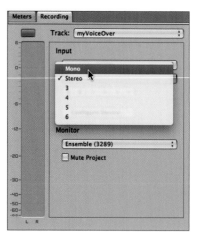

You'll now record one channel of audio only.

## Adjusting the Channel Setting

If your audio interface has more than one input, you can connect your microphone to any input on the audio interface. Soundtrack Pro will attempt to record from input 1 by default. To configure Soundtrack Pro to record from a different input, you'll use the channel buttons.

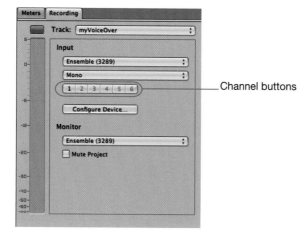

**NOTE ▶** If your audio interface lets you name inputs, those names will appear in the Channel Button pop-up menus. Check the manual for your specific audio interface to see if this is possible.

**1**   Click the first channel button.

A pop-up menu appears.

**2**   Choose the channel that your microphone is plugged into.

**NOTE ▶** The Apogee Ensemble used in these screenshots has 10 inputs. The number of inputs shown in your menu will depend on the hardware you're using. Many audio interfaces have only one or two inputs.

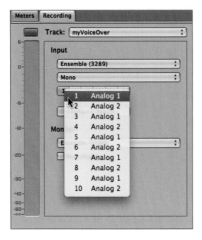

## Displaying Recording Settings in the Track Header

The settings you just configured in the Recording tab are also available in the track head-ers. However, you must have the Timeline track height set to medium or large for these settings to appear.

1   At the lower left of the Timeline, set the Timeline track height to medium.

The tracks become taller, and the input settings are now displayed directly in the track header.

## Recording a Single Take

In a moment you'll record your first dialogue take. But first, to ensure a successful recording, it's good to review basic recording protocol. Your speakers should be off or muted at this time. If you attempt to use your speakers to monitor your recording you're likely to encounter *feedback*. At its worst, feedback is a loud, shrill sound that will hurt both your ears and your speakers in addition to ruining the recording.

You should instead monitor through headphones, preferably a set that effectively blocks outside noise, as these will also help prevent sound from leaking out. By using appropriate headphones you'll be able to monitor the recording without allowing any unwanted sound to leak into the microphone and corrupt the take.

## Choosing a Recording Destination

By default, Soundtrack Pro saves all of your recordings in your Documents > Soundtrack Pro Documents > Recordings folder. If you want to record to a different folder, follow these steps.

1   Choose Soundtrack Pro > Preferences.

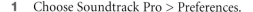

2   At the top of the Preferences pane, click the Recording button.

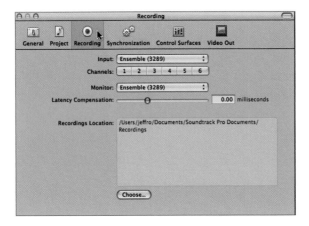

The Recording pane appears. At the bottom of the pane is a Recordings Location area.

**3**   Directly below the Recordings Location area, click the Choose button.

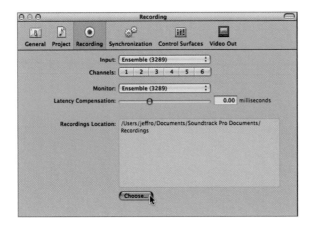

A Finder pane drops down from the top of the Recording pane.

**4**   Navigate to the folder where you want to save your recordings, and click Open.

The folder is selected as the destination for your newly recorded files.

**NOTE** ▶ For this lesson you may set the Recordings Location to any folder on your drive that you wish. In a later exercise you'll learn to collect your audio files for easy management and archiving.

**5**   Close the Preferences pane.

## Arming a Track for Recording

In order to record onto the myVoiceOver track you must first arm it. Only tracks that are record-armed will be recorded to, regardless of all the other settings you've made so far. This allows you to have as many tracks as you wish configured for recording, but during each pass, recording will occur only on the tracks you've chosen to arm.

> **NOTE** ▶ If you click Record without any tracks armed, Soundtrack Pro will create a new track and immediately begin recording to it. When it does this, the default options will be used for all recording settings.

1   On the myVoiceOver track, click the R (Arm for Recording) button, or select the track and press the R key.

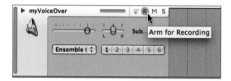

The track turns red, indicating that it's armed for recording.

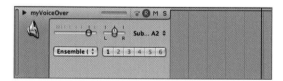

## Setting a Recording Level

With the track armed you'll see that the level meter in the Recording tab now displays the signal level for the input that you selected. You're now going to adjust the input level so that you can record the new dialogue track at the optimum level.

The audio quality will be at its best when you've properly set the gain on your recording equipment to record at the ideal level. To take full advantage of your hardware's capability, you should record a strong signal that doesn't clip or reach 0 dB.

It's good practice to set your recording level so that your audio peaks around –6 dB. This usually provides a strong signal but leaves enough *headroom* (margin between the peak level and 0 dB) so that any unexpected spikes don't cause clipping to occur.

1    Locate the input controls on your audio interface.

2    Say the words "Test, test, check, test" repeatedly at the same volume at which you intend to record yourself, and watch the Recording tab's input level meter.

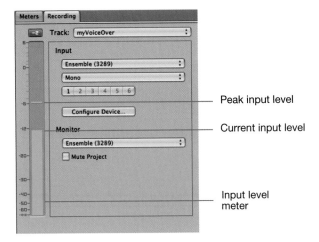

Peak input level

Current input level

Input level meter

> **NOTE** ▸ The input level meter is a peak-and-hold meter. The green bar displays the current (instantaneous) level while the thin white bar above it displays the highest level reached in the last few seconds.

3    Adjust the audio input until your test speech is peaking at approximately –6 dB.

> **NOTE** ▸ Input level is set on your audio hardware. If you you're using a third-party audio interface, refer to its user manual for input level adjustment. If you're using the built-in audio capability of your MacBook Pro or iMac, open System Preferences, select the Sound preference, select the Input tab, then adjust the Input Volume slider to set the input level.

## Resetting the Peak Indicator
The peak indicator is the small box located just above the input level meter. The peak indicator numerically displays the highest audio level incurred since the last time the

indicator was reset. If the level reaches 0 dB (or higher), the peak indicator changes from gray to red, giving you clear visual warning that the recording was clipped.

Peak indicator

1    To reset the peak indicator, click it once.

The indicator sets itself to the current peak in the signal.

## Recording a Take

The playhead is currently parked at 01:00:30:00, which is the start of the scene containing the male character whose dialogue you're about to replace. In the following steps, you'll record yourself saying "yes" in sync with the male actor's performance.

> **NOTE** ▶ You may want to review this scene to remind yourself of the content before returning the playhead to the project's 30-second mark.

1    Verify that your monitor speakers are off or muted, and put on headphones if you have them.

In the next steps you'll record a new audio file to the myVoiceOver track.

2    In the transport area at the bottom of the workspace, click the Record button.

The playhead moves along the Timeline, creating a new clip in the myVoiceOver track. This indicates that Soundtrack Pro is recording.

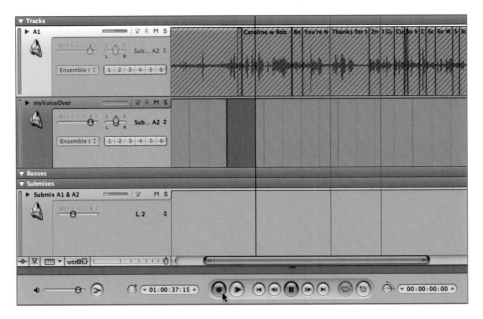

**3** Watch the action in the Video tab, and say *yes* when the male character says "yes."

**4** When the scene is finished, press the spacebar (or click the Record button a second time) to stop recording.

When the playhead stops, the red clip turns green and the waveform is visible.

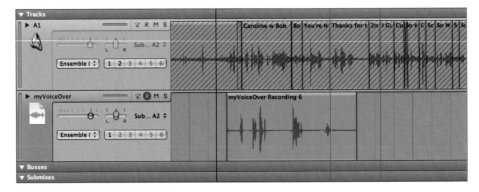

## Collecting the Project

Each take that you record in Soundtrack Pro creates a new audio file. These files are saved to the folder that you specified in User Preferences (see "Choosing a Recording Destination" earlier in this lesson). Over the course of a project, you may create dozens or even hundreds of new audio files. While you're working with the project, it's fine to keep these audio files in the default folder. At the end of a project, however, it's a smart practice to collect these audio files along with the project file and any associated video files so that they're in one easy-to-manage location.

Soundtrack Pro has a feature that makes this file management easy. *Collecting* the project places all the files associated with the project in one location. Once the project is collected, all future recordings made in the project will be recorded directly into the collected folder. Collecting the project is an ideal way to keep your media files properly organized.

1   From Soundtrack Pro's menu bar, choose File > Save As.

The Save As dialog appears. At the bottom of the dialog are options for handling associated media files.

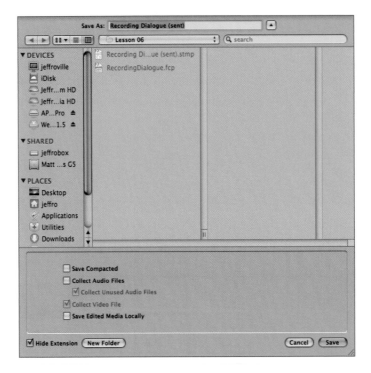

2   Click the Collect Audio Files checkbox to select it.

Selecting this checkbox tells Soundtrack Pro to gather all the audio files used for the project and place them with the saved project file. There are four additional options:

▶   **Save Compacted**—Choose this option to save the project without certain display data. This will reduce the amount of disk space the project requires but will cause the project to take longer to open.

▶ **Collect Unused Audio Files**—Keep this checkbox selected if you want Soundtrack Pro to include audio files that are not used in the Timeline but remain in the Bin, such as takes that you recorded but chose not to use, or clips that you deleted from the Timeline but didn't remove from the Bin.

▶ **Collect Video File**—Keep this checkbox selected if you want to collect the video file used in the project.

▶ **Save Edited Media Locally**—Select this checkbox to save any edited audio files into the collected project's folder. The files will be organized into a subfolder named *Media*. If this option is deselected, edited media will be saved to the location set in Preferences.

3   Deselect the Collect Unused Audio Files and Collect Video File checkboxes.

4   Navigate to the place where you want to save the collected project.

5   At the bottom of the Save As dialog, click the New Folder button.

**NOTE** ▶ If you don't see a New Folder button, click the disclosure triangle to the right of the Save As field to expand the dialog.

6   In the New Folder dialog that appears, type *myCollectedProject* and click the Create button.

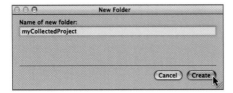

**7**   In the Save As dialog, click the Save button.

The Save As dialog is replaced by a progress bar showing Soundtrack Pro collecting the project.

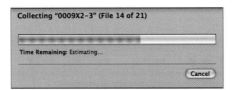

When the collection process is finished you'll find a new project file and a Media folder that contains all the audio files used in the project.

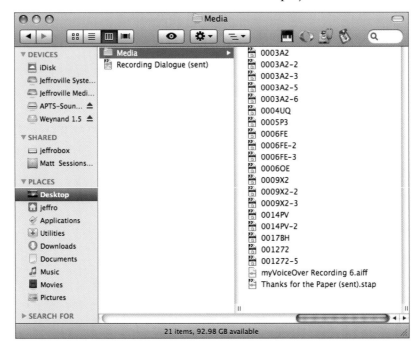

**8**   Click the File menu to open it and take a look at the options.

The Save command is now the Save (Collected) command. From this point forward, saving the project will collect all new audio files (such as recordings) to your collected project folder. This will be demonstrated in the next exercise.

## Using Punch Recording

*Punch recording* refers to the act of dropping one or more tracks into record mode while the playhead is already moving. The term originates from analog multitrack recording. When recording to multitrack tape, it was the engineer's or tape operator's job to press the Record button at precisely the right moment to record a new part over a previously recorded segment of tape. If the engineer pressed the Record button too soon, the new recording would permanently erase a desired piece of audio.

Punch recording is available in Soundtrack Pro, too. However, because Soundtrack Pro is a nondestructive audio editor, you never need worry about losing a previously recorded piece of audio. In this next exercise you'll use punch recording to rerecord the last two "yeses" in your voiceover.

Section to be punch-recorded

1   Verify that the myVoiceOver track is armed for recording.

2   Use the Timecode HUD to move the playhead to 01:00:40:00.

3   Start playback.

4   As the playhead nears the final two "yeses," click the Record button and say the *yeses* in sync with the male. This is called *punching in*.

5   Once you've recorded the two "yeses," click the Record button to stop recording. This is called *punching out*.

Note that the playhead continues to play. You could punch in and out as many more times as you need to without stopping the playhead.

A new clip appears on the Timeline where you punch-recorded. If you aren't happy with your performance you can Undo (Command-Z) it and try again.

**NOTE ▸** The clip you just recorded did not erase the audio beneath it on the original clip. You can drag the new clip to move it and you'll see that the audio on the original clip is revealed.

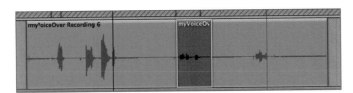

**6**   Save your project.

Because you've already saved as a collected project, the new recording is saved into the Media folder, along with the project's other audio files.

## Lesson Review

1.   What is the Timecode HUD?

2.   Where is the Recording tab located?

3.   True or false: In Soundtrack Pro, you can't record more than two channels of audio in the same clip.

4.   What level should you set as the peak for recording, and why?

5.   Why is it a good idea to collect a project after recording?

6.   When punch recording, how many times can you punch in and punch out of a track without stopping the playhead?

### Answers

1.   The Timecode HUD is a floating window that lets you see and adjust the playhead's timecode position.

2.   The Recording tab is in Soundtrack Pro's right pane.

3.   False. Depending on your audio interface, you can record up to six channels of audio (5.1 surround sound) in a single clip.

4.   Set a peak recording level of –6 dB. This level maximizes your signal-to-noise ratio while still leaving headroom for unexpected peaks.

5.   When you collect a project, all of the project's audio files are gathered together and placed in a Media folder beside the new project file. All of the project's future recordings will also be collected in the new Media folder each time you save the project.

6.   You can punch in and punch out as many times as you like without stopping the playhead while punch recording.

# 7

Lesson Files     Lesson Files > Lesson 07 > 07_EditingDialogue.stmp

Time     This lesson takes approximately 30 minutes to complete.

Goals     Work with Soundtrack Pro's audio editing tools

Utilize snapping modes

Arrange clips in tracks

Nudge clips in the Timeline

Use the File Editor tab

Time-stretch audio clips to match onscreen action

Work with cycle regions

Adjust track and clip volume

Set and apply an ambient noise print to fill in room tone

# Lesson **7**

# Editing Dialogue

In the preceding lesson you rerecorded dialogue to improve a scene. That audio now needs to be edited to fit seamlessly into the audio recorded on set. The new audio clips need to be trimmed to just their essential parts, placed, and time-stretched to precisely match the movement of the onscreen actor's lips, as well as adjusted to match the volume of the other clips in the Timeline. Ambient sound must also be added to the rerecorded clips to match the setting of the scene.

In this lesson you'll perform all of these tasks to properly edit and mix the rerecorded dialogue. In the process, you'll utilize some of Soundtrack Pro's advanced features to streamline the tasks. You'll also become extremely familiar with the use of all of Soundtrack Pro's editing tools.

## Using Soundtrack Pro's Editing Tools

Located in the upper-left corner of the Multitrack Editor's Project pane is a row of buttons. These are the Timeline editing tools. You'll recognize some of these tools, such as the Selection (arrow) and Blade tools, because they're used in Final Cut Pro. Others, such as the Timeslice and Lift tools, will be new to you. All of your Timeline editing work will be done using these tools. In this lesson you'll explore the functions of all of Soundtrack Pro's Timeline editing tools and learn to use them in the context of editing dialogue.

## Using the Selection Tool

The Selection tool, also known as the arrow, is the primary tool used in Soundtrack Pro. Just as in Final Cut Pro, the Selection tool is used to select and move clips as well as adjust edit points. In this exercise you'll explore the Selection tool's multiple functions.

1  In Soundtrack Pro, open the project titled **07_EditingDialogue.stmp** or continue working on the Soundtrack Pro project you had open at the end of Lesson 6.

2  Click the Selection tool, as shown below, or press the A key on your keyboard, just as you would in Final Cut Pro.

**3**   In the myVoiceOver track, select the large **myVoiceOver** clip.

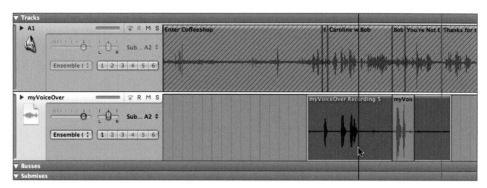

The clip turns dark green, indicating that it's selected. You'll notice that the small clip that you punch-recorded at the end of the previous lesson isn't highlighted. This is a separate clip from the one you just selected, and sits on top of the selected clip. Clips in Soundtrack Pro can overlap each other, but only the clip on top will be heard. What you see there is what you'll hear.

**NOTE ▶** Soundtrack Pro will play only the top audio clip, just as Final Cut Pro plays only the video clip in the top track.

There is a short section of silence before the first "yes" occurs in this clip. This section isn't truly silent, however; it contains ambient sound captured during the voiceover recording. This ambient sound doesn't match the ambient sound of the scene, so it should now be removed.

**4**   Position the pointer over the left edge of the clip you have selected.

The arrow turns into a Clip Resize pointer.

**5**   Drag toward the right to remove the "silence" at the beginning of the clip.

The edit you just performed should be made as tight as possible. In the next steps you'll improve on the edit's accuracy by zooming in tightly on the clip. Your edits will always be more precise if you zoom in to the point you're editing.

**6**   Make sure the myVoiceOver clip is still selected, and then press Option-Z.

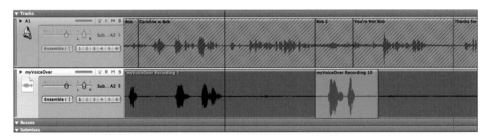

The Timeline centers the selected clip and the zoom level is automatically set so the clip fills the screen. At this zoom level you can see that the head of the clip can be trimmed a little more.

**7**   Drag the left edge of the clip until it stops at the beginning of the recorded vocal.

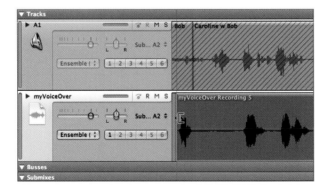

This process of trimming the clips to clean up the audio is one of the first steps in making new audio elements successfully blend into a scene. Later in this lesson you'll insert ambient noise from the scene into the gaps left by your edits, so that the viewer won't notice any difference in quality between the clips recorded on set and the clips recorded in the studio.

## Using the Blade Tool

The voiceover clip contains a long section of ambient noise between dialogue parts. This needs to be removed, just as you removed a similar section of dead air from the start of the clip in the previous exercise. One of the ways to remove audio from the middle of a clip is to split the clip.

The Blade tool is used to split clips in the Timeline.

1 Click the Blade tool, as shown below, or press the B key on your keyboard, just as you would in Final Cut Pro.

The pointer has now become the Blade tool.

2 Click the selected clip directly after the third "yes."

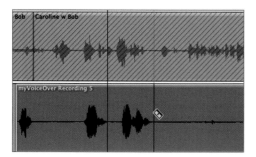

The clip is divided in two. You've just performed a split.

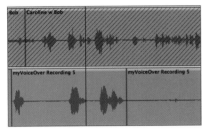

**NOTE ▶** Soundtrack Pro also contains the Blade All tool that splits clips across all tracks in the Timeline at once. The key command for this tool is BB (press the B key twice in quick succession).

## Deleting Clips

In Soundtrack Pro you can delete clips by selecting them with the Selection tool and then pressing the Delete key on your keyboard, or you can use the following trick to delete clips with any tool you currently have selected.

**1**  With the Blade tool still selected, Control-click or right-click the clip to the right of the split you made in the steps above.

A shortcut menu appears.

**2**  From the shortcut menu, choose Delete.

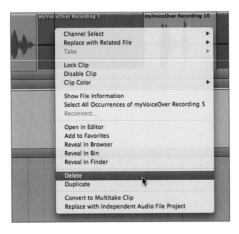

The selected clip is deleted.

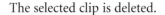

## Using the Timeslice Tool

The Timeslice tool is a special selection tool that allows you to select portions of a clip, or even portions of multiple clips in the same track or on different tracks. While the Selection tool is clip-based, meaning it can only select entire clips at once, the Timeslice tool's selections are time-based, making it possible to make precise edits to a specific section of a clip without affecting parts of the clip outside of the selection.

1   Click the Timeslice tool, as shown below, or press the W key on your keyboard.

2   In the Timeline, drag a selection range over the silence between the first and second sets of "yeses" in your recording.

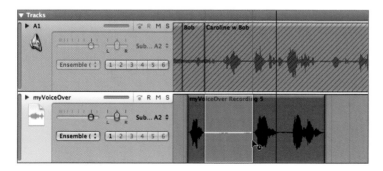

A portion of the clip is selected.

**3**    On your computer keyboard, press the Delete key.

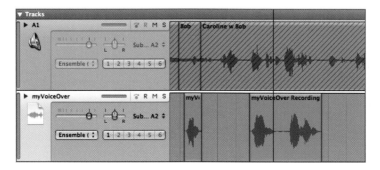

The selected portion of the clip is deleted.

### Editing Tools Exercise

These three tools, Selection, Blade, and Timeslice, are the primary editing tools in Soundtrack Pro, so it's important for you to be completely comfortable using them. Take a moment to exercise your editing skills by trimming the rest of the clips on the myVoiceOver track to remove any sound between the spoken words.

Use the editing techniques demonstrated in this section to edit your recording so that the clips in the myVoiceOver track look similar to the following figure.

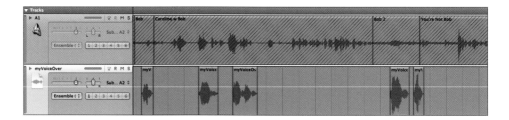

## Arranging Clips

In the previous section you used Soundtrack Pro's editing tools to cut out portions of your recording that aren't needed for your voiceover. However, unless you were spot on in your vocal recording, your words probably don't sync up precisely with the movement of the onscreen actor's lips. In this section, you'll explore techniques for moving clips in one track, and also across multiple tracks, to create a more exact arrangement.

## Disabling Snapping Mode

By default, Soundtrack Pro has snapping enabled. Snapping is useful when you need to perfectly align clips to one another, to a marker, or in the case of music to a specific beat. Later in this book you'll use snapping for all these purposes. In the following steps, however, you'll make very fine adjustments to the position of clips in your Timeline. For this type of editing it's best to disable snapping.

> **NOTE ▶** To temporarily reverse the snapping state, hold the Command key as you drag clips.

1   Move any clip left or right in the Timeline.

    Notice that the clip snaps from grid point to grid point.

2   Press Command-Z to undo the move.

3   Choose View > Snap (N) and make sure the snapping mode is off.

A checkmark next to the word "Snap" indicates that snapping is enabled. For the following steps you should not have snapping enabled.

4　Move a clip in the Timeline.

Notice that the clip now moves smoothly between grid points.

5　Press Command-Z to undo the move.

## Moving Clips in a Single Track

The waveform displayed within each clip makes many editing tasks quick and precise. In a previous exercise you removed the space between the words on your dialogue track by visually identifying the parts of the clips that should be removed. You must always check your edits by ear, of course—the sound of your work is all that truly matters—but the editing process is often a visual one.

If you look closely at the waveforms in the two tracks in this project you can clearly see the sections of sound that make up the spoken words. You'll also notice that the shape of the waveforms of your recorded "yeses" on the myVoiceOver track looks strikingly similar to the onscreen actor's recorded "yeses" in track A1.

In the next exercise you'll sync your voiceover to the actor's performance by moving the clips in the myVoiceOver track into the correct position. You'll perform these edits first by sight, and then check and possibly fine-tune them by ear.

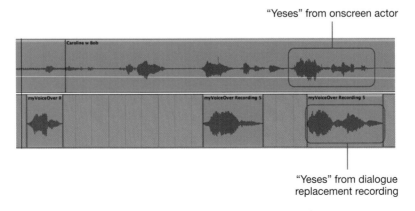

"Yeses" from onscreen actor

"Yeses" from dialogue replacement recording

**NOTE ▶** No two recordings are ever exactly the same. The waveforms in your recording will look slightly different from the recording in the figures that follow.

1   Look at the waveforms in your Timeline and determine which clips need to be moved to align the dialogue recordings.

2   Click the Selection Tool button (or press A on your keyboard).

3   Click a clip to select it.

4   Drag the clip left or right until its left edge begins at the same point as the beginning of the waveform it will eventually replace.

As you drag, notice that three alignment guides appear: one on the left edge of the clip, one on the right edge, and one directly aligned with the point on the clip you clicked when you initiated the drag. Use the left alignment guide to position the voiceover clip precisely at the beginning of the waveform on the A1 track that you're attempting to sync to.

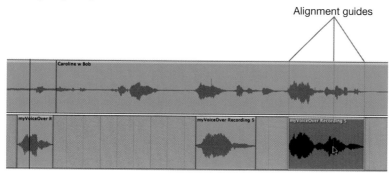

5   Click the Timeline just before the edit you've made to place the playhead.

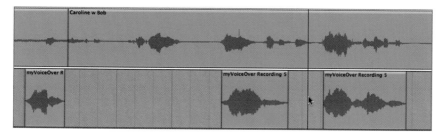

6   Press the spacebar to play the project and listen to the edit.

Listen to the synchronization between your voiceover recording and the actor's performance.

7   Press the spacebar again to stop playback.

8   Repeat steps 3 through 7 to adjust the position of the other dialogue clips in your recording.

Don't worry about positioning your clips perfectly at this point; you'll nudge the clips more precisely into place in the next exercise.

## Nudging Clips Frame by Frame

The precise synchronization of recorded dialogue and the onscreen lip movement of the actors is one of the most important parts of dialogue replacement. The smallest discrepancy can ruin a scene. To ensure that the viewer won't be able to detect any disconnect between what they're seeing and what they're hearing, you'll nudge the dialogue clips frame by frame, and even by sub-frames, until you've achieved perfect sync.

1   Choose a dialogue clip that's slightly out of sync with the onscreen actor's lip movement.

2   To nudge the clip, do one of the following:

▶   To nudge the clip to the left, press Command–Left Arrow.

▶   To nudge the clip to the right, press Command–Right Arrow.

The clip moves to the left or right by the default nudge amount, 1 frame.

3   To change the nudge amount, click the Nudge Amount pop-up menu.

4   Select the 1/4 Frame nudge amount.

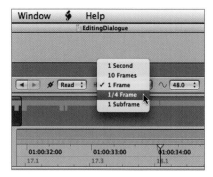

Now the nudge command moves the clip by 1/4 of a frame, giving you four times the accuracy in placing the clip.

Should you wish to place the clips even more precisely, select the 1 Subframe nudge amount and continue to use the nudge command to move the voiceover dialogue clips into sync with the actor's performance.

## Adjusting Clip Duration

Synchronizing the start of the voiceover clips with the onscreen performance gets you most of the way to a synchronized dialogue replacement. However, there's often a discrepancy between the length of the rerecorded dialogue and the performance it's intended to replace. Looking at your recorded dialogue clips, you'll notice that they start at the same point as the waveforms in the A1 track but end either sooner or later than the actor's performance.

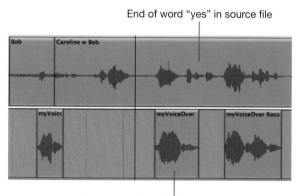

Soundtrack Pro's Time Stretch capability makes correcting differences in length a simple process. Time-stretching audio clips allows you to adjust a clip's duration without altering its pitch. To do this, you'll work in the File Editor tab.

1   If the lower pane isn't visible, click the Lower Pane button in the upper-right corner of the Toolbar.

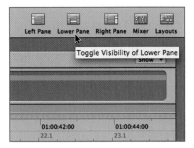

2    In the Timeline, select a clip with a duration that needs adjusting.

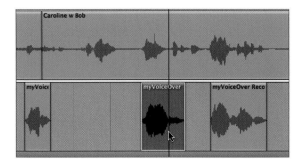

3    In the lower pane, click the File Editor tab.

The File Editor tab is nearly identical to the File Editor you already know from your work in Audio File Projects in Lesson 1. The File Editor tab provides all the same functions that you remember from the previous lesson, right here in the lower pane of the Multitrack Editor.

**4**    From the File Editor tab's toolbar, select the Audio Stretching tool (T).

**5**    With the Audio Stretching tool, drag a selection range over the audio you want to stretch.

A selection range appears, with purple lines at its left and right edges.

**6**    Position the Audio Stretching tool over the purple line on the right edge of the selected audio.

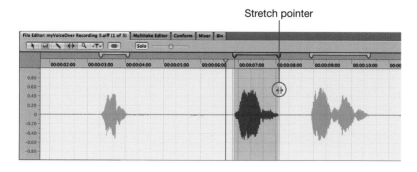

The arrow turns into the Stretch pointer.

**7**   Drag left or right to stretch the selected portion of the audio file.

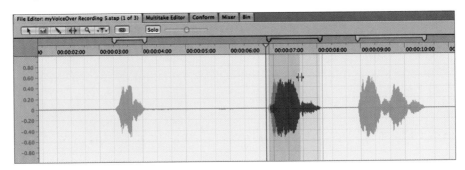

The selected area of the audio file is stretched. Back in the Timeline, you can clearly see the results of your edit and judge if your edit is correct.

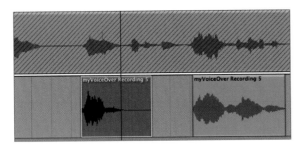

**8**   In the left pane, click the Actions tab.

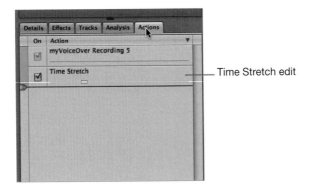

The Time Stretch edit has been added to the Actions list. As with any action, you can adjust a Time Stretch process you have already performed by double-clicking it in the

Action list. You can also undo this action at any time by toggling it off or just deleting it from the Actions list.

**NOTE ▶** You can also perform time stretch functions by making a selection and then choosing Process > Time Stretch. This opens the Time Stretch window, which you can use to make precise adjustments to the selected audio, such as setting an exact duration.

9   Play your project and listen to the edit you've made.

10   If necessary, repeat steps 5 through 7 above until the clip is exactly the correct duration.

11   If there are other clips in your project that need to be time-stretched, select them and repeat steps 5 through 7 until they're all perfectly aligned with the original source audio.

## Setting the Default Time Stretch Algorithm

Soundtrack Pro includes three different Time Stretch algorithms. Each excels at stretching different types of audio. You can choose which algorithm the Audio Stretching tool will use in Preferences.

1   Press Command-Comma (,) to open the Preferences window.

2   Click the General tab if it isn't already displayed.

3   In the General tab, look for the preference called Default Time Stretch.

The three built-in Time Stretch algorithms are as follows:

▶   **Universal**—This is a highly adaptive algorithm that is built for excellent application with nearly every type of source audio. If you're unsure of which setting to pick, choose this one.

▶   **Complex**—This algorithm may produce better results with music tracks.

▶   **Percussive**—This algorithm may produce better results with beat-based loops.

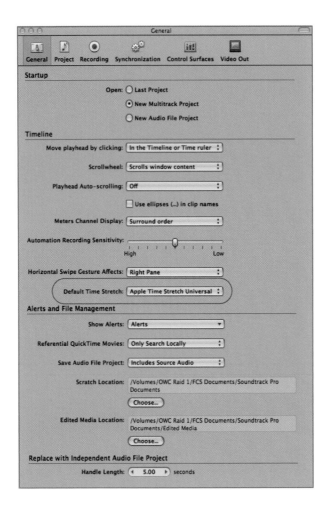

In addition, Soundtrack Pro supports the following third-party Time Stretch plug-ins: Serato Pitch 'n' Time, Sound Toys Speed, and iZotope Radius. If you have any of these plug-ins installed on your system, you'll be able to use it as the default audio stretch algorithm by choosing it in the Default Time Stretch pop-up menu.

## Truncating Overlapping Clips

You now have your rerecorded dialogue clips nudged into place and time-stretched to the same duration as the source audio. This should accurately synchronize your new audio clips to the actor's performance. The next step is to remove the original dialogue so it isn't heard along with your rerecorded dialogue. You could accomplish this by using the Blade tool to split the original audio clips, and then deleting the sections of the clips that you recorded replacement audio for. But there is a faster method: using the replacement dialogue clips themselves to truncate the clips in track A1.

First, a little cleanup is necessary. When you time-stretched your audio clips in the previous exercise, some "dead air" space was probably added to the end of your tightly edited clips. You need to remove this silence prior to moving these audio clips up to the A1 track to truncate the original audio.

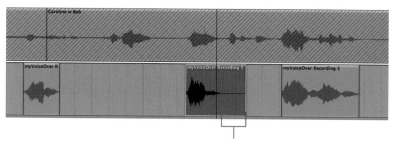

Silence added to end of clip by time-stretching

**1**   Click the Selection Tool button (A).

**2**   Adjust the right edge of any clip that needs the silence removed (for more information about working with clips, see the earlier exercise "Using the Selection Tool").

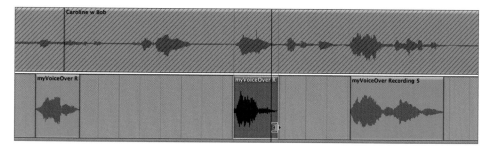

NOTE ▶ If you still have the File Editor tab open, it will display the resize action as you perform it in the Multitrack Editor. This can be useful for getting a precise view of your edits as you make them.

3    Using the Selection tool, drag across all of the clips in the myVoiceOver track to select them.

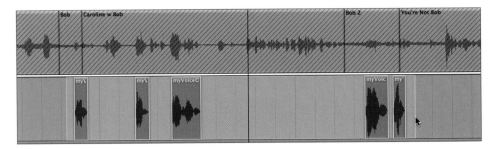

4    At the top of the Timeline, click the Truncate button.

Soundtrack Pro's default mode, Crossfade, will place fade transitions on overlapping clips. For this exercise, you'll have Soundtrack Pro truncate the clips, automatically performing split edits where the clips overlap.

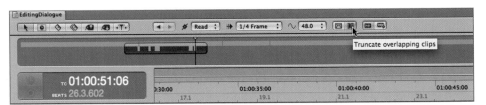

You may need to unlock the A1 track so you can replace the audio in it with your rerecorded dialogue clips.

5    If necessary, Control-click or right-click the header of track A1, and choose Unlock Selected Track from the shortcut menu.

The diagonal lines across track A1 are removed, indicating that the track is no longer locked.

**6**   Hold down the Shift key, and then drag the selected clips from your dialogue recording track up to track A1.

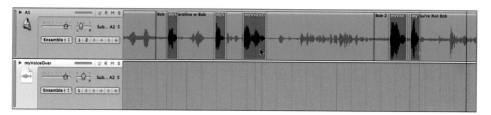

Holding down the Shift key while you drag the clips forces the clips to move only in the direction that you first drag them. In this instance you dragged them vertically, so by holding the Shift key you restrict them to moving between tracks and don't allow them to slip forward or backward in time. This ensures that the clips stay perfectly in sync as you drag them to the A1 track.

Performing this edit in Truncate mode causes Soundtrack Pro to split the audio clips originally on track A1 at the points where the new clips are dragged onto them.

**7**   Hold down the Shift key and move the selected clips back down to the myVoiceOver track.

The clips in the A1 track that were truncated now have empty space where you placed the new dialogue clips.

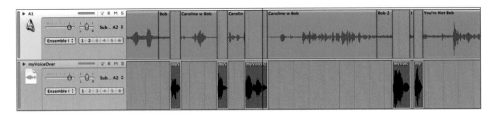

**NOTE** ▶ Keeping audio from different sources on separate tracks makes your work easier when you get to the mixing process. Having the rerecorded clips on their own track makes them easier to identify. Also, by returning the rerecorded dialogue to its own track, you'll be better able to utilize track-based processing in your mixing session (see Lesson 11, "Mixing Multitrack Projects").

8    Play the project and listen to the edits you've made.

There are a few more steps to take to finesse this sequence into a seamless-sounding dialogue track. The absence of ambient sound from the on-set location in the new dialogue recordings makes them sound unnatural. Also, the volume of your dialogue recordings probably doesn't match the volume of the dialogue in the original recording. In the next exercises you'll perform the necessary adjustments to make this dialogue replacement sound convincing.

## Blending the Rerecorded Dialogue into the Scene

The replacement dialogue has been recorded and edited. In the following exercises you'll learn techniques for mixing the rerecorded dialogue into the scene.

## Creating a Cycle Region

When working on a mix, it often helps to create a *cycle region*. A cycle region is a section of the sequence that will loop repeatedly on playback. This allows your ears to adjust to the sound and lets you focus on the mix without interruption.

1    In the Time ruler at the top of the Timeline, drag from left to right to create a cycle region around the area of the Timeline that contains the first three "yeses." You must drag in the lower half of the Time ruler to create a cycle region.

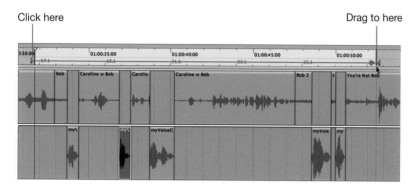

Soundtrack Pro sets In and Out points in the Timeline.

2    Press the spacebar to play your project.

As the project plays, notice that it automatically loops from the Out point back to the In point.

3    Press the spacebar to stop playback.

**NOTE ▶** To disable cycle playback without clearing your cycle region, press the C key or click the Cycle button in the transport area at the bottom of the workspace. Press the C key or click the Cycle button again to enable cycle playback again.

## Adjusting Track Volume

The volume of your rerecorded dialogue needs to be adjusted so that it blends with other audio clips. This is the point where you really must put on your audio engineer's hat and depend on your ears more than your eyes. Listen carefully as you work through the steps below.

1    Press the spacebar to start the playback of your cycle.

2   As the cycle plays, adjust the volume slider on the track header.

Moving the slider left decreases the volume, whereas moving the slider right increases the volume.

3   When you've set the volume so that the recorded dialogue blends evenly with the source audio, press the spacebar to stop playback.

The track volume slider is useful for setting an overall level, but you're going to use other techniques to mix the dialogue tracks now. Remember the value that the volume slider is set at because in the next steps you'll use an action to make the same adjustment.

4   Double-click the volume slider to reset it to 0 dB. Double-clicking any slider resets it to its default value.

## Using Actions to Adjust Clip Volume

In addition to using the track volume slider to adjust the volume, you can use actions to apply volume adjustments. Both are useful techniques for setting clip volume.

1   In the Timeline, select the first clip on the myVoiceOver track.

The File Editor tab is still open in the lower pane, so the audio file appears there; the region representing the clip is selected. However, the volume change we applied to the track affects every clip in the track, and several clips are part of this one audio file. Consequently, we need to apply the volume change to the *entire file* to ensure that each clip's volume is properly adjusted.

**2**   Click anywhere on the File Editor tab to make sure it's in focus.

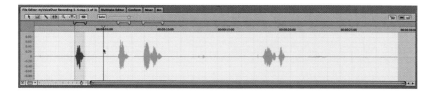

**3**   Press Command-A to select the entire audio file.

**4**   Choose Process > Adjust Amplitude.

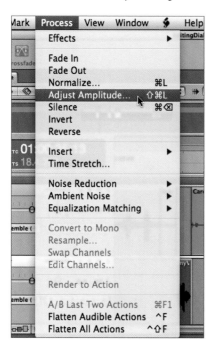

The Adjust Amplitude dialog appears. Through actions, you can use this function to adjust the volume of the audio file.

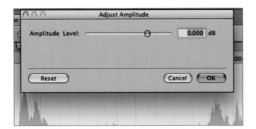

**5**    In the number field on the right of the Adjust Amplitude dialog, enter the value that was set on the volume slider from step 1, and click OK.

> **NOTE ►** If you attenuated, or lowered, the volume of your track, make sure you put a minus (–) in front of the input volume so Soundtrack Pro knows to decrease the volume. Positive values will increase the volume.

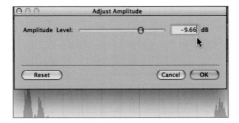

Soundtrack Pro adjusts the volume of the entire audio file, which includes all Timeline clips that are part of the audio file. To prove this, follow the next step.

**6**    In the Timeline, select any of the first three audio clips in the myVoiceOver track.

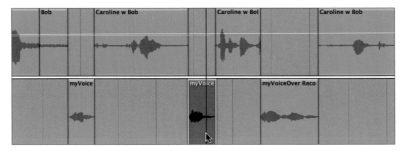

**7**   Click the Actions tab in the left pane.

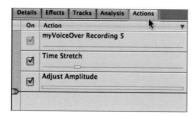

The Adjust Amplitude action has been applied to the clip. Furthermore, the bar representing the part of the clip to which the action has been applied spans the entire clip, not just a section, indicating that the action was applied to the whole clip.

**8**   Press the spacebar to play the cycle region.

You can hear that the volume has been adjusted for all three clips.

**NOTE** ▸ You can change the volume assigned to this action by double-clicking the Adjust Amplitude action in the Actions list and changing the volume assigned to the action.

## Working with Ambient Noise

With the volume adjusted, you can now hear clearly how your dialogue clips lack the ambient noise of the source audio stream. This change in ambience between your rerecorded dialogue recordings and the source audio is abrupt and noticeable.

It's important that the ambient sound be consistent throughout the scene. When dialogue is rerecorded, as you've done in this exercise, ambient sound recorded in the original setting needs to be mixed with it as well. Soundtrack Pro provides a way to do this very quickly.

**1**   In track A1, use the Time Slice tool to select the end of the first clip. Select from a point after the woman has said "Bob" to the end of the clip.

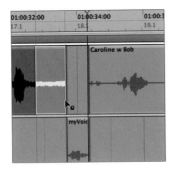

**2**  Choose Process > Ambient Noise > Set Ambient Noise Print (Control-Command-Y).

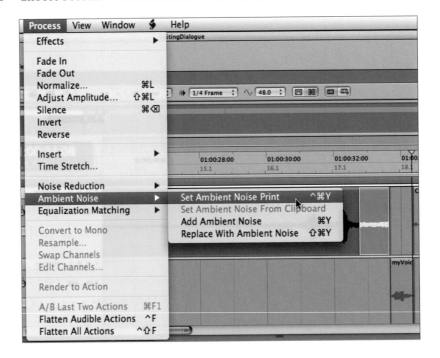

Soundtrack Pro uses the sound in the clip as the basis for an *ambient noise print*.

**NOTE** ▶ You can also select a portion of a file for an ambient noise print in the lower pane's File Editor tab.

**3**  Switch back to the Selection tool and select the first "yes" clip in the myVoiceOver track.

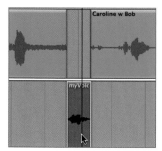

**4**  Choose Process > Ambient Noise > Add Ambient Noise (Command-Y).

**5**  Play the project and listen to the results of the Add Ambient Noise process.

The ambient noise lifted from the first clip has been applied to the second clip, and the transition into the recorded dialogue clip is now seamless.

Add Ambient Noise is now listed in the Actions tab. If you need to remove the action at any time you can delete or disable it here.

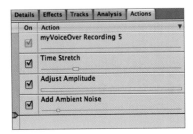

**TIP** The Process > Ambient Noise menu contains a command called Replace With Ambient Noise. Choosing this option directly replaces the selected clip (or portion of a clip) with the sound contained in the ambient noise print. This can be useful, for example, if you have a scene with several expletives you need to bleep out. Just import a "bleep" sound somewhere in your project, set it as the noise print, and then select and replace all the words you need to bleep out with the ambient noise print.

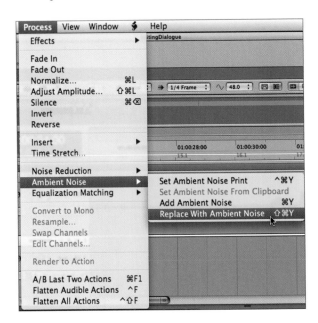

# Lesson Review

1.  What are the key commands for the Selection (arrow) and Blade tools, respectively?

2.  True or false: The Timeslice tool can be used to select portions of clips, whereas the Selection tool can select only entire clips.

3.  How do you time-stretch an audio clip?

4.  How do you create a cycle region?

5.  What is an ambient noise print?

## *Answers*

1.  A for the Selection tool, and B for the Blade tool.

2.  True.

3.  Select the clip to open it in the File Editor, and then use the Audio Stretching tool to select a portion (or all) of the clip. Finally, use the Stretch pointer to drag the edges of the selected clip to the correct duration.

4.  Drag horizontally in the Time ruler at the top of the Timeline to create In and Out points defining the cycle region, and then click the Cycle button (C) in the transport controls to activate the cycle region.

5.  An ambient noise print is a section of audio you define and set by choosing Process > Ambient Noise > Set Ambient Noise Print. Once the ambient noise print is set, you can apply it to any clip in your project, and Soundtrack Pro will mix the ambient noise print with the sounds already contained in the selected clip.

# 8

Lesson Files     Lesson Files > Lesson 08 > 08_MultitakeEditing.stmp

Time     This lesson takes approximately 40 minutes to complete.

Goals     Create a guide track

Create a multitake clip

Cycle record directly into the Multitake Editor

Manage takes in the Multitake Editor

Split, slip, and arrange takes

Create a composite multitake clip

Add crossfades between takes

# Lesson 8
# Automated Dialogue Replacement Using the Multitake Editor

Dialogue replacement is a key feature of Soundtrack Pro, and the latest version of the software makes it easier than ever to sync studio-recorded dialogue with field-recorded video. In the previous two lessons, you used a manual method of dialogue replacement that involved recording a take and then using cutting, shifting, nudging, time-stretching, and other techniques to match the rerecorded audio to the performance. As you may have discovered, this process can be time-consuming. On a positive note, the experience taught you to work with all of Soundtrack Pro's editing tools and showed you the editing techniques that make up the core of all audio editing work. In most other *DAWs* (digital audio workstations), this relatively tedious method of replacing dialogue is the only available option. Soundtrack Pro, however, provides a far more advanced method of replacing dialogue: The Multitake Editor.

The Multitake Editor allows you to record multiple takes into one clip in the Timeline. These synchronized recordings can be adjusted, and then mixed and matched to produce one perfect take called a *composite*. The industry term for this is *automated dialogue replacement*, or ADR for short.

Once the ADR is complete, the multitake clip is collapsed and treated as a single, easy-to-work-with clip in the Timeline. And the whole process is nondestructive.

## About Multitake Editing

Cycle recording, the process of using looped playback to record multiple takes of a performance, is one of the most powerful features in any DAW. The process is simple: Create a cycle region (as you did in Lesson 7) and then record. As the cycle loops from its end to the beginning, the DAW creates a new take for each pass through the cycle. In most other DAWs, each new take is created on its own individual track, which results in several, or dozens, of tracks in the Timeline, each of which must be individually managed. Soundtrack Pro provides a more advanced, yet easier to manage, cycle recording process which places all the takes inside a single clip. This is the foundation of multitake editing.

## Setting Up for Multitake Editing

Before you start cycle recording, you'll want to create an empty track to record on.

1 In the Lesson 08 folder, open **08_MultitakeEditing.stmp**, or continue working on your project from the previous lesson.

2 On the myVoiceOver track, click the mute (M) button.

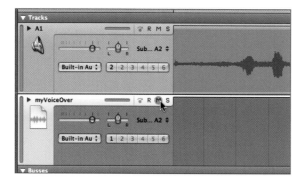

The track is now muted and will no longer be heard. You don't need to hear this track because you're about to record new dialogue takes for these parts.

**3**   Control-click or right-click the track header for the myVoiceOver track, and choose Insert Track Before in the shortcut menu that appears.

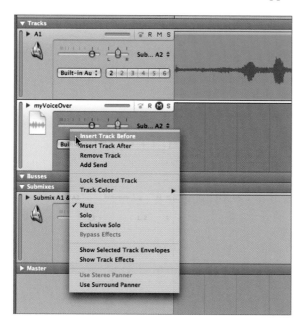

Soundtrack Pro creates a new track above the myVoiceOver track.

**4**   Name the new track *Multitake*.

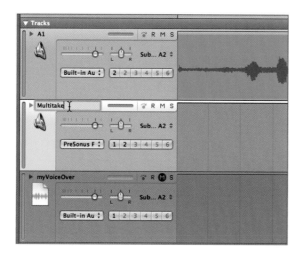

You now have a track prepared for recording. In the next step you'll create a guide take to serve as a blueprint for the replacement dialogue you're about to record.

## Creating a Guide Take

A *guide take* is a master take for a voiceover session. Most often its origin is the audio that was recorded on set. For one reason or another, the on-set audio can't be used—perhaps too much background noise was recorded, or an actor stumbled over a word, or some other faux pas has ruined an otherwise great performance. Rerecording the dialogue offers the opportunity to fix these problems, but to keep the audience in their seats you must be sure the rerecorded dialogue lip syncs with the original performance. A guide take makes this easier for the talent and the engineer alike.

> **NOTE ►** In some voiceover sessions it isn't necessary to use a guide take. For example, when recording voiceover that isn't tied to an onscreen actor (such as narration), you can skip the creation of the guide take and begin by cycle recording. When you use cycle recording to record multiple passes, Soundtrack Pro automatically creates a multitake clip and loads it into the Multitake Editor, as explained below.

1   Find the **GuideTrack.aiff** audio file, located in the Lesson 08 folder.

This audio file contains the on-set sound recording of the portion of the scene you're working on.

2   Drag this audio file to the Soundtrack Pro Timeline. Position it over the track named Multitake that you created, and place the clip so that the left edge of the clip is roughly just to the left of the first "yes" that you rerecorded in the last lesson.

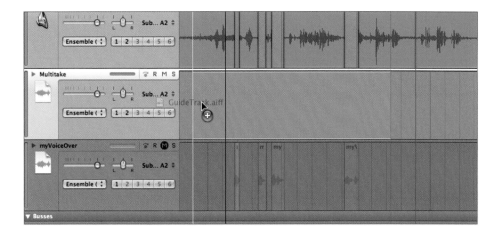

The clip is placed on the track. When the waveform appears you should notice the similarity between the GuideTrack clip and the clips on the A1 track.

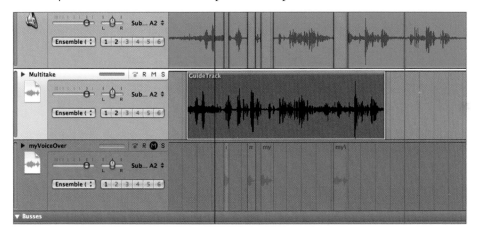

**3**   Play the sequence from the start of the GuideTrack clip.

You'll hear the dialogue echo because the two tracks are not quite in sync. Depending on where you dropped the GuideTrack clip, you may hear it play either before or after the audio in the A1 track. You need to align the GuideTrack to the A1 track. Because the two tracks are adjacent to each other, it's easy to do this by sight. A good reference mark to use for this is the very beginning of the clip where the female actor says, "Hello, Bob?"

4 Zoom in on the beginning of the GuideTrack clip.

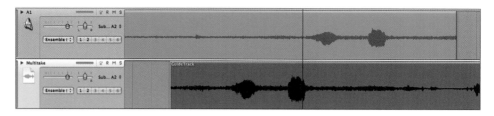

The waveforms clearly indicate the words "hello" and "Bob."

5 Move the GuideTrack clip to align its waveforms with those in the A1 track.

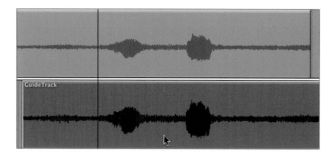

You should be able to get the waveforms closely aligned without too much difficulty. If you'd like to synchronize them even more precisely, zoom in, and then fine-tune the GuideTrack clip's position. You can use the Nudge commands (Command–Left Arrow and Command–Right Arrow) you learned in Lesson 7 to do this very precisely if you wish.

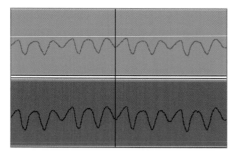

The A1 track and the Multitake track, zoomed in to the maximum level to verify sync

Now that the GuideTrack clip is synced to the video, you'll turn it into a multitake clip, and then cycle record dialogue in the Multitake Editor.

## The Multitake Editor

The Multitake Editor is like a multitrack editor built into a single audio clip. It's specifically designed for the task of building a *comp*, or *composite take*. A comp is a performance built by selecting the best parts from multiple takes and editing them together to become a single, ideal performance. The Multitake Editor makes it easy for you to select the good parts of a take, omit the bad parts, slip the audio to perfect the sync, and then apply crossfades between the comped takes to smooth them into the illusion of a single take performed flawlessly.

## Converting a Clip into a Multitake Clip

You've established a guide take for the dialogue replacement session, so now you can convert the guide take clip into a multitake clip and begin working in the Multitake Editor.

1   Control-click or right-click the GuideTrack clip and select Convert to Multitake Clip in the pop-up menu.

The clip is converted to a multitake clip. In the lower pane, the Multitake Editor tab jumps into focus.

The guide take is currently the only take in the Multitake Editor, but you're about to record several new dialogue takes very quickly. Before adding new takes you should rename the guide take for easy reference.

## Naming Takes

As your takes list grows, it becomes a smart idea to name each take for easy reference.

**1** In the header of the guide take, click the name.

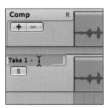

A text field appears.

**2** Type *Guide Take* and press Return.

The take is renamed.

## Cycle Recording in the Multitake Editor

There are two ways to use cycle recording in Soundtrack Pro. The first is to do so in the Timeline, much like the recording you did in Lesson 7. To cycle record in the Timeline you simply set a cycle region, arm a track, and click the Record button, at which point Soundtrack Pro will record multiple passes of the cycle as new takes. It will then collect those takes into a multitake clip that you can edit in the Multitake Editor. However, if you already have a multitake clip, as you've just created in the previous exercises, Soundtrack Pro allows you to record new takes directly in the Multitake Editor. Because you have a guide take to follow for your current dialogue replacement task, this is the ideal workflow for the recording you're about to perform.

1   In the upper-left corner of the Multitake Editor, click the Arm for Recording button.

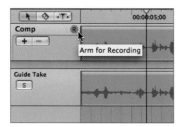

The Multitake Editor is now armed for recording. In the Timeline, the Multitake track is also now armed. The Multitake Editor and the track that the multitake clip lives on are linked together. When the Multitake Editor is used for cycle recording, no track other than the one the multitake clip resides on can also be armed for recording.

In the Timeline, Soundtrack Pro has set a cycle region to the start and end points of the multitake clip that is now armed for cycle recording.

**NOTE ▸** The recording settings for the Multitake Editor are taken from the track the multitake clip lives on. If you need to make changes to your hardware's input settings you should do so prior to arming the Multitake Editor for recording. Select the track where the multitake clip resides, and then configure your hardware in the right pane. (See Lesson 6 for detailed instructions on configuring input settings for recording.)

Soundtrack Pro automatically sets a cycle region to
the start and end points of the multitake clip.

**2**   In the transport controls, click the Record button (or press Command-R).

Soundtrack Pro begins recording. Watch the video in the left pane's Video tab, listen
to the guide take, and record your voiceover "yeses." Perform at least three passes so
you have a good selection of takes to work with.

**3**   When you've finished recording three to five takes, press the spacebar to stop
recording.

**NOTE** ▸ You can also press Command-R or click the Play/Pause button in the transport controls to stop recording.

When you stop the transport, the new takes immediately appear in the Multitake
Editor.

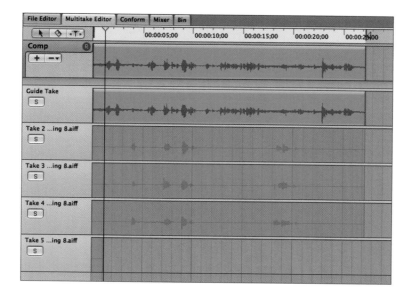

4    Click the Arm for Recording button in the upper-left corner of the Multitake Editor (or press the R key) to unarm the track.

NOTE ▶ A multitake clip is similar to a nested sequence in Final Cut Pro. The clip in the Timeline is like the nested clip, whereas the Multitake Editor is like stepping into the nest, where you can see the stacked tracks that make up the nested clip. Like other types of nested sequences, the edits performed inside the nest are reflected in the parent clip in the Timeline.

## Deleting a Take

Before you start compositing your takes, you may need to perform a little cleanup. If the cycle recording looped around to start a new take before you stopped the transport, you may have a take at the bottom of the take list that's empty (see Take 5 in the figure at the end of the previous exercise). To clean up the window you can delete this take.

NOTE ▶ If you don't have a blank take at the bottom of your take list, you may skip this step.

1  In the upper-left corner of the Multitake Editor, hold down the Remove Take button.

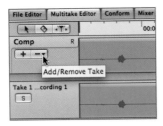

2  Select the take you wish to remove.

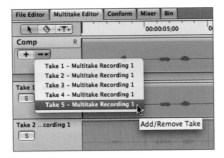

The take is removed from the list.

## Adding a Prerecorded Take

Occasionally you'll need to add a prerecorded take to your multitake clip. You might do this to add a guide take to a multitake clip that already exists or, as in this example, to add a dialogue take that was recorded in another studio so it can be included in the comp.

1  Click the Add Take button in the upper-left corner of the Multitake Editor.

2  Select the **myVoiceOver Recording 5** file and click Open.

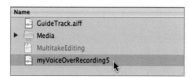

A new take is added to the bottom of the Multitake Editor.

**NOTE** ▸ You can also add a take by dragging an audio file from the Finder to the Multitake Editor.

3    Rename the take you just added *Prerecorded Take*.

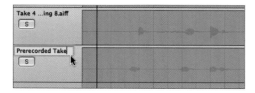

The take is renamed.

## Reordering Takes

The Prerecorded Take track is currently at the bottom of the Multitake Editor. Let's move it up in the takes list so that it's just below the guide take.

1    Drag the header of the Prerecorded Take track until it's just below the Guide Take header.

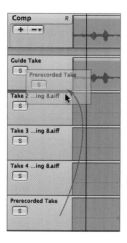

The take is moved into position just below the guide take.

## Auditioning Takes

The active take, or the one that's playing, always appears in a brighter green, whereas the muted takes are a faded green, indicating that they won't be heard. By default, the first take in the Multitake Editor is the one that plays, but you can choose to play any take by simply clicking it. Select the guide take now so that it's the track that will be heard.

1   In the Multitake Editor, click the Guide Take track.

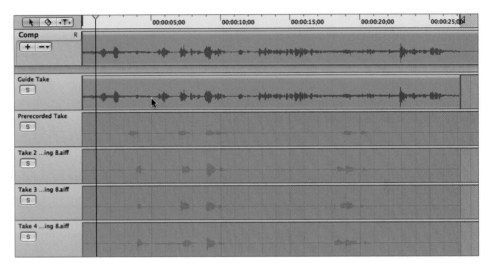

The guide take is selected and the other takes become muted.

2   Press the spacebar to play the cycle region.

Because the guide take is the active track in the Multitake Editor, its waveform is visible in the multitake clip in the Timeline.

3   Click the Prerecorded Take track to select it.

If the transport was still in motion when you clicked the Prerecorded Take track, Soundtrack Pro immediately mutes the Guide Take track and begins playing the track you have selected.

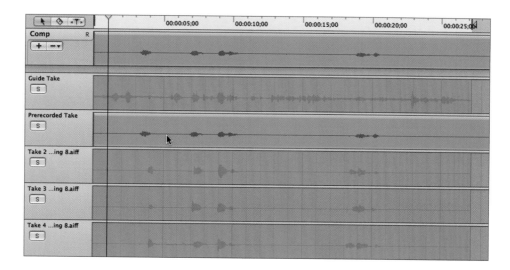

With the Prerecorded Take track playing, you should notice that the "yeses" in this take don't sync up with the Guide Take track very well. Particularly, the first "yes" comes in much earlier than the onscreen actor's performance.

## Slipping Takes

Currently, the Prerecorded Take track is out of sync with your recorded takes.

To move the Prerecorded Take track into closer sync, you need to *slip* it along the Multitake Editor Timeline. In video editor's jargon, a slip edit is one that shifts the position of the media left or right inside a clip, without changing the In or Out points of the clip itself. In other words, the clip stays in its same time position in the Timeline, but the media inside the clip change position. To perform a slip edit, follow these steps.

1   Hold down Command-Option and drag the Prerecorded Take clip left or right until the first "yes" waveform roughly syncs with the "yes" waveform in the Guide Take track.

2   Continue holding down Command-Option and drag the take track left or right until the first "yes" waveform in Take 1 roughly aligns with the "yes" waveform in the Guide Take track.

You don't need to sync the takes exactly; just get it close. You'll refine this for a more accurate lip sync as you work through the rest of this lesson.

## Creating a Composite Take

The purpose of the Multitake Editor is to assemble a composite take, or master take, from regions of the takes in the takes list. The Comp track, located at the top of the Multitake Editor, always displays the take that will play in the Timeline. To create a composite take, you split, slip, and select portions of your takes to place them into the Comp track so that they'll be played in the Timeline exactly as you wish.

## Splitting Takes

Splitting a take enables you to separate the portion of the take that you want from the unwanted portion. You'll use the Multitake Editor's Blade tool to perform a split.

1    In the Multitake Editor, select the Blade tool (B).

2    With the Blade tool, click after the first "yes" in the Guide Take track.

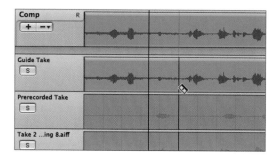

A transition point is created, and each take track, including the Guide Take track, is split into two regions.

**NOTE ▸** The Blade tool in the Multitake Editor acts like the Razor Blade All tool in Final Cut Pro, cutting a vertical line through all the takes.

3  Using the Blade tool, click before the third "yes" in the Guide Take track.

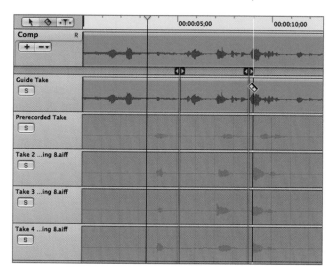

Each take is split into three regions.

4   In the Multitake Editor, click the Selection Tool button (A).

5   Slip the "yeses" region of each take track until each is roughly in sync with the "yeses" in the Guide Take track (for more information, see the earlier exercise "Slipping Takes").

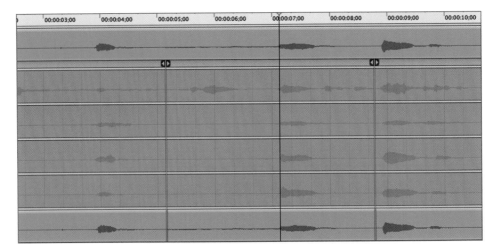

You can now see, visually, that the "yeses" in your recorded takes are roughly aligned with the "yeses" in the Guide Take track. You could refine these edits further, but for now let's move on to the next step in the process.

## Selecting Takes

You've split the takes into regions and slipped the recorded take tracks so that they're roughly synced with the Guide Take track. Next, you'll select the part of each take to be used in the final composite.

1   Press the spacebar to play the cycle region.

The cycle region begins playing.

2   As the cycle plays, click each region of each take, listen closely, and watch the Video
tab to see which takes sound the best and are in closest sync with the performance of
the onscreen actor.

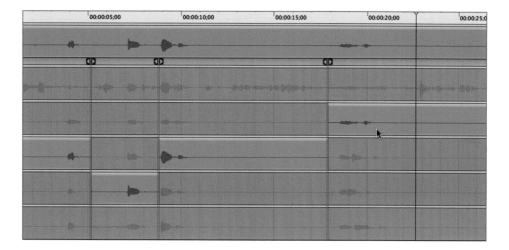

As you select different regions of the takes, each one in turn becomes the "active" take
and the Comp track at the top of the Multitake Editor updates to display the waveform of the combination of selected regions. The Multitake Editor makes it extremely
easy to evaluate and arrange multiple takes to piece together the best possible track.

NOTE ▸ The multitake clip in the Timeline also updates to show the waveform of the
Comp track.

3   Where necessary, slip the selected regions to fine-tune their sync with the onscreen
actor (for more information, see the earlier exercise "Slipping Takes").

## Using Transitions

You've now recorded multiple voiceover takes, synced them with a guide track, edited
them, and selected the best regions from each take to create a composite. The final step in

finishing the comp is applying transitions to smooth the edits. This helps hide any sign that the finished track is a composite, and convinces the audience that what they're hearing is natural sound.

## Adding Transitions

A transition is a smooth fade between two pieces of audio. Transitions can make the difference between sketchy, Frankenstein edits and undetectable edits that sound indistinguishable from audio recorded flawlessly on set. Transitions are applied to multitake clips directly in the Multitake Editor.

1  At the top of the first transition point, where you split the take with the Blade tool, drag the arrow handles left and right to spread them apart.

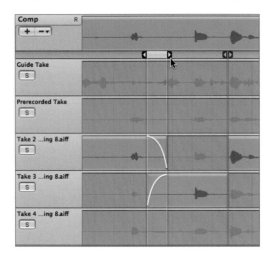

This creates a crossfade. The fade lines show you that the end of the first region will fade into the beginning of the second region. You'll work with these fades in more detail in the next section. First, apply transitions to the other splits.

2  At the top of the second transition point, drag the arrow handles left and right to spread them apart.

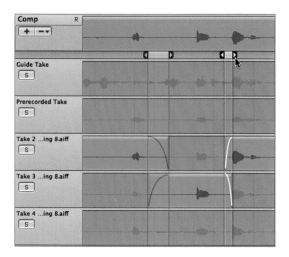

## Working with Fades

The transitions you applied in the previous steps were the default crossfade. Soundtrack Pro provides several different types of fades. One fade type may sound better than another for a certain transition, so it's important to be familiar with Soundtrack Pro's Fade Selector.

1   Double-click directly under the fade line in the first crossfade.

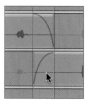

The Fade Selector appears. Down the left edge of the Fade Selector are four types of fades.

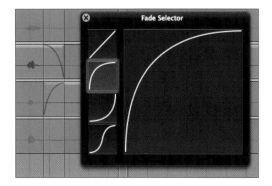

2   Select the type of fade you want (for more information about fade types, see Lesson 9).

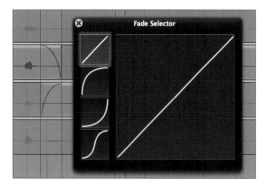

3   In the upper-left corner of the Fade Selector, click the close button.

The Fade Selector closes.

4   Repeat steps 1 through 3 to adjust the remaining fades in the Multitake Editor.

NOTE ▶ You can change the length of your fades at any time by positioning the pointer over the fade's left or right edge, and dragging.

When you're satisfied with your transitions in the Multitake Editor, play the entire sequence in the Timeline and evaluate how your dialogue replacement blends into the scene.

## Lesson Review

1.  How do you convert a regular clip to a multitake clip?

2.  What does cycle recording do?

3.  What is the function of the Multitake Editor?

4.  What does slipping a clip do?

5.  How do you slip a clip in Soundtrack Pro?

6.  In the Multitake Editor, what is a transition?

7.  True or false: You can't change the default fade in the Multitake Editor's transitions.

### *Answers*

1.  Control-click or right-click the clip and choose Convert to Multitake Clip.

2.  Each time the cycle loops from the Out point back to the In point, Soundtrack Pro records a new take into the clip. These takes are stacked in the Multitake Editor.

3.  The Multitake Editor lets you mix and match regions of different takes to produce a composite take.

4.  Slipping maintains the clip's position in the Timeline, but moves the media in the clip forward or backward in time.

5.  Hold down Command-Option while dragging the clip left or right.

6.  A transition is a smooth fade from one take to the next.

7.  False: You can select from four types of fades for Multitake Editor transitions.

# 9

**Lesson Files**     Lesson Files > Lesson 09 > 09_Leverage_Promo.fcp

**Media**     Leverage

**Time**     This lesson takes approximately 40 minutes to complete.

**Goals**     Use several techniques to spot sound effects to the Timeline

Explore the Bin and the Browser

Use the Multipoint Video HUD to sync audio clips to video

Create a three-point edit

Use the Search tab to find sound effects by keyword

Reset the End of Project marker

# Spotting Sound Effects

The previous lessons have focused a lot on working with dialogue in Soundtrack Pro. Dialogue is the main sound element in most video productions. However, sound effects and music also play vital roles in immersing your viewers in your video. Sound effects inform your viewers about the environment in which the onscreen action is taking place. Music directs your viewers' emotional response to what they're seeing.

In this lesson you'll explore techniques for *spotting*, or placing, sound effects at specific points in the Timeline. You'll also explore new tabs in the Soundtrack Pro interface that help you organize and find media files on your system.

## Setting Up for Spotting

In the remaining chapters of this book you'll be working with media from the television show *Leverage*.

**1**   In the Lesson 09 folder, open the **09_Leverage_Promo.fcp** project file in Final Cut Pro.

A sequence opens in Final Cut Pro.

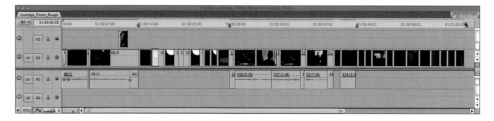

**2**   Play the sequence to familiarize yourself with the media you'll be working on.

This material from *Leverage* has been roughly cut into a 1-minute promotional piece, much like a trailer. Although the video is in place, the only audio present is the dialogue. The sequence lacks sound effects and music. In this lesson you'll add the sound effects. In the next lesson you'll create a musical score for the sequence.

**3**   In the Browser, Control-click or right-click the *Leverage_Promo_Rough* sequence and choose Send To > Soundtrack Pro Multitrack Project from the shortcut menu.

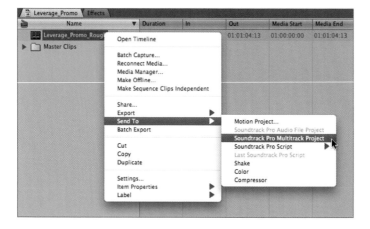

A Save dialog appears.

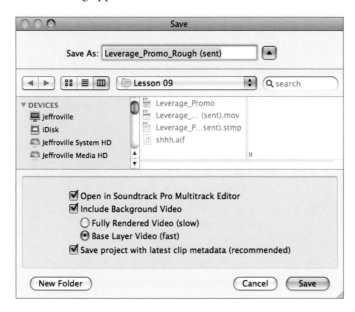

The clips in this sequence have color correction and fades applied. For this lesson it's beneficial to retain these effects by rendering the video as it's sent to Soundtrack Pro.

4    Select Fully Rendered Video (slow).

5    Save the new Soundtrack Pro project to the location you prefer on your hard drive.

The project opens in Soundtrack Pro.

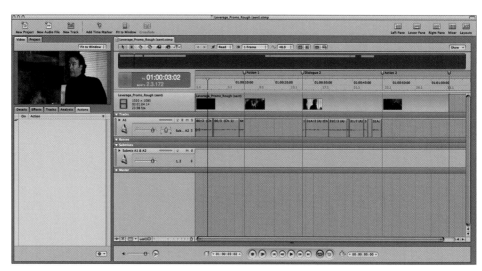

## Exploring the Bin and the Browser

Soundtrack Pro's Bin is your project's library. Any media used in the open project is listed in the Bin. The Bin also lists properties for each file, such as sample rate, channel configuration, and where in the Timeline the clip is located.

### Opening the Bin

The Bin is located in Soundtrack Pro's lower pane.

1   If the lower pane isn't open, click the Lower Pane button in the Toolbar.

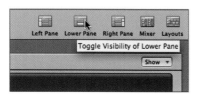

The lower pane opens.

**2**   Click the Bin tab.

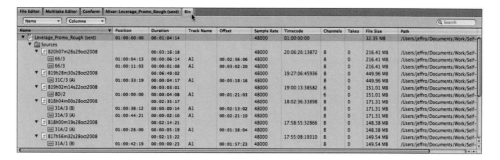

The Bin is a hierarchical list of the items referenced by the open project. At the top of the list are the project files. Within each project file, a list of the media files used in the project appears. Within each media file is a list of all the clips that reference that file.

## Previewing Files in the Bin

Files can be auditioned in the Bin. This is useful when you're uncertain which file contains the sound you're looking for.

**1**   Click the file named 31/7 (A) in the Bin.

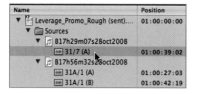

The file automatically plays, allowing you to identify it by ear.

**2**   Click the Pause button in the lower-left corner of the Bin.

Playback stops.

To the right of the Play/Pause button is a slider that controls the volume of the preview.

## Opening the Browser

The Browser is like a miniature Finder built into Soundtrack Pro. You'll use it to quickly find files on your hard drives and add them to your project.

1   If the right pane is not currently displayed, click the Right Pane button on the Toolbar.

The right pane opens.

2   In the lower portion of the right pane, click the Browser tab.

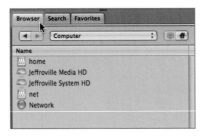

## Locating Files in the Browser

When you first open the Browser it displays the disks mounted on your system. You can double-click a disk to open it, and then navigate through the folders to find the media files you're interested in adding to your project. There's a sound effect file located in the Lesson 09 folder that you'll now add to this project.

**1**   In the Browser, double-click through the file hierarchy to find the **shhh.aif** file, located in the Lesson 09 folder.

**NOTE** ▶ If you navigate to the wrong folder, use the navigation buttons in the upper-left corner of the Browser tab to back your way up the folder hierarchy, or use the menu located at the top of the Browser tab to jump up several folders quickly.

**2**   Click the **shhh.aif** file to audition it.

The file plays. Media files can be previewed in the Browser in the same way they can be previewed in the Bin. The same controls you saw in the Bin for play/pause and volume control are also located at the bottom of the Browser.

## Adding Browser Files to Your Project

Once you've located a file in the Browser, you can simply drag it to the Timeline. To make it easier for you to spot this effect, markers were added to the project in Final Cut Pro. Those markers remained in the project when you sent it to Soundtrack Pro. The video editor created a marker to designate where in the Timeline this sound effect should be placed. You'll now spot this sound effect to that marker.

1    Position the playhead at the marker labeled "Shhh" (the 2nd marker in the Timeline) by pressing Shift-M until the playhead jumps to the marker.

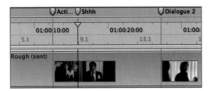

**NOTE** ▶ Shift-M jumps the playhead to the next marker in the Timeline; Option-M jumps the playhead to the previous marker in the Timeline. These key commands are the same in Final Cut Pro.

2    Press Command-T to add a new track to the Timeline.

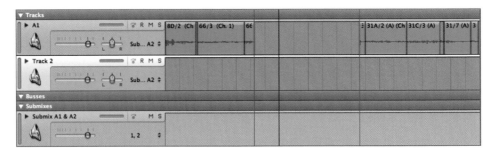

A new audio track is created.

3    Click the Track 2 in the new track's header.

4    Name the track *SFX*, and then press Return.

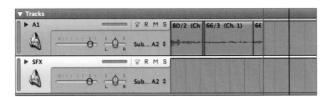

You now have a new track named SFX, and it should already be selected.

5   In the Browser, Control-click or right-click the **Shhh.aif** file and choose Spot to Playhead.

The sound file is placed in the SFX track at the playhead's position.

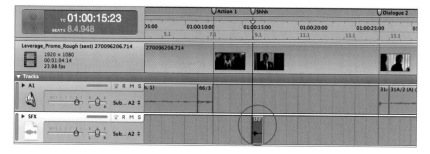

6   Press the spacebar to hear the sound effect in the Timeline and watch the Video tab.

You'll notice that the sound effect is not quite synchronized with the action in the video. In the next exercise you'll use the Multipoint Video HUD (heads-up display) to place the sound clip precisely in sync with the video in the Timeline.

**NOTE ▶** You can also add files to the Timeline by dragging them from the Bin or Browser. Alternatively, you can drag a file directly from the Finder to the Timeline to add it to your project.

## Using the Multipoint Video HUD

The Multipoint Video HUD is a powerful tool for placing audio clips in precise sync with the video. You'll use it to reposition the clip you added to the Timeline in the previous exercise so that it aligns with the onscreen action.

**1** Choose Window > HUDs > Multipoint Video, or press V on your keyboard.

> **NOTE ▶** Pressing V toggles the Multipoint Video HUD display. If the HUD isn't onscreen when you press V, it appears, but if the Multipoint Video HUD is already onscreen, it disappears.

The Multipoint Video HUD opens.

The Multipoint Video HUD contains three video windows. You need to be able to see them easily. If the HUD is too small for you to clearly view the video you should resize the HUD.

**2**  Drag the lower-right corner of the Multipoint Video HUD to make it bigger.

## Spotting with the Multipoint Video HUD

The Multipoint Video HUD displays several frames of video, each with a timecode value. This HUD's primary purpose is to provide context as you edit in Soundtrack Pro by showing you exactly which frames of video the audio clip you're working on will sync to.

This HUD behaves in different ways depending on what you have selected in the workspace. For example, if you select a marker (with no duration) at the top of the Timeline, the Multipoint Video HUD shows only a single frame of video, because markers with no assigned duration represent only a single moment in time, and thus are attached to one frame of video. (Markers, and marker duration, will be discussed in more detail in Lesson 10.)

Single marker displayed in the Multipoint Video HUD

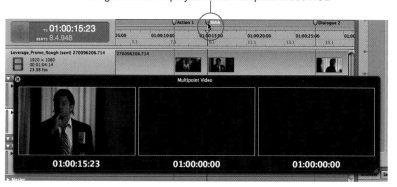

On the other hand, when you select a clip that has duration, the left frame of the HUD shows the first frame of video in the selected clip, while the right frame of the HUD shows the last frame of video in the selected clip. The frame in the middle of the HUD displays the frame of video directly under the pointer's position when you select the audio clip. Zoom in on the clip you added to the Timeline so that you can use the HUD to accurately sync it to the video.

1   Press Shift-M to move the playhead to the "Shhh" marker (or Option-M if the play-head is after the marker in the Timeline).

2   Press Command-Equal Sign (=) to zoom in until you can clearly see the audio clip added in the last section.

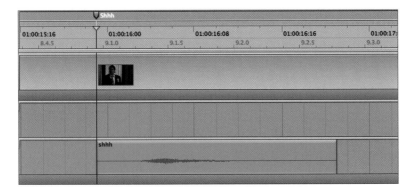

At this closer zoom level, you can see that there's a section of silence at the beginning of the clip. This means that you can't simply sync the beginning of the clip to the frame of video in which the action occurs.

3   Position the pointer over the part of the clip where the sound begins, and then hold down the mouse button.

A thin blue line extends vertically across the Timeline from the pointer's position. This line gives you a visual reference of the clicked point in the audio clip that extends to the Time ruler as well as through the clips on any other tracks. The middle frame of the HUD updates to show you the frame of video directly under this blue line as well.

4   Drag the clip left or right until the clicked point of the clip lines up with the "Shhh" marker. Watch the middle frame of the HUD as you do so.

Release the clip where the actor's finger comes up to his lips to make the shushing sound.

5   Move the playhead to a point before the clip, and play the sequence to evaluate the clip's spotting.

You can continue to fine-tune the clip's placement by dragging the clip left or right. By zooming in on the clip more, you'll make more precise movements as you drag. When you're satisfied with the clip's placement, press V to close the HUD.

**NOTE** ▸ You can also nudge the clip by pressing Command–Left Arrow or Command–Right Arrow. Refer to Lesson 7 for instructions on how to set the nudge amount.

## Three-Point Edits

In the world of video editing, three-point edits provide a common technique for adding selections to the Timeline. In a three-point edit, you specify an In point and an Out point in a clip, and then add the selected section to the Timeline at the playhead's current position.

If you're familiar with the three-point editing workflow in Final Cut Pro you'll quickly learn the technique in Soundtrack Pro. The major difference is that instead of selecting your In and Out points in Final Cut Pro's Viewer, you select them in Soundtrack Pro's File Editor.

In the steps below, you'll use the three-point editing technique to isolate a part of a sound effect from a sound file and spot it to the appropriate video frame.

1    In the lower pane, click the File Editor tab.

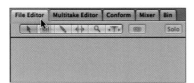

2    From the Browser, drag the **electric sync.caf** file into the File Editor.

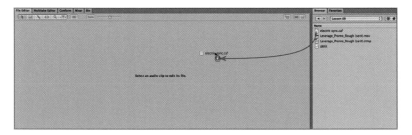

**3** Press the spacebar to play the file.

This is a long sound effect. You'll only need to use about 1/4 of it.

**4** In the File Editor, make sure that the Selection tool is selected, and then drag to create a selection from about 01:00:01:07 to the end of the file.

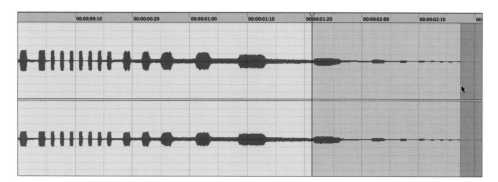

**5** Press the spacebar to play the sound.

It's a warbling electronic tone. Now you'll spot this sound to each place in the project that a phone shows a time syncing application.

**6** In the Multitrack Editor, move the playhead to timecode 01:00:52:06.

How you move the playhead is up to you. You can enter the timecode directly into the Timecode display, drag in the upper half of the Time ruler, or use any other technique you've learned.

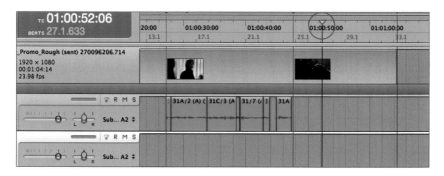

**7** In the Multitrack Editor, select the SFX track header if it isn't already selected.

**8** In the upper-right corner of the File Editor, click the Spot to Playhead button, or press Command-Backslash (\).

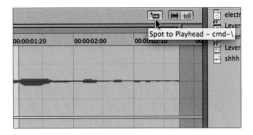

The selected part of the audio file is added to the SFX track as a clip, with the beginning of the selection spotted to the playhead's position in the Timeline.

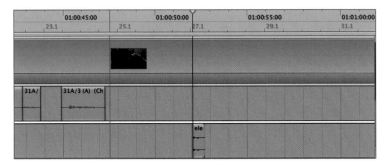

**9** Play the project from slightly before the newly added clip, listen to the effect, and watch the Video tab to evaluate the sound effect's sync.

**10** Move the playhead to timecode 01:00:54:09.

**11** Press Command-Backslash (\) to spot the selection to the playhead.

**12** Find the next place where a phone appears and park the playhead on the video frame in which a timer appears (approximately 01:00:57:21).

**13** Press Command-Backslash (\) to spot the selection to the playhead.

**14** Spot the same sound effect for the final character's part in the sequence. Place the playhead where you think the sound fits best between 01:00:59:02 and 01:01:00:16.

**15** Press Command-Backslash (\) to spot the selection to the playhead.

You've now placed the selected portion of the sound effect in four carefully spotted locations in the project. Your Timeline should look similar to the figure below.

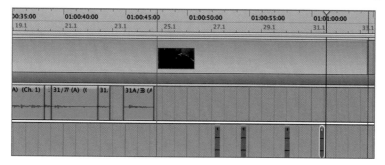

## Using the Search Tab to Find and Spot Sound Effects

Soundtrack Pro comes with an immense library of sound effects and music loops. The Search tab makes it easy to find just the audio file you're looking for in the thousands of audio files Soundtrack Pro provides. In the following exercise you're going to use the Search tab to find a sound effect and spot it to the Timeline. In the next lesson you'll make more extensive use of the Search tab to find music loops you'll use to compose a score for this project.

**1** Position the playhead at approximately 01:00:59:00.

**2** Press the spacebar and watch the video until the end of the Timeline is reached.

At the very end of the sequence, the actor slams his phone closed and walks off. Finding a dramatic sound effect to place here will help drive the closing of this sequence.

**3**    In the right pane, click the Search tab.

The Search tab can be viewed in two different ways: column view and button view. In this lesson you'll use column view; in Lesson 10 you'll use button view.

**4**    Click the Column View button.

The most useful feature of the Search tab is its ability to let you narrow your searches to only the types of sounds you're interested in. Right now you're interested in a sound effect, so you'll narrow the options shown to only that type of audio file.

**5**    In the pop-up menu, choose Sound Effects.

In the column view, the Search tab displays two columns. On the left is Keywords, and on the right is Matches. The Keywords column shows the categories of sound types that are available in your current search. The Matches column displays the total number of files that meet the search requirements and the subcategories those files belong to.

You're currently looking for an impact sound to place where the character slams his phone closed.

**6**    Click the Impacts & Crashes category in the left column of the Search tab.

Instantly, three subcategories appear in the Matches column. The matching audio files, hundreds of them, appear in the lower section of the Search tab.

Just as in the Bin and the Browser, clicking an audio file in the Search tab will audition it. You can use the Up Arrow and Down Arrow keys to quickly audition each audio file in order. To speed the process you can enter text to search for.

**7**   Click the Search Text field.

**8**   Type *Metal* to narrow the search to sound effects that have been tagged as having a metal sound.

As you type, the list of matches is refined. You can audition this smaller list of matches if you like.

**9**   Select **Impact Metal Hit Reverb 01.caf** to audition it.

This sound effect will work nicely in your project.

**10**   In the Multitrack Editor, position the playhead in the Timeline on the frame that shows the phone being closed (01:01:03:04).

**11**   The SFX track should still be selected. If it's not, click its header to select it.

**12**   In the Search tab, Control-click or right-click the **Impact Metal Hit Reverb 01.caf** file and choose Spot to Playhead.

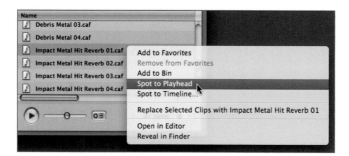

The selected audio file is added to the Timeline on the SFX track.

**NOTE ▶** You can also drag audio files from the Search tab to the Timeline, or to the File Editor.

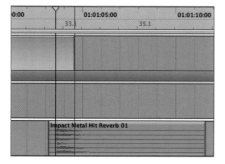

You'll notice that this clip looks different. Many of the audio files in Soundtrack Pro's sample library are surround sound clips. These audio files are capable of playing back in 5.1 surround sound, so they contain six discrete channels of audio. If you aren't currently mixing in surround sound, these audio files will work just fine in stereo as well. No adjustment is necessary.

13 Play the project from a position a few seconds prior to the audio clip you just placed in the Timeline.

Two things are obvious. First, the silence at the beginning of the audio clip has caused it to play too late to sync with the onscreen action in the video. Second, Soundtrack Pro stops playback (or loops back to the beginning of the project) before the end of the sound effect is heard. You'll fix the first problem by syncing the sound effect to the video, and then you'll address the second problem.

**14** Return the playhead to the frame that shows the phone being closed (01:01:03:04).

**15** Zoom in so the waveform in the impact sound effect is easily visible.

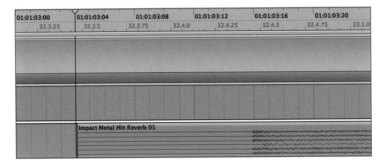

**16** Press and hold down the mouse button in the audio clip where the waveform shows the sound begins.

**17** Drag the clip so the start of the waveform aligns with the playhead. Use the Multipoint Video HUD (press V to toggle it on/off) as a guide.

**18** Play the sequence from a few seconds prior to the start of the impact clip. Watch the Video tab to check its sync.

The impact sound should now happen simultaneously with the closing of the phone.

## Setting the End of Project Marker

You've worked with some markers in Soundtrack Pro already, and you'll explore advanced uses of markers in the next lesson. There's also a special marker called the End of Project marker. This marker tells Soundtrack Pro where the end of the project is. When the play-head reaches the End of Project marker it will stop playback. Also, when you export the project (See Lesson 11 for more information on exporting projects), Soundtrack Pro will export only the portion of the Timeline that precedes the End of Project Marker. This is why it's important to set this marker correctly. When you send a multitrack project to Soundtrack Pro from Final Cut Pro, an End of Project marker is automatically inserted at the end of the last clip in the sequence. It's the only red marker in the Timeline.

The End of Project marker

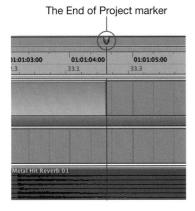

When you create a new multitrack project in Soundtrack Pro there's no End of Project marker. You can create one. In the next steps, you'll delete the End of Project marker in this project and create a new one.

**1**   Click the End of Project marker.

**2**   Press the Delete key.

Soundtrack Pro deletes the End of Project marker.

**3**   Position the playhead in the Timeline after the waveform in the last clip ends (approximately 01:01:08:00).

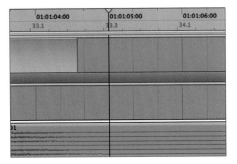

**4**   Choose Mark > Set End of Project.

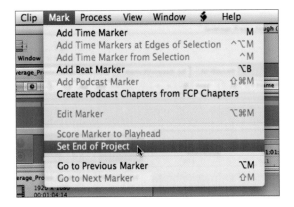

The End of Project marker is placed at the playhead's position.

**NOTE ▸** You can also drag the End of Project marker to reset its position.

**5**   Play the sequence.

Soundtrack Pro now plays to the end of the impact sound effect clip before cycling back to the beginning of the project.

## Additional Practice

If you'd like to get some additional practice spotting sound effects to the Timeline and syncing them to the video, take the time to do so now. Use the Search tab to find audio files located in the Sound Effects category and place them in appropriate places in the Timeline, and then fine-tune their positioning by using the Multipoint Video HUD. In the next lesson, you'll compose a score for this sequence by using the Search tab to find Apple Loops.

## Lesson Review

1. What does the Bin do?
2. What does the Browser do?
3. True or False: You can audition audio files in the Bin, but not in the Browser.
4. What is the function of the Multipoint Video HUD?
5. True or False: You can only spot entire audio files to the playhead.
6. When will a Soundtrack Pro Multitrack Project contain an End of Project marker?

### Answers

1. The Bin shows you all of the media referenced in your project.
2. The Browser lets you search your hard disk for media that you'd like to add to the project.
3. False: Selecting an audio file in either the Bin or the Browser allows you to preview the file.
4. The Multipoint Video HUD provides context for your edits by showing you the frame of video at the beginning of the clip in its left window, the frame of video at the end of the clip in its right window, and the frame of video directly under the pointer's position in the middle window, and updates in real time as you move the clip. This helps you align the beginning, end, or sync point to precise video frames.
5. False: Use a three-point edit to select a portion of an audio file in the File Editor, and then spot just that selection to the playhead in the Multitrack Editor.
6. When Final Cut Pro sends a sequence to a Soundtrack Pro Multitrack Project, an End of Project marker is automatically placed at the end of the last clip in the sequence. For all other projects, if you want to have an End of Project marker, you'll need to create it manually.

# 10

| | |
|---|---|
| **Lesson Files** | Lesson Files > Lesson 10 > 10_Leverage_Promo_Rough (sent).stmp |
| **Time** | This lesson takes approximately 60 minutes to complete. |
| **Goals** | Set the Time ruler to beats-based units |
| | Set the tempo of the project |
| | Use the Search tab to find Apple Loops |
| | Use snapping to place clips on beat |
| | Arrange Apple Loops to create an original musical score |
| | Apply and adjust a crossfade |
| | Use markers and the Master tempo envelope to create a tempo change |
| | Synchronize the music to events in the video |

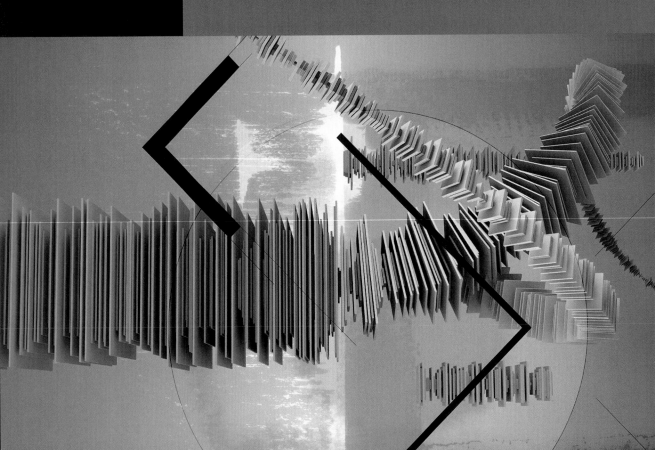

# Scoring Using Loops

Video tells the viewer what's happening, but music tells the viewer how to feel about what they're seeing. An effective soundtrack will add a powerful dimension to the viewer's experience of a feature or documentary. A bad soundtrack can make serious moments seem laughable, or sincere characters appear suspicious.

Soundtrack Pro is designed to make creating an original music score easy, even if you have little or no knowledge of songwriting or composition. The included (and expandable) Apple Loops automatically conform to musical key and tempo, making composing as simple as selecting the instruments and performances that best match the music you hear in your head.

In this lesson you'll use Soundtrack Pro's included Apple Loops to compose music for the *Leverage* trailer for which you spotted sound effects in the previous lesson. You'll layer instrument parts to create an entirely original music score, and you'll use advanced techniques to make the score sync perfectly with the onscreen cues in the video.

## Setting Up for Music Production

So far you've been working in Soundtrack Pro with rulers that measure time using SMPTE timecode. As previously mentioned in Lesson 3, the SMPTE format displays time in hours: minutes: seconds: frames, and is the standard way of looking at time when working with video. In music it's more common, and useful, to measure time in musical bars and beats. Soundtrack Pro displays both SMPTE time-based and beats-based rulers simultaneously; however, one ruler is designated the primary unit base and the other is a secondary display. By default, projects are time-based, which is ideal for editing dialogue, spotting sound effects, and many other tasks that benefit from placement on the same absolute time scale that the video references. When you're scoring the project, however, you'll need to switch the project to beats-based units. Later in this lesson you'll also set the time base on a track-by-track basis.

## Switching the Project to the Beats-Based Ruler

With the ruler set to display timecode, the gridlines in the project align to frames in the video. When you set the ruler to display beats, the gridlines show musical measurements, bars and beats, which is necessary for arranging loops and other musical elements to compose a score.

1    In the Lesson 10 folder, open the file **10_Leverage_Promo_Rough (sent).stmp**.

> **NOTE ▶** This is the same sequence you worked on in the last lesson, but a new SFX track has been added and additional sound effects have been placed. You may have made similar additions if you worked beyond the last exercise in Lesson 09. The new sound effects on the SFX2 track are from the Apple Loops library included in Soundtrack Pro. They haven't been mixed into the project yet; you'll create a mix in Lesson 11.

2    In the left pane, click the Project tab.

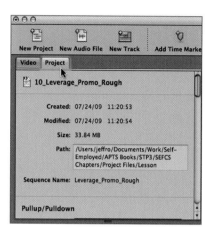

**3**  Scroll down the Project tab to the Properties area.

**4**  In the Ruler Units pop-up menu, select Beats.

In the Timeline, the beats ruler moves to the top of the Time ruler and the grid now aligns to music beats. The SMPTE timecode values are still visible, now located in the lower half of the Time ruler.

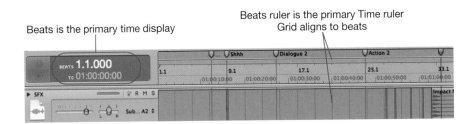

Beats is the primary time display

Beats ruler is the primary Time ruler
Grid aligns to beats

**5**    Click the Video tab so that the video is visible while you continue to work.

Setting the Ruler Units to Beats also causes all new tracks to default to the beats time base. You'll see in the next exercise that when the tempo is changed, clips on a beats-based track will stay locked to the bar and beat they're placed on, whereas clips on time-based tracks will stay locked to the minutes: seconds: frames that they're placed on.

## Searching the Apple Loops Library

In the previous lesson, you used the Search tab to find sound effects, and then spot them to the Timeline. In this lesson you'll use the Search tab to find music samples in the Apple Loops library. The Search tab has features designed to help you locate just the type of music loop you're looking for.

## Opening the Search Tab

As you learned in the previous lesson, the Search tab is located in the bottom section of Soundtrack Pro's right pane.

**1**    If the right pane isn't showing, click the Right Pane button.

**2**    In the bottom section of the right pane, click the Search tab.

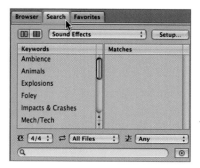

In the previous lesson you used the Search tab in column view. This time, you'll use button view.

**3**    Click the Button View button.

The Search tab switches to Button View mode.

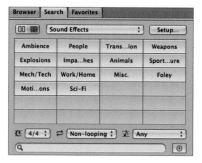

Button view presents you with a grid of buttons. In each button is the name of a keyword you can use to narrow the search results.

**4**    Click the keyword pop-up menu and select Music Beds.

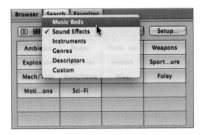

The Search tab now shows available Apple Loops tagged with the keyword Music Beds. The Mixed button should be active by default (if it's not, click it to activate it).

**NOTE ▶** The Mixed category of audio files includes samples of multi-instrument music passages. These are generally complete music passages, like mini songs, that are ready to be placed in a project. They're ideally suited for use in projects for which taking the time to compose an original score is not necessary or practical. They can also be used as music temp tracks, music beds that serve as placeholders in the project until the real score is completed.

The number of audio files listed in the current results is shown in the lower-right corner of the Search tab. There are quite a few audio files that match the search parameters, so you should narrow the search. You're looking for a style of music that will fit the action sequence in this project, starting at the Action 1 marker.

5    Command-click the Grooving button.

Clicking a keyword button while holding down the Command key retains the previous button selections and adds the new keyword to further refine the search results.

**NOTE ▶** To deselect a keyword button, Command-click it a second time. To deselect all keyword buttons, click any one of the selected buttons.

6    Hold down the Command key and click the Urban button.

The results list is now narrowed to a reasonable number of audio samples.

7    Click the first audio file in the results list to audition it.

8    Use the Down Arrow key to audition each audio file in the results list.

Because of the keywords you used to narrow the search, all the audio files you audition will be complete musical passages, with multiple instruments, groove-oriented rhythm, and an urban feel.

## Looping Versus Non-looping Files

Soundtrack Pro supports two types of audio samples: looping and non-looping.

*Looping files* are audio elements that can be arranged into more complex musical parts. Looping files will loop seamlessly when resized on the Timeline. Looping files usually have tempo and key information embedded in them that allows them to conform to tempo and key parameters, including adapting to scoring markers, set in the Soundtrack Pro Timeline. This type of Apple Loop will conform to a change in tempo without changing pitch, or to a change in key without changing tempo.

*Non-looping files* are audio samples that don't have tempo and key information embedded in them, so they don't conform to the tempo or key of the project they're placed in. When a non-looping file is resized in the Timeline it can be shortened or lengthened, but if you resize it beyond the length of the original file, Soundtrack Pro will add silence to the end of the clip.

**NOTE ▶** You can convert a non-looping audio file to a looping audio file by using the Apple Loops Utility, included with Final Cut Studio. The Apple Loops Utility will also let you turn a looping file into a non-looping file.

## Using Snapping to Place Clips in the Timeline

In the previous lesson you spotted files to the playhead. In this exercise you'll drag the audio file from the Search tab to the Timeline. You'll place the clip precisely on beat by using snapping.

1   Choose Multitrack > Add Track, or press Command-T to create a new track.

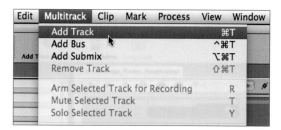

2   Click the new track's header to rename the track. Name the track *Music1*.

**3** Click the Snapping On/Off toggle button in the lower-left corner of the Multitrack Editor to turn snapping on.

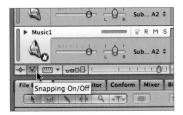

**NOTE** ▸ You can also toggle snapping on and off by pressing the N key, just as in Final Cut Pro.

Snapping forces edits to occur on the grid lines. When placing music loops, setting the project's ruler to Beats mode and turning on snapping helps guarantee that the music loops stay on beat when you place them in the Timeline.

**4** Drag the **Looping Music Bed 10.caf** file to the Music1 track and release it at exactly 7.1 (the first beat of the seventh measure).

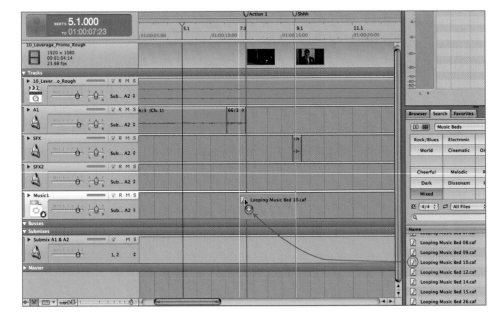

The clip is added to the Music1 track.

**NOTE ▶** Be certain that the start of the clip is positioned at exactly 7.1 in the Timeline. When you have the clip in the right place you'll see the white guide marker that denotes the edge of the clip snap to 7.1 in the Time ruler.

5   Play the project from a position before the music clip you just placed.

The music starts a little early and cuts off the last line of dialogue. The music bed is also too short to fill the section of the project it was intended for. In an upcoming exercise, you'll extend the loop to play until the next section of dialogue occurs in the sequence. But first, you'll set the project's tempo.

## Setting the Tempo of the Project

One of the most powerful aspects of Apple Loops is their ability to automatically match the tempo of the project they're placed into. This makes it easy to layer Apple Loops in the Timeline to build a score because, regardless of a loop's native tempo, once placed into the Timeline all Apple Loops play back at the project's tempo. Soundtrack Pro projects default to a tempo of 120 beats per minute (bpm), but you'll now change that to a tempo that will better match the pace at which this video was cut. Later in this lesson you'll also change the tempo of just one section of the project.

1   Click the Project tab in the upper-left corner of the Project pane.

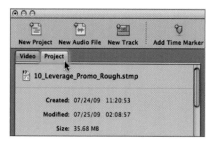

2   Scroll down to the bottom of the Project tab.

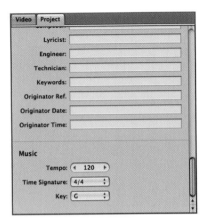

You'll find the project's music properties here.

**3**    In the Tempo text field, click the left arrow 5 times to lower the tempo to 115 bpm. As you click the arrow, watch the Timeline.

As you change the tempo, you'll see the Looping Music Bed 10 clip stay anchored at the beginning of bar 7, while the Time ruler adjusts to reflect the new tempo.

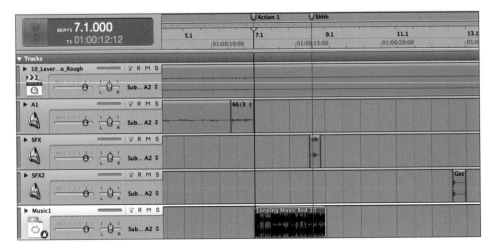

This section of the video was cut with a tempo of 115 bpm in mind. With the project set to the intended tempo, the music clip now begins playback just after the last line of dialogue. However, this music is intended to play until the second section of dialogue and currently ends much too soon. In the next exercise you'll resize the Apple Loop to fill the section of the project between the Action 1 and Dialogue 2 markers.

**NOTE ▶** You can change the tempo while playing the project. Soundtrack Pro will adjust to the new tempo in real time as you make the changes and you'll instantly hear the effect of your tempo change. To try this, simply set a cycle region, click Play, and then change the tempo using the technique you just learned in this exercise.

## Resizing Looping Files

The music bed you just placed in the Timeline is too short to fill the section that it's intended to score; however, it is a looping file. Looping files will loop, or repeat, perfectly on beat when resized beyond their original length.

1   Move the pointer to the right edge of the Looping Music Bed 10 clip. Position the pointer over the lower-right corner of the clip.

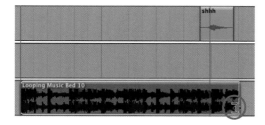

The pointer turns into the Resize tool.

2   Drag the right edge of the clip to the Dialogue 2 marker.

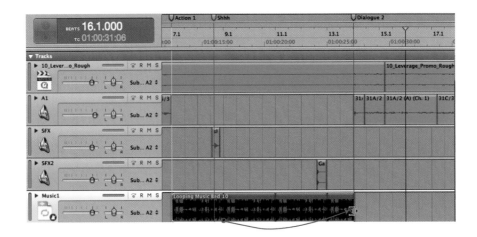

The audio file is looped as you resize it.

**3**   Play the project, paying attention to the music bed you just placed.

The music clip now plays for the entire section between the Action 1 and Dialogue 2 markers.

With a little mixing and a fade-out to transition the end, this Apple Loop could serve very well as a score for this section of the video. Soundtrack Pro comes with many of these ready-to-go music beds that are perfect when used as incidental music in a scene, a short spot, or a cue for a graphic or title sequence.

The real power of the Apple Loops library is in the thousands of instrument loops you can use to build your own original scores. In the next exercise you'll replace the current music bed with Apple Loops to create an entirely original musical composition.

> **NOTE** ▶ Soundtrack Pro comes with thousands of Apple Loops. GarageBand and Logic Studio also utilize the Apple Loops format, so if you have either of those applications installed on your system you'll have access to their substantial libraries, too. If you'd like to further expand your Apple Loops library you can purchase Jam Packs from Apple. A number of third-party libraries are available in the Apple Loops format as well.

# Creating an Original Score Using Apple Loops

Consider the music bed you placed in the previous exercise to be a temp track. It's an example of the style of music you're working toward, but it isn't exactly what you want. By carefully selecting from the thousands of Apple Loops in the library, you'll produce an original score of your own design.

1   Play the project between the Action 1 and Dialogue 2 markers one more time to get a feel for the style of music. You'll be creating something similar, though original, in the next steps.

2   With the Selection tool, click the **Looping Music Bed 10** clip to select it.

3   Press the Delete key to remove the clip.

The Music1 track is now clear and ready for you to place new Apple Loops to create the new score.

The music bed you're replacing had a funk, urban feel to it. You'll be searching for loops that match that style. In the following steps you'll build a new score, one instrument at a time.

4   In the Search tab in the right pane, click the Keywords pop-up menu, and then select Instruments.

The buttons in the Search tab now display keywords that will let you refine your search by musical instrument. You'll start with the drums.

5   Select the Drum Kit button.

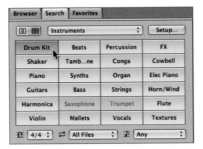

In the search results, only drum loops are displayed. You may audition a few if you like; then continue to the next step.

6   In the search results, find the audio loop called **Live Edgy Drum Kit 35.caf** and drag it to the Music1 track. Release the clip at exactly 7.1 in the Timeline.

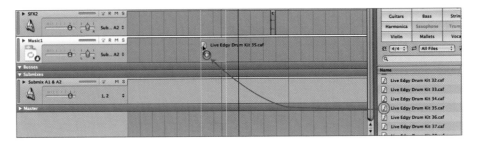

The drum loop is placed in the Timeline.

7   Position the pointer over the lower-right corner of the clip. When you see the Resize tool, drag the right edge of the clip to 14.1.

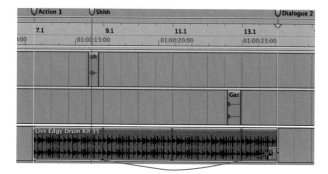

The drum loop is extended.

As you continue to layer your music tracks, it will be helpful to create a cycle region.

8  With the Live Edgy Drum Kit 35 clip selected, Control-click or right-click the Time ruler, and then choose Cycle Region > Create Cycle Region From Selection.

A cycle region is created from bar 7.1 to bar 14.1.

9  Lower the volume slider for the Music1 track to around –12 dB so it isn't too loud.

10  Select Multitrack > Add Track, or press Command-T, to add a new track.

**11** Name the new track *Music2*.

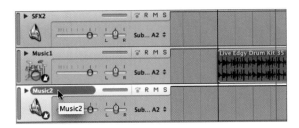

**12** Press the spacebar to play the cycle region.

**13** Lower the volume slider for the Music2 track to the same level you set for Music1.

**14** In the Search tab, click the Bass button to bring up a list of bass loops.

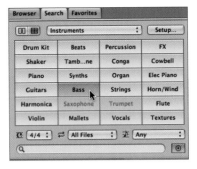

**15** Select a loop in the search results to audition it.

The loop you selected is auditioned and Soundtrack Pro automatically syncs the auditioned loop's playback to the tempo and position of the Apple Loop that's playing back in the Timeline. This lets you quickly audition loops in the Search tab while simultaneously hearing how the auditioned loop will blend with the loops you've already placed into the Timeline.

**16** Drag the **Acoustic Double Bass Groove 09.caf** audio file to the Music2 track and release it at exactly 7.1.

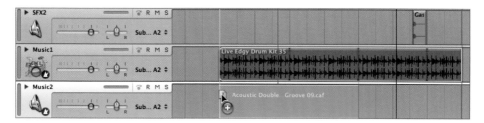

**17** Resize the bass clip so that it ends at 13.1.

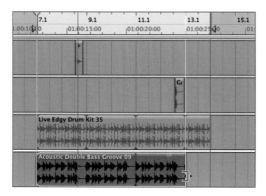

The bass now plays perfectly in time with the drums. By ending the bass loop a measure before the drums, you create a break that will help lead into the next section of the score. Next, you'll add the last instrument loop to this section.

**18** Select Multitrack > Add Track, or press Command-T, to add a new track.

**19** Name the new track *Music3*.

**20** Lower the volume slider for the Music3 track to the same level you set for Music1 and Music2.

**21**  In the Search tab, select the Guitars button.

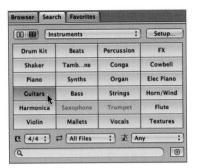

The results list now shows all of the guitar Apple Loops available on your system. You're specifically looking for funky guitar loops. Use the search text box to refine the results.

**22**  In the Search tab's keyword text field, type *funk*.

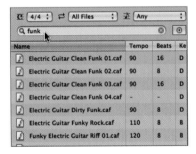

As you type, the list of Apple Loops shown in the results box is reduced to only those that include the keyword you're typing.

**23**  From the Search tab's results list, drag the **Funky Electric Guitar Riff 37.caf** audio file to the Music3 track and release it at exactly 9.1.

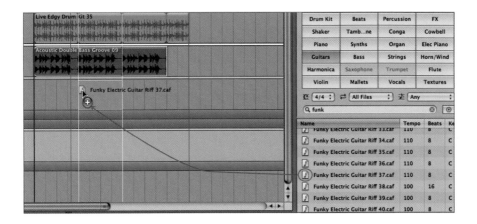

**24**  Resize the guitar clip so that it ends at 13.1, just like the Bass clip.

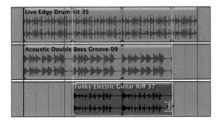

**25**  Play the cycle region to listen to your score.

The instruments are unmixed at this point; you'll perform a proper mix in the next lesson. However, with just three loops arranged on the Timeline you've created an original score. There are thousands of other Apple Loops to choose from, so when you've finished this lesson you may want to spend some time composing an alternative score. First, you need to place some background music to carry the video through the next dialogue section. The passage of music you just created needs to flow smoothly into the music you place in the subsequent section. This is easily accomplished using a crossfade.

## Using Crossfades

In the next part of the video there's a section of dialogue. You'll continue a piece of music under the dialogue, but you'll need to select music that isn't quite as intense as the score you created for the action sequence. You don't want the music to interfere with the dialogue. You also need the two pieces of music to flow seamlessly together.

In Lesson 7, you used Soundtrack Pro's Truncate mode to replace sections of dialogue clips with new clips that you recorded. Truncate mode causes the deletion of any part of a clip that is overlapped by another clip. In Crossfade mode, Soundtrack Pro applies fades to blend the transition between the two clips, allowing both to be heard during the section in which they overlap. In the next exercise you'll place a new Apple Loop into the Music1 track, and then use a crossfade to blend between it and the drum loop that occurs before it.

**1**    At the top of the Multitrack Editor, click the Crossfade Mode button.

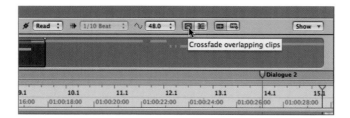

**2**    In the Search tab, select the Drum Kit keyword button.

**3**    Drag the **Drummers of Motown 07.caf** audio file to the Music1 track and place it at 14.1.

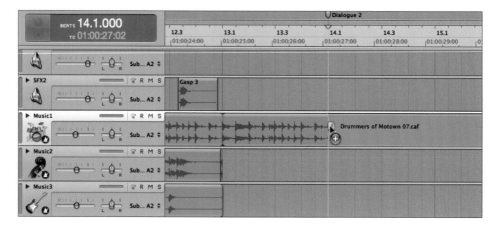

4   Use the Resize tool to extend the Drummers of Motown 07 clip to 24.1 in the Timeline.

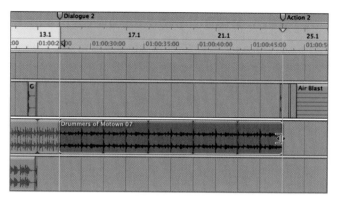

5   In the Time ruler, drag the cycle region to 24.1.

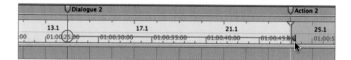

6   Play the cycle region and listen to the transition between the two music sections.

The transition from the first drum beat to the second is a little abrupt for the purpose intended here. A crossfade will improve this transition.

7   Position the pointer over the left edge of the Drummers of Motown 07 clip, and then use the Resize tool to drag the edge of the clip back to 13.1 (drag to the left one measure).

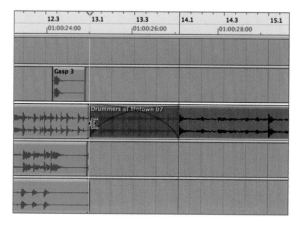

As you resize the Drummers of Motown clip over the Live Edgy Drum Kit clip, you'll see that a crossfade symbol stretches over the section of the clips that overlap. The waveform of both clips is visible in the overlapped section as well.

8   Play the project from a position just before this overlapped section and listen to the crossfade that Soundtrack Pro automatically created.

The transition is smoother, but still sounds a little too abrupt. This is due to the type of fade curves that were applied. In the next step, you'll adjust the type of crossfade to achieve a more gradual-sounding transition.

## Choosing the Fade Type

By default, the crossfade that Soundtrack Pro applies when you overlap clips in Crossfade mode is the +3dB fade. This type of fade works great for many transitions, but it isn't ideal for the transition you're attempting to create here.

1   Position the pointer over the crossfade.

The crossfade symbol in the clip is highlighted.

2   Double-click the clip to open the Fade Selector HUD.

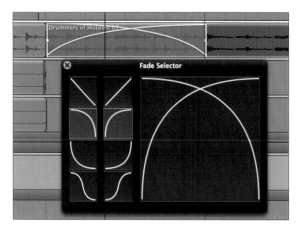

The Fade Selector HUD was introduced in Lesson 2, "Sound Mixing Basics." As you did in that lesson, you may select each of the fade types and listen to how each affects the sound of the crossfade. You can also drag the left or right edges of the crossfade to change its duration and midpoint.

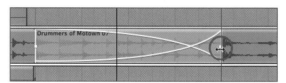

Crossfading clips is a powerful technique audio engineers use to transition between two sounds without causing an abrupt change that may distract the viewer. When you're satisfied with the results of your work on this crossfade, continue to the next exercise to score the final section of the project using an advanced technique to set a tempo change.

## Using Markers to Set Tempo

At the beginning of this lesson you changed the tempo of the project from the default 120 bpm to 115 bpm. This change affected the entire project. Soundtrack Pro also allows you to define tempo changes throughout the project. When creating a music score for a long video it's common to write distinctive music passages for different scenes. Often, each piece of music will have a different tempo. In Soundtrack Pro you create tempo changes using the Master tempo envelope.

## Using the Master Tempo Envelope

Envelopes are a type of automation. Working with envelopes may be familiar to you from working in Final Cut Pro, where they're used to automate changes in parameters like volume (on audio clips) or opacity (on video clips), or in the Motion tab properties. In the next lesson you'll work with envelopes to set the volume and pan of individual tracks in Soundtrack Pro.

Master envelopes work the same way, but instead of affecting a single track, they affect all the tracks in the project.

**1** In the Multitrack Editor, scroll to the bottom of the track list.

The Master bus becomes visible below the Submixes area.

**2** If the Master bus area is closed, click the disclosure triangle to open it.

The Master bus area opens and reveals the Master volume envelope.

**3** In the Show Envelopes pop-up menu, choose Tempo.

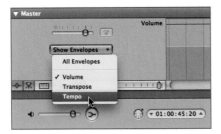

The tempo envelope is revealed.

**4**   Click the first envelope point at the beginning of the tempo envelope.

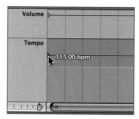

The project's tempo is displayed.

You can use the Master tempo envelope to create tempo changes throughout your projects by double-clicking any point along the tempo envelope to create a new breakpoint, and then dragging the breakpoint to set the new tempo.

> **NOTE ▶** Apple Loops that contain tempo tags will play back at the tempo set by the Master tempo envelope, but clips without tempo information embedded in them will continue to play at their native speed.

You can use the Master tempo envelope to set the tempo for sections of a project when you know what the tempo you want to set is. In the next exercise you'll use markers, along with the Master tempo envelope, to set a tempo change for a section without knowing what the target tempo needs to be to properly fit the music to events in the video.

## Adapting Tempo to Onscreen Video Cues

The final section of this project, the second action sequence, still needs music. The music you built for the first action sequence can also be used in the second action sequence. First you'll copy the music clips to the second action sequence in the Timeline, and then you'll set a tempo change for this section of the project so the music ends at the right moment.

**1**   Using the Selection tool, select the Live Edgy Drum Kit clip. Then hold down the Shift key and select the Acoustic Double Bass Groove clip and the Funky Electric Guitar Riff clip.

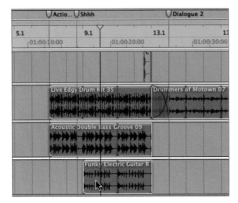

All three clips should be selected.

2    Hold down the Option key and drag the clips to the right. Drop them so that the drum and bass clips both start at exactly 24.1 on the Timeline.

NOTE ▶ Holding down the Option key when you drag with the Selection tool causes the clip (or clips) to be copied.

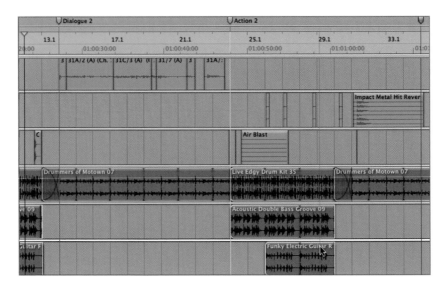

The Drummers of Motown clip was copied as well because it overlaps with the Live Edgy Drum Kit you copied. We don't want this clip to play a second time, so we'll need to remove it.

3   Select the second instance of the Drummers of Motown clip, and then press Delete to remove it.

4   At the Action 2 marker, double-click the Master tempo envelope to create an envelope point.

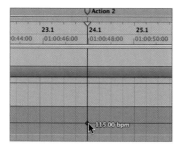

This point sets the beginning of the tempo change.

5   Position the playhead where the Impact Metal Hit Reverb 01 clip's waveform begins. You may need to zoom in or disable snapping to do this accurately.

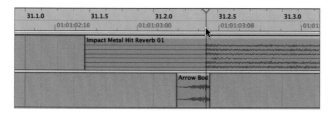

6   Press the M key to place a marker at the playhead.

This marker indicates the frame of video that you'll be syncing to.

**7**  Position the playhead at the end of the Live Edgy Drummer clip.

> **NOTE ▶** Remember that you can quickly move the playhead to the edge of a clip by pressing the Up Arrow or Down Arrow keys.

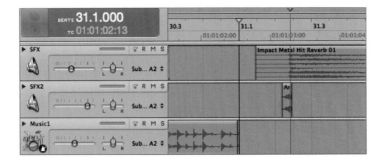

The position of the playhead indicates the place in the Timeline that you'll be syncing to the marker you placed in the previous step.

**8**  Select the marker that you placed over the Impact Metal Hit Reverb clip.

**9**   Choose Mark > Score Marker to Playhead.

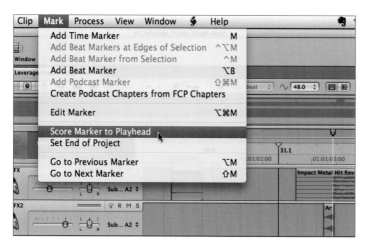

Soundtrack Pro calculates the tempo necessary to make the position of the playhead sync to the selected marker and inserts the appropriate envelope point into the Master tempo envelope.

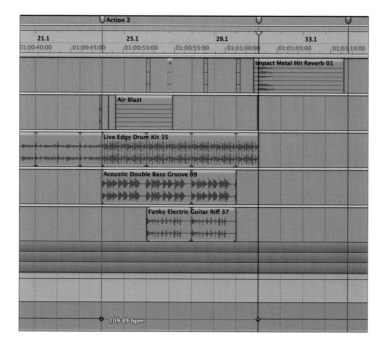

**10** Play the project and listen to the timing of the final piece of music.

The new tempo, inserted at the Action 2 marker, makes the final section of music end perfectly at the dramatic impact sound.

Score Marker to Playhead is a very useful technique for fitting a passage of music to a section of video that wasn't cut with a specific tempo in mind.

Play the project from the beginning and evaluate your work so far. You now have a video project with sound effects spotted at all the necessary points and original music scored throughout, synced to key events in the video. All of the elements are in place; however, they're not yet mixed. In the next lesson you'll utilize Soundtrack Pro's mixer, busses, and DSP effects to create a professional mix.

## Lesson Review

1. How do you set the Time ruler to beats-based units?

2. What does the Search tab do?

3. How do you loop Apple Loops in the Timeline?

4. True or false: Once you set a crossfade, you can't change its duration.

5. How do you set a marker?

6. Where do you set changes to tempo for a section of a project?

### Answers

1. Visit the Project tab's Properties area, and set the Ruler Unit menu to Beats.

2. The Search tab lets you quickly locate and audition indexed Apple Loops, music beds, and audio effects files on your hard disk.

3. Drag the right edge of the Apple Loop audio clip, and Soundtrack Pro will automatically loop the clip as many times as you need.

4. False: You can adjust the duration of a crossfade by dragging its edges to resize it.

5.  Position the playhead where you want to place the marker, and then press the M key.

6.  In the Master tempo envelope, located in the Master bus.

# 11

| | |
|---|---|
| **Lesson Files** | Lesson Files > Lesson 11 > 11_Leverage_Promo_Rough (sent).stmp |
| **Time** | This lesson takes approximately 45 minutes to complete. |
| **Goals** | Use the Soundtrack Pro Mixer to set level and pan |
| | Create submixes for dialogue, sound effects, and music |
| | Use Voice Level Match to set dialogue levels |
| | Apply real-time effects to a track |
| | Use the Tracks tab channel strip |
| | Apply effects to busses and route signal through them |
| | Configure tracks for surround mixing |
| | Return the project to Final Cut Pro for final output |

# Advanced Mixing Techniques

Mixing is the art of balancing the sound in the project to achieve the greatest impact. A good mix makes the program both clear and compelling. In addition to balancing levels, the sound mixer applies pans and effects to create perspective and depth in the mix. In this lesson you'll expand on the basic mixing practices you learned in Lesson 2. You'll use busses to apply effects such as reverb to groups of tracks. You'll also make use of dynamic compression, automation, and a tool unique to Soundtrack Pro to create a clear and consistent dialogue level throughout the project.

You'll begin by accomplishing one of the most important tasks in preparing a good mix: organizing mix elements into dialogue, sound effects, and music stems by using submixes.

## Preparing for Mixing

The Mixer tab was introduced to you in Lesson 2, "Sound Mixing Basics." If you need to refresh your memory regarding using the Mixer to set or automate levels and pan, it's suggested that you revisit that chapter now. We'll expand on those techniques in this lesson.

One of the first tasks in producing a great mix is preparing the project by organizing the tracks and submixes.

1   Open the file **11_Leverage_Promo_Rough (sent).stmp** in the Lesson 11 folder.

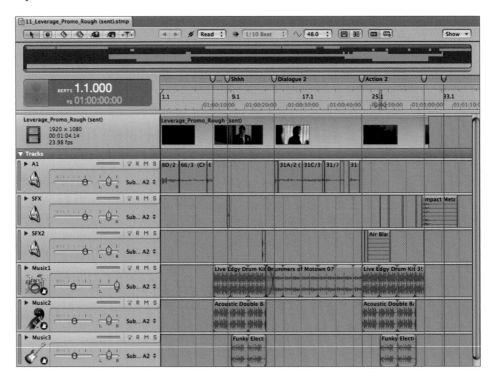

The project opens. This project continues from where you left off at the end of Lesson 10. All of the elements are in place, but the project hasn't been mixed.

2   Click the header of the A1 track's name to rename the track.

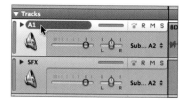

**3**  Rename the track *Dialogue*.

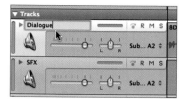

There are three main elements to a mix: dialogue, sound effects, and music. All of the tracks in this project are now named to make identifying them by category easy. In the next exercise you'll create a submix for each element type.

## Naming Submixes

There are six audio tracks in this project: one dialogue, two sound effects, and three music tracks. These tracks are all being mixed together to create the overall sound that you hear. In Soundtrack Pro, all audio tracks are always routed first through a submix, and then to the Master bus. Presently, all six tracks are being routed through one submix.

**1**  In the track list, click the Submixes disclosure triangle.

The submixes are revealed.

**2**    Click the Mixer button to open the lower pane (if it wasn't already open) and select the Mixer tab all at once.

The Mixer opens in the lower pane. The Mixer will always contain the same tracks that appear in the Project pane. Signal from the tracks flows into submixes; submixes, in turn, feed the Master bus.

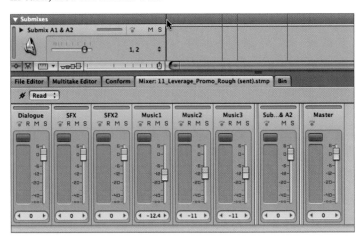

**3**    In the track header, click the name of the submix track to rename it.

**4**    Rename the track *Dialogue*.

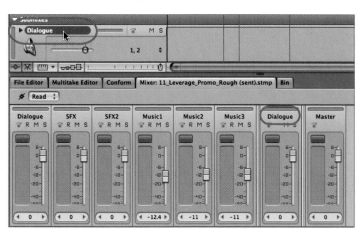

The submix is renamed and the change is reflected in both the Project pane and the Mixer tab.

## Routing Tracks to Submixes

Because the Dialogue submix is the only submix in the project right now, all of the audio tracks are being routed through it. You want the sound effects and music tracks to be routed to their own submixes, however, so you'll now create new submixes and reroute audio tracks to them.

**1**    Choose Multitrack > Add Submix, or press Command-Option-T.

A new submix is created.

**2**    Name the submix *SFX*.

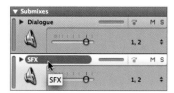

**3**    In the SFX track's header, click the submix menu.

**4**    Select the SFX submix.

The SFX audio track is now routed to the SFX submix.

**5**    Route the SFX2 audio track to the SFX submix as well.

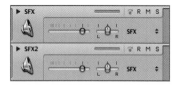

**6**    Create a new submix.

**7**    Name this submix *Music*.

**8**    Route each of the three music tracks to the music submix.

In the Mixer tab, the new submixes appear between the audio tracks and the Master bus.

Dialogue, SFX, and Music each have their own submix now. You can control the overall level of any of these elements by adjusting the appropriate submix's fader. For example, you can fade out music without affecting the mix of the individual music tracks, by simply lowering the fader of the Music submix.

## Mixing the Project

The project is prepared for you to mix it now. You'll start by setting a consistent dialogue level, then mix the music and set its level in relation to the dialogue, and finally blend the SFX in as well. In addition to setting and automating levels to accomplish this, you'll use real-time effects on the tracks.

## Adding Real-Time Effects to Mixer Tracks

In previous lessons you've used process effects to individually affect clips in a track. That's the ideal method of applying effects localized to individual clips of audio. To apply an effect to a track, submix, or even the output of the whole project (the Master bus), you use a real-time effect on the track, submix, or bus.

Real-time effects don't render their actions to disk; they use your computer's CPU to perform the effect processing in real time while the project plays.

1    Select the Dialogue audio track in either the Project pane or the Mixer tab.

**2** Click the Effects tab in the left pane.

The Effects tab opens.

The Effects tab displays the categories of real-time effects in the left column, and the effects available in the selected category in the right column.

**3** Select Dynamics.

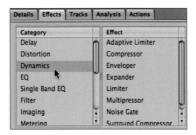

The right column of the Effects tab displays all the dynamics processing effects available on your system. You're going to apply a compressor to the Dialogue track.

**4** In the right column of the Effects tab, double-click Compressor to add it to the selected track.

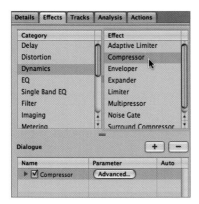

The Compressor effect is added to the track's effects chain and the Compressor effect's HUD appears.

You'll use this compressor to make the dialogue track's volume more consistent before you set level changes.

5   Create a cycle region from the beginning of the project to the Action 1 marker.

It's helpful to use cycle regions when mixing so you can hear the part of the project you're working on repeatedly as you're making your adjustments.

6   Play the cycle region.

7   In the left pane, click the Tracks tab.

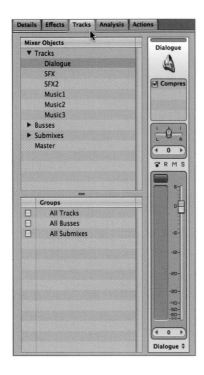

The Tracks tab displays a list of all the tracks, submixes, and busses in the project. On the right, it also displays an expanded version of the selected track's channel strip. This is very useful, especially when using a smaller monitor that can't display a large Mixer tab and the Project pane simultaneously. The Tracks tab channel strip gives you a large meter and fader to work with regardless of the size of the Mixer tab.

The Tracks tab channel strip also displays the real-time effects that have been inserted on the track, such as the Compressor effect that you placed in the track. Double-click the name of the effect when you need to reopen its HUD.

**8**  With the cycle region playing, adjust the compressor's Ratio to 2.5:1 and the Compressor Threshold to –24dB.

The dynamic range of the track is decreased, resulting in a louder apparent volume (see Lesson 2 for more information about using compressors).

**NOTE ▶** For detailed information on the function and use of every effect, see the Soundtrack Pro Effects Reference document, available in Soundtrack Pro's Help menu.

When making adjustments to effects it's very useful to evaluate your work by referencing the preprocessed sound. You can do this by bypassing the effect while the project plays.

**9**  Click the Bypass button in the lower-left corner of the effect's HUD to toggle the Compressor effect on and off.

Effects can also be bypassed in the Mixer (or in the Tracks tab channel strip) by deselecting the checkbox next to the name of the effect.

The compressor helped raise the level of the quieter parts of the track to the target level of about −12dB, but parts of the track are a little too loud. The first clip in the sequence is noticeably louder than the subsequent clips, even after the compressor has been applied. In the next step you'll use a special process to match the levels of the dialogue in these clips.

## Using Voice Level Match

Soundtrack Pro features a unique process called Voice Level Match. It's specifically designed to match the dialogue level in one clip to the level in another clip. Its specialized algorithm isolates the sound of the human voice from any extraneous sounds, analyzes its average amplitude, and saves it in the Sound Palette. You then stamp the Voice Level print onto any the clips whose level you wish to match the source clip. This feature makes matching dialogue levels an extraordinarily fast process.

1   Zoom in on the first two clips in the Dialogue track.

    The waveform in the first clip, 8D/2, is noticeably larger than the waveform in the second clip, 66/3.

2   Play this section of the project, paying attention to the difference in levels.

3   In the toolbar, select the Lift Tool.

The pointer turns into the Lift tool , and the Sound Palette HUD appears. Make sure that Lift Voice Level is checked.

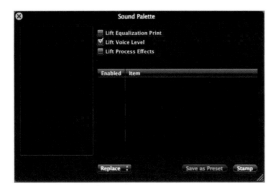

4    With the Lift tool, click the 66/3 clip.

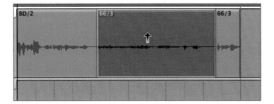

The Sound Palette HUD shows that Level Match properties were lifted from the 66/3 clip.

The pointer has automatically changed from the Lift tool to the Stamp tool. The Stamp tool is used to paste the lifted properties onto clips.

5    Using the Stamp tool, click the 8D/2 clip.

The Voice Level print lifted from 66/3 is stamped onto the 8D/2 clip. The waveform in the stamped clip is made noticeably shorter. The Level Match process appears in the Actions list.

6   Play this part of the project, paying particular attention to the levels of the two clips.

The two clips now have the same average level.

The Lift and Stamp tool has two additional functions: It can create and transfer an Equalization Print that will match the sound of two clips by analyzing a clip's equalization curve and applying it to the clip it's stamped onto, and it can be used to copy and paste process effects from clip to clip.

## Blending Music and SFX

There are three music tracks in this project: Music1, Music2, and Music3. Music1 has the drum loops, Music2 has the bass loops, and Music3 has the guitar loops. Use the track faders in the Mixer to set levels for these instruments that blend them together to your taste. Automation shouldn't be necessary (though you can automate them if you wish), and the overall level of the music can be controlled with the Music submix. Set a level for the music that doesn't obstruct the dialogue. The drums should peak around –6dB. When you're satisfied with the sound of the music mix, move to the sound effects tracks.

The two sound effects tracks, SFX and SFX2, also need to be blended into the project. Now that you have the dialogue level set and the music mixed and set at a level just below the dialogue, it will be very easy to determine the proper place in the mix for the SFX elements.

1   Play the project, paying particular attention to the level of the SFX clips.

The Shhh clip is already at an appropriate level, but the Gasp 3 clip is too loud.

2   Select the Gasp 3 clip with the Selection tool.

3   Choose Process > Adjust Amplitude (Command-Shift-L).

4   Reduce the clip's amplitude to around –16dB.

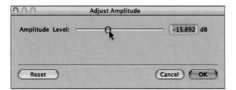

The Gasp 3 clip now blends more appropriately.

**5**   Select the first Click Off FX clip and adjust its amplitude to about –9dB.

**6**   Select the second Click Off FX clip and adjust its amplitude to about –12dB.

Setting the two identical clips to different levels helps make them seem more realistic to the viewer.

**7**   Select the Impact Metal Hit Reverb 01 clip.

This clip is much louder than the other elements in the project. It's so loud, in fact, that it's causing clipping.

**8**   Use the Adjust Amplitude process to lower the Impact Metal clip's level by –10 dB.

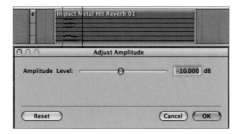

The sound effects are now at approximately the appropriate levels; however, they aren't blending into the scene quite as well as they could. To help place these sounds into the environment, you'll use a reverb effect. Reverb is best placed on a bus.

## Using Busses and Sends

Busses are primarily used in Soundtrack Pro in conjunction with sends to apply real-time effects to multiple tracks simultaneously. For example, if you want to place multiple tracks in the same room ambience created by a reverb, rather than placing that reverb on every track and matching the settings on each one, you'd place the reverb on a bus and use sends to add signal from each track to the reverb bus. *Sends* allow you to control the amount of reverb generated by each track independently, giving you complete control over the effect. In the next exercise you'll create a bus, place a reverb effect on it, and route tracks to the bus to apply the reverb to them.

> **NOTE** ▸ Busses can also be used to create alternate mixes—for example, a discrete headphone mix. To accomplish this, you would assign the output of the bus to the outputs on your hardware interface that you've connected to your headphone amplifier.

## Creating a Bus

1    From the Multitrack menu, choose Add Bus (Control-Command-T).

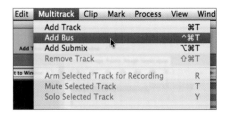

A new bus is added to the Mixer, and it also displays in the Tracks tab.

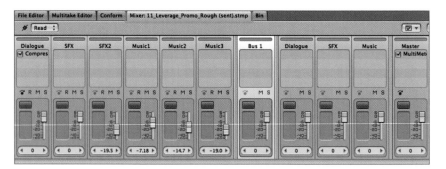

## Naming Busses

Busses are named the same way tracks and submixes are. This bus is going to contain a reverb.

1    In the Mixer, click the name at the top of the bus channel strip.

A text field appears.

2  Name the bus *Reverb*.

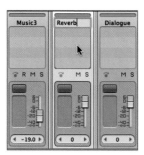

## Working with Effects on Busses

You now have a bus in your mixer. The next step is to insert a reverb effect in the bus.

1  In the Mixer tab, select the Reverb bus.

2  In the Tracks tab, select the Reverb category, and then double-click Space Designer.

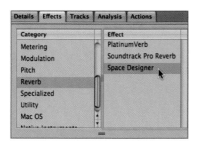

The Space Designer reverb is inserted on the Reverb bus. The Effects HUD appears.

Now that you have a reverb waiting on a bus, you need to send signal from the audio tracks to the bus so they can be affected by the reverb. To do this, you use a send.

## Using Sends

A send connects an audio track to a bus. Sends have level sliders to control the amount of signal that's being sent to the bus, which determines how strong the effect is.

1   Select the SFX audio track.

2   In the Effects tab, click Add Send.

The send is created. Because the Reverb bus is the only one in the project, the send automatically connects to it.

3   Select the SFX2 audio track.

4   In the Effects tab, click Add Send.

A send is added to the SFX2 track. This send is connected to the Reverb bus just like the send you added for the SFX track.

**5** Create and play a cycle region around the Shhh and Gasp 3 clips (approximately 8.1 to 14.1).

**6** In the Space Designer HUD, set the Dry Output to 0 (Mute).

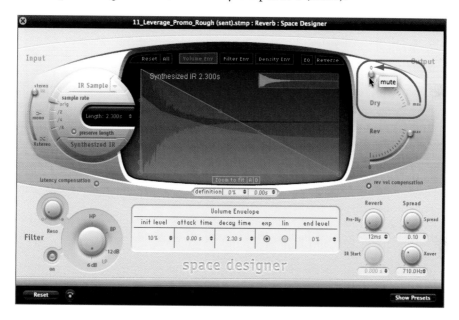

The dry feed is already coming directly from the audio track, so including more dry signal on the Reverb bus is unnecessary and can potentially cause issues like phase cancellation.

**7** Increase the Rev Output to Max.

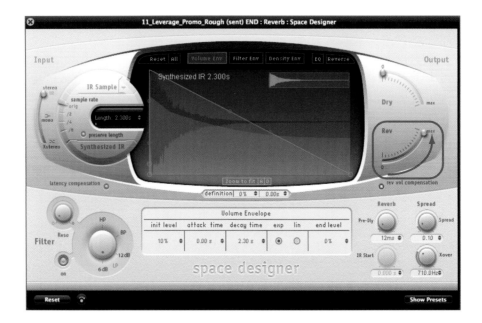

The Space Designer reverb is now set to output 100% of the wet (affected) signal and none of the dry (unaffected) signal.

**8**    In the Mixer tab, select the Reverb send in either the SFX or SFX2 channel strip to bring up the Send parameters in the Effects tab.

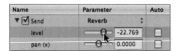

The Level slider in the Send parameters will control the amount of reverb generated by the signal on this track. Try playing with this control to find the optimum reverb setting for this project. You can also create sends in other tracks and experiment with adding reverb for the dialogue or music elements as well.

The advanced routing techniques you've learned in this lesson are vital to properly setting up and delivering a professional mix. Soundtrack Pro features dozens more professional-quality effects. In your free time, experiment with Soundtrack Pro's other effects to get a feel for all that Soundtrack Pro has to offer.

> **NOTE** ▶ Soundtrack Pro also works with any Core Audio–compatible audio plug-in. There are hundreds of Core Audio effects plug-ins available from third-party manufacturers.

If time permits, use the techniques you've learned in this lesson and in Lesson 2 to mix the project to your taste. Then move on to the next exercise to learn how to mix this project in 5.1 surround sound.

> **TIP** ▶ Soundtrack Pro supports the use of a variety of hardware control surfaces and has extremely tight integration with the Euphonix EuCon Ethernet control protocol. See the Soundtrack Pro User Manual for information on setting up control surfaces for use with Final Cut Studio.

## Setting Up for Surround Mixing

Soundtrack Pro is built for designing surround sound mixes, which makes it extremely easy to switch from stereo to 5.1 surround mixing at any point in your workflow. There are a few basic requirements to meet, and then a few simple configuration changes to make.

To produce a 5.1 surround mix, you'll need a hardware interface with at least 6 outputs connected to the appropriate speakers. Soundtrack Pro uses the SMPTE/ITU standard for surround speaker assignment:

| Audio Interface Output | Speaker |
| --- | --- |
| 1 | Left |
| 2 | Right |
| 3 | Center |
| 4 | LFE |
| 5 | Left Surround (Ls) |
| 6 | Right Surround (Rs) |

When you have your speakers properly connected, there are only two changes to make in your multitrack project. First, you reassign the output of your submixes to the surround outputs.

**1**   In the Mixer tab, click the Output menu at the bottom of the SFX submix track.

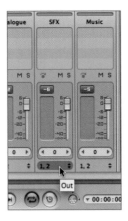

**2**   In the Output pop-up menu, select Surround > 1-6.

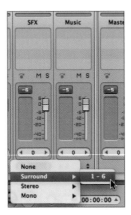

The SFX submix is now set to output in 5.1 surround. The only remaining step is to switch the SFX audio tracks from stereo panners to surround panners.

**3**  Select the SFX audio track in either the track list or the Mixer.

**4**  Choose Multitrack > Use Surround Panner.

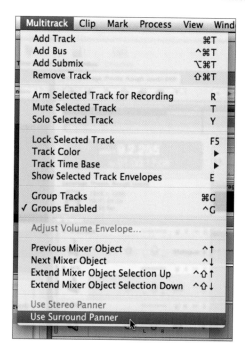

The SFX track switches to surround panning mode and the stereo panner is replaced by the mini surround panner.

**NOTE ▶** You can also switch the panner mode by Control-clicking the panner and choosing the desired pan type.

You can position the track in the surround field by dragging the mini surround panner with the pointer. However, there's an easier way to set the pan on a surround track.

**5** Double-click the mini surround panner in the SFX track to open the Surround Panner HUD.

The Surround Panner HUD appears.

The Surround Panner HUD gives you complete control over the placement of the track in the surround space. It also graphically displays the ratio of sound level coming from each speaker.

If you have a surround speaker system already configured at your workstation, you may wish to take a few minutes to play with the Surround Panner HUD.

## Returning to Final Cut Pro

When you're finished with your sound mix, it's time to move back to Final Cut Pro in preparation for final output.

**1**  Clear any cycle region you have by double-clicking in the lower half of the Time ruler.

**2**  Choose File > Export.

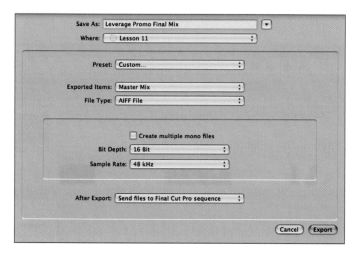

The Export dialog opens.

**3**  Name the file *Leverage Promo Final Mix*.

**4**  To export the complete mix, select Master Mix in the Exported Items menu.

**5**  If necessary, set After Export to "Send files to Final Cut Pro" sequence so that the project will be sent directly back to Final Cut Pro for final output.

**6**  Click Export.

The mix is exported to an XML file, and Final Cut Pro is automatically brought forward (or launched if it wasn't currently open) and the Import XML dialog appears.

**7**    Leave all the settings at their default values, and click OK.

A Save dialog appears, asking you to save a project.

**8**    Navigate to the directory of your choice and click Save.

A new Final Cut Pro project is created. The A1 and A2 audio tracks are the new mixed tracks from Soundtrack Pro. The A3 audio track, which has been disabled, is the original sequence audio.

The project is now ready for final export.

## Lesson Review

1.    Why does a cycle region help when mixing?

2.    What are submixes used for?

3.    What are busses used for?

4.    If you apply a reverb to a bus, what should the dry setting be set to?

5.    What types of sound will Voice Level Match analyze and adjust volume for?

6.    True or false: If your project contains one or more busses, the signal always travels through the Master channel *before* it's fed to a bus.

7.    What are the three steps necessary to mix in surround?

*Answers*

1. Using a cycle region, you can play a certain section of the song repeatedly, which allows you to become familiar with the sounds it contains as you mix.

2. A submix is a collection of similar tracks. You can use a submix to control the volume and pan, or apply effects to several tracks at one time.

3. Busses let you apply a single instance of a real-time effect to multiple tracks at once.

4. If a reverb is applied to a bus, you should set the dry setting to 0.

5. Voice Level Match works only on the human voice and will ignore any other sounds that may be present in a clip.

6. False. Signal passes from left to right through the Mixer, starting at tracks, and then progressing to busses, submixes, and finally the Master channel.

7. Connect the hardware outputs to the speakers, assign the submix to the surround outputs, and select the surround panner for each audio track you wish to mix in surround.

# 12

**Lesson Files**

**Time**

This lesson takes approximately 60 minutes to complete.

**Goals**

Understand the parallel workflows of picture and sound editors

Send revised picture edits to Soundtrack Pro from Final Cut Pro

Conform a sound edit to a revised picture edit

Review and approve clip changes

Learn how to compare projects

Manage the conform process

# Conforming Multitrack Projects

The editorial process, by definition, involves change. On large productions in which editorial chores are split between "picture editor" and "sound editor," any change introduced into the process can become time-consuming and costly.

Consider this scenario: You're the sound editor on a television show and you're working feverishly to sweeten and mix the show before your looming deadline. You've been told "the picture is locked" (meaning that no further changes to the picture will be made). However, while you're working on the sound mix you're told that the director has ordered a re-edit of a scene to tighten up the performance. This means that you'll have to adapt your sound mix to the new edit of the picture, a process called "conforming." Manually conforming a project involves importing the picture editor's new sequence into the existing multitrack project, and then painstakingly comparing the placement of the clips in the new edit to the clips in the sound mix. Clips in the old mix are then adjusted to match the position of the clips in the new edit, and clips may have to be deleted or added if shots were cut or added.

Fortunately, Soundtrack Pro benefits from its tight integration with Final Cut Pro, and is able to automate the conform process. This makes conforming edits much more efficient, and also helps eliminate the potential for mistakes.

## Working in Parallel

One of the benefits of working in Final Cut Studio is that the picture editor and sound editor can work in parallel, as opposed to requiring the picture editor to finish work before the sound editing begins. With Final Cut Studio, each editor can continue to refine his or her work, and then use Conform to merge the results. In this lesson, you'll experience the conform process first-hand by conforming the mix you made in the previous lesson to a new picture edit.

1   Navigate to the Lesson 12 folder and open **12_Leverage_Promo_FINAL_MIX.stmp**.

   The Leverage Promo project that you've been working on through the last three lessons opens. Play the project if you wish to see it again.

2   Place the playhead at the end of the video clip (enable snapping to do this easily).

3   Note the duration of the picture edit by looking at the time displayed in the timecode window as a reference to the original picture edit's length.

   The video ends at 01:01:04:14.

## Importing Changes from Final Cut Pro

While you've been working on the sound mix in Soundtrack Pro, the picture editor has been re-cutting the video in Final Cut Pro. You'll need to open the revised picture edit in Final Cut Pro to see the changes, and then send a new multitrack project to Soundtrack Pro and conform the two projects.

1   In the Lesson 12 folder, open the file **12_Leverage_Promo_RE-EDIT.fcp**.

   The revised edit of the project opens in Final Cut Pro.

2   Play the project and note the changes in timing during the second dialogue sequence.

3   Press the End key to move the playhead to the end of the last video clip.

4   Note that the timecode is 01:01:03:22.

   The edits in the middle of the sequence have shortened the duration of the video by 16 frames. This may not seem like a huge difference to the casual viewer, but it will push all the sound effects and music cues out of sync by half a second.

## Sending the Revised Edit to Soundtrack Pro

The revised picture edit must now be sent to Soundtrack Pro for conforming.

1   In the Browser, Control-click or right-click the *Leverage_Promo_Revised_Edit* sequence, and from the shortcut menu, choose Send To > Soundtrack Pro Multitrack Project.

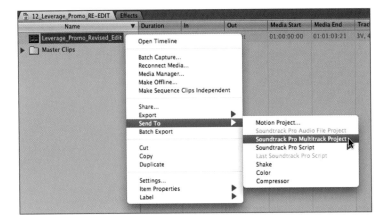

A Save dialog appears.

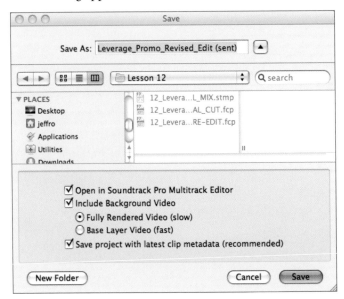

**2**    As you did last time, select Fully Rendered Video (slow) to retain the color correction filters that were applied to the clips in this project, and then click Save.

NOTE ▸ The checkbox labeled "Save project with the latest clip metadata (recommended)" is very important for the conform process to work correctly. The clip metadata that's saved in the exported project provides Soundtrack Pro with crucial information regarding the changes that have been made in the project you're sending.

## Conforming Projects

In Soundtrack Pro you should now see two project tabs side by side in the Project pane for Leverage_Promo_MIX.stmp and Leverage_Promo_Revised_Edit (sent).stmp.

The **Leverage_Promo_Revised_Edit.stmp** project is dialogue only, just as the Final Cut Pro project it was sent from was. As the sound editor, your job is to integrate the changes from this revised Final Cut Pro project with your original sound mix project.

1    In the lower pane, click the Conform tab.

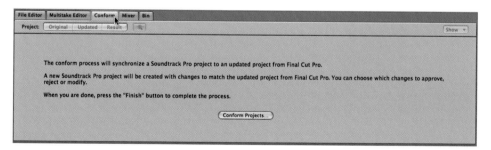

In the Conform tab, a notice appears telling you what will happen when you click the Conform Projects button.

2    Click the Conform Projects button.

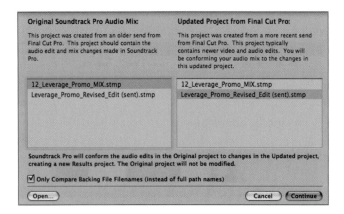

The conform process is initiated and a dialog appears. In the left box, the **Leverage_Promo_MIX.stmp** project is selected by default. Projects selected in the left box are projects that contain the desired audio edit. In the right box, the **Leverage_Promo_Revised_Edit (sent).stmp** project is selected. Projects in the right box are projects that contain the revised or updated project that was sent from Final Cut Pro.

**3** Click the Continue button.

Soundtrack Pro compares the clip positions in the original audio mix project to the clip positions in the revised picture edit project, and then determines the best resulting clip position and duration for each clip by attempting to conform the audio mix to the updated video edit.

A new project, currently untitled, is created with the results of the conform process.

**4** Play the project from start to end.

You'll notice that the position and duration of some audio clips have been adjusted because of changes to the picture edit.

In the Conform tab, a list of clips that may have been moved or altered appears. This is called the Conform worklist. In the following exercises you'll review the changes in the Conform worklist and approve or reject them.

## Reviewing Changes

Although Soundtrack Pro will automatically adjust clips to fit the new edit, you need to make sure that the adjustments it made to the position and/or duration of the clips are appropriate.. The review and approval process can be approached in different ways depending on the project's complexity. In one approach, the sound editor simply plays back the conformed Timeline to make sure that no audio files have been altered inappropriately. If audio clips aren't in their proper locations relative to the picture, changes can be made directly in the Timeline using Soundtrack Pro's editing tools.

In another approach, the sound editor uses both the worklist and the Timeline to verify one another's accuracy. In this approach, the worklist presents changes to the audio more objectively, giving the editor critical feedback as to how Soundtrack Pro executed a given change. This method allows the sound editor to make editorial changes directly in the worklist rather than in the Timeline.

In the following steps, you'll use the second approach to approve the changes to the clips.

Before doing so, you may find it helpful to maximize the size of the lower pane so you can easily read all the data in the columns.

1   Press Control-D.

    The left pane is hidden.

    **NOTE** ▶ Control-A will hide the right pane.

2   Select the first clip in the worklist, **66/3**.

    The clip is selected in the Timeline.

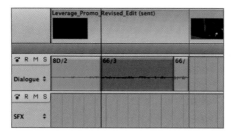

This is a helpful feature for quickly locating and identifying clips in the Timeline that you're reviewing.

**NOTE** ▸ You can Command-click in the worklist to add to your selection in the Timeline. Additionally, selected clips also appear in yellow in the Global Timeline view.

## Viewing Clip Details

To see how a clip was changed, you'll need to load the clip into the Details section of the Conform tab.

**1**   Select the **Impact Metal Hit Reverb 01** clip in the worklist.

The Details section displays the name of the clip and the changes that Soundtrack Pro made to the clip.

There are two basic types of changes: Position/Duration changes and Media changes. The position of this clip was changed, as was the clip's media. To see why Soundtrack Pro made these choices you'll need to look in the worklist.

In the Impact Metal Hit Reverb's row, the Position D column has a value of –00:00:00:16, informing you that the clip was moved 16 frames earlier in time. However, in the Duration D column, you'll see that the clip's duration did not change. (The delta D symbol denotes a change in value.)

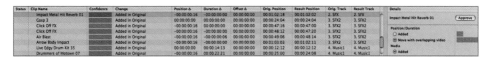

As you may recall from the beginning of this lesson, the revised picture edit shortened the overall length of the project by 16 frames. This is why this clip, which is located at the end of the sequence, was moved forward by 16 frames.

## Approving Changes

Now that you've reviewed and verified the changes that were made to the clip, you're ready to approve the clip.

1    Click the **Air Blast** clip in the worklist.

The worklist indicates that the clip's position has moved forward 16 frames and its duration has been shortened by 6 frames.

2    Move the playhead to around the Action 2 marker and press the spacebar to play the clip.

Playing the clip in the Timeline is necessary to verify that the conform process made the change correctly. If all looks and sounds as it should, approve the change.

3    Click the Approve button for the **Air Blast** clip.

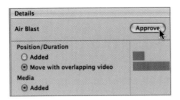

After you approve the clip, a checkmark appears in the Status column and the clip's details are dimmed. Approving a clip simply flags the clip to remind you that it's been reviewed. Once you click Approve, the button changes to an Edit button.

The approval process is entirely for your reference. Ultimately, when you click the Finish button, the changes are applied to the clips whether you've approved all of the changes or not. Reviewing the clips in the worklist gives you the opportunity to assess the changed clips and flag them appropriately in an organized manner. This saves you from having to review clips more than once as you refine the results of the conform.

## Filtering, Sorting, and Grouping Clips

At the bottom of the Conform tab are options for hiding and grouping clips. These controls help you organize the worklist.

### Filtering

You can hide unchanged or already approved clips by selecting the filter checkboxes.

1   Select the Hide Approved checkbox.

    Selecting this option will remove from view any clips that have checkmarks by them. As you approve clips they'll automatically disappear from the worklist.

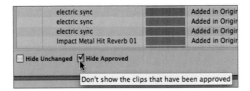

**2**   Select the Hide Unchanged checkbox to remove from the worklist any clips that were not modified.

## Sorting

**1**   To sort the worklist, click a column header.

## Grouping

You can also create groups of clips. Grouping clips allows you to approve clips in batches, making the review and approval process faster.

**1**   Drag the Group slider to the right.

Groups of clips are created.

**2**   Select a group.

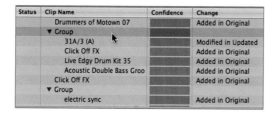

All clips in the Timeline that belong to that group are selected. This makes it easier to approve a batch of clips that you're confident are correct.

**3**   Click the Approve button, and all clips within the group are flagged in the Status column with a checkmark.

**4**   Drag the Group slider to the left to return all clips to individual listings.

## Finishing

When you've reviewed all the changes, you're ready to finish the conform.

**1**  Click the Finish button in the lower-right corner of the Details section.

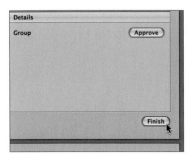

A dialog will appear verifying that you wish to complete the conform process.

**2**  Click OK.

Soundtrack Pro completes the conform process.

You now have a new Soundtrack Pro project containing your original sound edits reconciled with the changed picture edit.

You can continue editing the audio in Soundtrack Pro. If further picture edits are required, you can then conform any new edits with this conformed sequence as the new "original" project.

## Lesson Review

1.  Why is it important to save project metadata during the conform process?

2.  Does the conform process create a new Soundtrack Pro project?

3.  What is the Conform worklist?

4.  True or false: Only by clicking the Approve button can you instruct Soundtrack Pro to save changes to a project made in the Conform process.

5.  Is it possible to approve more than one clip at a time?

*Answers*

1.  The metadata provides Soundtrack Pro with crucial information about what's changed in the multitrack project you're sending.

2.  Yes, the sound editor can approve, reject, or modify changes nondestructively and then save the resulting project.

3.  The Conform worklist is a sound-change list in which Soundtrack Pro displays all the clips that may have been moved or changed in some way by the conform process.

4.  False. When you ultimately click the Finish button, the changes are executed whether you've approved them all or not. The approval process is for tracking and management purposes only.

5.  Yes, by using the Group slider to create groups of clips to make reviewing and approving easier to manage. This is helpful in projects in which the editor may have hundreds of clips to conform.

# Glossary

**16-bit** A standard bit depth for digital audio recording and playback.

**5.1** A common surround sound format, typically comprising five full-frequency speakers, which are fed by five independent channels, plus one dedicated low-frequency subwoofer.

**A/D converter box** Equipment that changes an analog signal into a digital signal.

**add edit** Working like the Razor Blade tool, adds an edit point to all clips in the Timeline at the current position of the playhead.

**AIFF (Audio Interchange File Format)** Apple's native uncompressed audio file format created for the Macintosh computer, commonly used for the storage and transmission of digitally sampled sound.

**affiliate clip** A copy of a clip that shares properties with the original, or master, clip.

**ambience** A type of sound that includes background room noise, traffic noise, and atmospheric sound effects.

**animation** The process of changing any number of variables such as color, audio levels, or other effects over time using keyframes.

**arming** Enabling a track to be recorded.

**audio interface** A device that provides audio inputs and outputs to your computer.

**audio meters** A graphic display of the audio level (loudness) of a clip or sequence. Used to set incoming and outgoing audio levels and to check for audio distortion and signal strength.

**audio mixing** The process of adjusting the volume levels of all audio clips in an edited sequence, including the production audio, music, sound effects, voice-overs, and additional background ambience, to turn all of these sounds into a harmonious whole.

**audio peaks** The highest audio levels in a track. Peaks that exceed 0 dB will be *clipped*.

**audio sample rate** The rate or frequency at which a sound is sampled to digitize it. 48 kHz is the standard sampling rate for digital audio; CD audio is sampled at 44.1 kHz.

**audio waveform** A graphical representation of the amplitude (loudness) of a sound over a period of time.

**automation** The ability to record, edit, and play back the movements of all knobs and switches, including volume faders and pan, EQ, and aux send controls.

**Autosave Vault** A function that automatically saves backup copies of all your FCP open projects at regular intervals. It must be turned on, and you can specify the intervals.

**AVI** A PC-compatible standard for digital video no longer officially supported by Microsoft but still frequently used. AVI supports fewer codecs than QuickTime. Some AVI codecs will not play back in QuickTime and will thus be inaccessible in Final Cut Studio without prior format conversion.

**B**

**backtiming** Using In and Out points in the Viewer and only an Out point in the Timeline. The two Out points will align, and the rest of the clip will appear before (to the left) of this point.

**bar** A measure of music, containing a specified number of beats, that establishes the rhythmic structure of the composition.

**bars and tone** A series of vertical bars of specific colors and an audio tone used to calibrate the audio and video signals coming from a videotape or camera to ensure consistent appearance and sound on different TV monitors.

**Bezier handle** The "control handles" attached to a Bezier curve on a motion path that allow you to change the shape of the curve.

**bin** A file folder in the Browser window used to keep media clips grouped and organized. Derived from film editing where strips of film were hung over a cloth bin for sorting during the editing process.

**bit depth** The resolution (number of 0s and 1s) of a digital audio sample, which influences the dynamic range of a digital audio recording.

**bounce** To combine several tracks of audio into one file.

**Browser** An interface window that is a central storage area where you organize and access all of the source material used in your project.

**bus** A virtual audio cable to route audio between channel strips, for processing or submixing tasks.

**C**

**cache** An area of the computer's memory (RAM) dedicated to storing still images, digital audio, and video in preparation for real-time playback.

**Canvas** The window in which you can view your edited sequence.

**capture** The process of digitizing media in the computer.

**capture card** Hardware added to a computer (often an internal circuit board) to enhance video-acquisition options, such as enabling the capture of analog video formats.

**channel** A path used to transport a signal.

**clip** Media files that may consist of video, audio, graphics, or any similar content that can be imported into Final Cut Pro.

**clipping** Distortion during the playback or recording of digital audio due to an overly loud level.

**codec** Short for *compression/decompression*. A program used to compress and decompress data such as audio and video files.

**compression** The process by which video, graphics, and audio files are reduced in size. The reduction in the size of a video file through the removal of redundant image data is referred to as a lossy compression scheme. A lossless compression scheme uses a mathematical process and reduces the file size by consolidating the redundant information without discarding it. See also codec.

**Core Audio** The standardized audio driver for a computer running Mac OS X 10.2 or higher. Allows the connection of all audio interfaces that are Core Audio-compatible.

**Core MIDI** The standardized MIDI driver for a computer running Mac OS X 10.2 or higher. Allows the connection of all MIDI devices that are Core MIDI-compatible.

**cross fade** A transition between two audio clips where one sound is faded out while the other is faded in. Used to make the transition between two audio cuts less noticeable.

**cut** The simplest type of edit where one clip ends and the next begins without any transition.

**cutaway** A shot that is related to the current subject and occurs in the same time frame; for instance, an interviewer's reaction to what is being said in an interview or a shot to cover a technically bad moment.

**data rate** The speed at which data can be transferred, often described in megabytes per second (MB/sec). The higher a video file's data rate, the higher quality it will be, but it will require more system resources (processor speed, hard disk space, and performance). Some codecs allow you to specify a maximum data rate for a movie during capture.

**D**

**decibel (dB)** A unit of measure for the loudness of audio.

**decompression** The process of restoring a video or audio file for playback from a compressed video, graphics, or audio file. Compare with *compression*.

**device control** A cable that allows Final Cut Pro to control a video deck or camera. Three protocols are used most frequently to control video devices: serial device control via the RS-422 and RS-232 protocols, and FireWire for DV camcorders and decks.

**digital audio workstation (DAW)** A computer that records, mixes, and produces audio files.

**digital signal processing (DSP)** The mathematical process of manipulating digital information to modify sound.

**dithering** A process of reducing an audio signal from a higher-bit resolution to a lower one.

**driver** A software program that allows your computer to communicate with another piece of hardware.

**drop frame timecode** NTSC timecode that skips ahead in time by two frame numbers each minute, except for minutes ending in 0, so that the end timecode total agrees with the actual elapsed clock time. Although timecode numbers are skipped, actual video frames are not skipped. See *timecode*.

**dub** Making a copy of an analog tape to the same type of format.

**DV** A standard for a specific digital video format created by a consortium of camcorder vendors, which uses Motion JPEG video at a 720 x 480 resolution at 29.97 frames per second (NTSC) or 720 x 546 resolution at 25 fps (PAL), stored at a bit rate of 25 MB per second at a compression of 4:1:1.

**dynamic range** The difference, in decibels, between the loudest and softest parts of a recording.

**Easy Setup** Preset audio/video settings, including capture, sequence, device control, and output settings.

**E**

**edit point** (1) Defines what part of a clip you want to use in an edited sequence. Edit points include In points, which specify the beginning of a section of a clip or sequence, and Out points, which specify the end of a section of a clip or sequence. (2) The point in the Timeline of an edited sequence where the Out point of one clip meets the In point of the next clip.

**Edit to Tape** The command that lets you perform frame-accurate insert and assemble edits to tape.

**EDL (Edit Decision List)** A text file that uses the source timecode of clips to sequentially list all of the edits that make up a sequence. EDLs are used to move a project from one editing application to another, or to coordinate the assembly of a program in a tape-based online editing facility.

**effects** A general term used to describe all of Final Cut Pro's capabilities that go beyond cuts-only editing. See *filters, generators,* and *transitions.*

**extend edit** An edit in which the edit point is moved to the position of the playhead in the Timeline.

**fade** An effect in which the picture gradually transitions to black.

**F**

**faders** In the Audio Mixer, vertical sliders used to adjust the audio levels of clips at the position of the playhead.

**favorite** A frequently used customized effect. You can create favorites from most of the effects in Final Cut Pro.

**filters** Effects you can apply to video and audio clips or group of clips that change some aspect of the clip content.

**finishing** The process of fine-tuning the sequence audio and video levels and preparing the sequence for output to tape or other destination, such as broadcast, the Web, or DVD. Finishing may also involve recapturing offline clips at an uncompressed resolution.

**FireWire** Apple's trademark name for the IEEE 1394 standard used to connect external hard drives and cameras to computers. It provides a fast interface to move large video and audio files to the computer's hard drive.

**fit to fill edit** An edit in which a clip is inserted and retimed into a sequence such that its duration matches a predetermined amount of specified track space.

**frame** A single still image from either video or film. For video, each frame is made up of two interlaced fields (see *interlaced video*).

**frequency** The number of times a sound or signal vibrates each second, measured in cycles per second, or hertz.

**gain** In video, the level of white in a video picture; in audio, the loudness of an audio signal.

**G**

**gap** Locations in a sequence where there is no media on any track. When output to video, gaps in an edited sequence appear as black sections.

**handles** Extra frames of unused video or audio that are on either side of the In and Out points in an edit.

**H**

**head** The beginning of a clip.

**headroom** Refers to the available dynamic range before clipping, or distortion, occurs.

**incoming clip** The clip that is on the right-hand side, or B-side, of a transition or cut point.

**I**

**In point** The edit point entered either in the Viewer, Canvas, or Timeline that determines where an edit will begin.

**insert edit** To insert a clip into an existing sequence into the Timeline, which automatically moves the other clips (or remaining frames of a clip) to the right to make room for it. An insert edit does not replace existing material.

**jog** To move forward or backward through your video one frame at a time.

**J**

**jump cut** A cut in which an abrupt change occurs between two shots.

**keyframe** In Final Cut Pro, a point at which a filter, motion effect, or audio level changes value. There must be at least two keyframes representing two different values to show a change.

**K**

**kilohertz** A measure of audio frequency equal to 1000 hertz (cycles per second). Abbreviated kHz.

**labels** Terms that appear in the Label column of the Browser, such as "Best Take" and "Interview." Labels can also be assigned to clips and media to help distinguish and sort them. Each label has an associated color that is also applied to clips.

**L**

**lift edit** An edit function that leaves a gap when material is lifted from the Timeline.

**link** (1) To connect audio and video clips in the Timeline so that when one item is selected, moved, or trimmed, all the items linked to it are affected. (2) The connection between a clip and its associated source media file on disk. If you move source media files, change their names, or put them in the Trash, the links break and associated clips in your Final Cut Pro project become *offline clips.*

**linked selection** An option in the Timeline that, when enabled, maintains connections between linked clips. When linked selection is turned off, linked items behave as if they are not connected.

**locked track** A track whose contents cannot be moved or changed. Crosshatched lines distinguish a locked track on the Timeline. You can lock or unlock tracks at any time by clicking the Lock Track control on the Timeline.

**log and capture** The process of playing clips from a device and logging and capturing the clips you want to use in editing.

**Log bin** A specific bin where all the logged or captured clips go when using the Log and Capture window.

**logging** The process of entering detailed information, including the In and Out points from your source material, log notes, and so on, in preparation for a clip to be captured.

**M**

**markers** Location indicators that can be placed on a clip or in a sequence to help you find a specific place while you edit. Can be used to sync action between two clips, identify beats of music, mark a reference word from a narrator, and so on.

**Mark In** The process of indicating with a mark in the Viewer, Canvas, or Timeline the first frame of a clip to be used.

**Mark in Sync** A command in the Modify menu that marks a selected audio clip from one source as being in sync with a selected video clip from another source. Mark Out The process of indicating with a mark in the Viewer, Canvas, or Timeline the last frame of a clip to be used.

**Mark Out** The process of indicating with a mark in the Viewer, Canvas, or Timeline the last frame of a clip to be used.

**Marquee** The rectangular lasso of dotted lines that the pointer generates as it is dragged in the Browser or Timeline to select items.

**master clip** The status given to a clip the first time that clip is used in a project. It is the clip from which other affiliate clips, such as sequence clips and subclips, are created.

**Mastering mode** A mode in the Edit to Tape window that lets you output additional elements such as color bars and tone, a slate, and a countdown when you output your program to tape.

**master shot** A single, long shot of some dramatic action from which shorter cuts such as close-ups and medium shots are taken in order to fill out the story.

**Match Frame** A command that looks at the clip in the Timeline at the playhead and puts that clip's master into the Viewer. The position of the playhead in the Viewer matches that of the playhead in the Canvas, so both the Canvas and the Viewer will display the same frame, and the In and Out points of the clip in your sequence will be matched to those of the copy in the Viewer. In addition, all the original source material for this clip will also be displayed.

**media file** A generic term for captured or acquired elements such as QuickTime movies, sounds, and pictures.

**Media Manager** A tool that helps you manage your projects, media files, and available disk space quickly and easily in Final Cut Pro without the Finder.

**MIDI** Musical Instrument Digital Interface. An industry standard that allows devices such as synthesizers and computers to communicate with each other.

**mono audio** A single track of audio.

**MPEG (Moving Picture Experts Group)** A group of compression standards for video and audio.

**multicam editing** This feature lets you simultaneously play back and view shots from multiple cameras and cut between them in real time.

**multiclip** A clip that allows you to group together multiple sources as separate angles and cut between them. Up to 128 angles can be synced, of which 16 can be played back at a time.

**natural sound** The ambient sound used from a source videotape.

**N**

**nest** To place an edited sequence within another sequence.

**non-drop frame timecode** NTSC timecode in which frames are numbered sequentially and run at 30 fps. NTSC's frame rate, however, is actually 29.97 fps; therefore, non-drop frame timecode is off by 3 seconds and 18 frames per hour in comparison to actual elapsed time.

**noninterlaced video** The standard representation of images on a computer, also referred to as "progressive scan." The monitor displays the image by drawing each line, continuously one after the other, from top to bottom.

**nonlinear editing (NLE)** A video editing process that uses computer hard disks to randomly access the media. It allows the editor to reorganize clips very quickly or make changes to sections without having to re-create the entire program.

**nonsquare pixel** A pixel whose height is different from its width. An NTSC pixel is taller than it is wide, and a PAL pixel is wider than it is tall.

**NTSC (National Television Systems Committee)** Standard of color TV broadcasting used mainly in North America, Mexico, and Japan, consisting of 525 lines per frame, 29.97 frames per second, and 720 x 486 pixels per frame (720 x 480 for DV).

**offline clip** Clips that appear in the Browser with a red slash through them. Clips may be offline because they haven't been captured yet, or because the media file has been moved to another location. To view these clips properly in your project, you must recapture them or reconnect them to their corresponding source files at their new locations on disk.

**O**

**offline editing** The process of editing a program at a lower resolution to save on equipment costs or to conserve hard disk space. When the edit is finished, the material can be recaptured at a higher quality, or an *EDL* can be generated for re-creating the edit on another system.

**OMF (Open Media Framework)** An edit data interchange format.

**outgoing clip** The clip on the left-hand side of the cut point or the A-side of the transition.

**Out of sync** Said of the audio of a track when it has been shifted horizontally in the Timeline, causing it to no longer match the video track.

**Out point** The edit point entered in the Viewer, Canvas, or Timeline where an edit will end.

**overwrite edit** An edit where the clip being edited into a sequence replaces an existing clip. The duration of the sequence remains unchanged.

**P**

**PAL (Phase Alternating Line)** The European color TV broadcasting standard consisting of 625 lines per frame, running at 25 frames per second, and 720 x 546 pixels per frame.

**patch panel** The section of the Timeline containing the Audio, Source, Destination, Track Visibility, Lock Track, and Auto Select controls.

**peak** Short, loud bursts of sound that last a fraction of a second and can be viewed on a digital audiometer that displays the absolute volume of an audio signal as it plays.

**PCM** Pulse-code modulated audio. This is simply uncompressed digital audio, including AIFF, WAV, and SDII files.

**playhead** A navigational element that shows the current frame you are in the Timeline, Canvas, or Viewer.

**plug-in** A small software application that adds functions to a main program.

**post-production** The phase of film, video, and audio editing that begins after all the footage is shot.

**post-roll** The amount of time that a tape machine continues to roll after the Out point of an edit, typically between 2 and 5 seconds.

**pre-roll** A specified amount of time, usually 5 seconds, given to tape machines so they can synchronize themselves to the editing computer before previewing or performing an edit.

**preview** To play an edit to see how it will look without actually performing the edit itself.

**Print to Video** A command in Final Cut Pro that lets you *render* your sequence and output it to videotape.

**proc amp (processing amplifier)** A piece of equipment that allows you to adjust video levels on output.

**project** In Final Cut Pro, the top-level file stores the editing information associated with a program, including sequences and clips of various kinds.

**punch in, punch out** A technique that allows you to interrupt playback and record audio as the sound is playing.

**Q**

**QuickTime**  Apple's cross-platform multimedia technology. Widely used for editing, compositing, CD-ROM, Web video, and more.

**QuickTime streaming**  Apple's streaming media addition to the QuickTime architecture. Used for viewing QuickTime content in real time on the Web.

**R**

**real-time effects**  Effects that can be applied to clips in an edited sequence and played back in real time, without requiring rendering first. Real-time effects can be played back using any qualified computer.

**record monitor**  A monitor that plays the previewed and finished versions of a project when it is printed to tape. A record monitor corresponds to the Canvas in Final Cut Pro.

**redo**  To reverse an undo, thus restoring the last change made to a project.

**render**  To process video and audio with any applied effects, such as transitions or filters. Effects that aren't real time must be rendered in order to be played back properly. Once rendered, your sequence can be played in real time.

**render file**  The file produced by rendering a clip to disk. FCP places it in a separate hidden folder so it does not show up in the Browser but is referenced and played in the Timeline.

**render status bars**  Two slim horizontal bars, in the Timeline ruler area, that indicate which parts of the sequence have been rendered at the current render quality. The top bar is for video, and the bottom for audio. Different colored bars indicate the real-time playback status of a given section of the Timeline.

**replace edit**  Allows you to replace an existing shot in a sequence with a different shot of the same length using the playheads in the Viewer and sequence as reference points.

**RGB**  An abbreviation for red, green, and blue, which are the three primary colors that make up a color image.

**ripple edit**  An edit that trims the In or Out point of a sequence clip, and repositions (or "ripples") subsequent clips, while lengthening or shortening the entire sequence.

**roll edit**  An edit that affects two clips that share an *edit point*. The Out point of the outgoing clip and the In point of the incoming clip both change, but the overall duration of the sequence stays the same.

**RT Extreme**  Real-time effects processing that scales with your system.

**S**

**sampling**  The process during which analog audio is converted into digital information. The sampling rate of an audio stream specifies how many samples are captured. Higher sample rates yield higher-quality audio. Examples are 44.1 kHz and 48 kHz.

**scratch disk**  The hard disk designated to hold your captured media, rendered clips, and cache files.

**scrub**  To move through a clip or sequence by dragging the playhead with the mouse. Scrubbing is used to find a particular point or frame or to hear the audio.

**scrubber bar**  A bar below the Viewer and the Canvas that allows you to manually drag the playhead in either direction to playback.

**send**  An output on an audio channel that splits a portion of a channel's sound and sends it through a bus to another audio channel strip.

**sequence**  An edited assembly of video, audio, or graphics clips. A sequence can contain your entire edited program or be limited to a single scene.

**sequence clip**  A clip that has been edited into a sequence.

**sequencer**  A computer application that allows you to record both digital audio and MIDI data and blend the sounds together in a software mixing console.

**shuttle control**  The slider located at the bottom of the Viewer and the Canvas. This control is useful for continuous playback at different speeds, in fast and slow motion. It also shifts the pitch of audio as it plays at varying speeds.

**slate**  A small clapboard, placed in front of all cameras at the beginning of a scene, which gives basic production information such as the take, date, and name of scene. A slate or clapper provides an audio/visual cue for synchronization of dual-system recordings.

**slide edit**  An edit in which an entire clip is moved, along with the edit points on its left and right. The duration of the clip being moved stays the same, but the clips to the left and to the right of it change in length to accommodate the new positioning of the clip. The overall duration of the sequence and of these three clips remains the same.

**slip edit**  An edit in which the location of both In and Out points of a clip are changed at the same time, without changing the location or duration of the marked media. This is referred to as *slipping* because you slip a pair of In and Out points inside the available footage.

**slug**  A solid black video frame that can be used to represent a video clip that has not yet been placed in the Timeline.

**SMPTE (Society of Motion Picture and Television Engineers)**  The organization responsible for establishing various broadcast video standards like the SMPTE standard time-code for video playback.

**snapping**  A setting that affects the movement of objects in the Timeline, such as the playhead, clips, and markers. With snapping enabled, when dragging these objects close together, they "snap," or move directly, to each other to ensure frame accuracy.

**solo**  An audio monitoring feature in which one audio track from a group may be isolated for listening without having to be removed from the group.

**SOT**  Acronym for *sound on tape.*

**sound bite**  A short excerpt taken from an interview clip.

**split edit**  An edit in which the video track or the audio track of a synchronized clip ends up being longer than the other; for example, the sound may be longer than the video at the head of the clip, so it is heard before the video appears. Also referred to as an *L-cut.*

**spread** An audio control that allows you to adjust the amount of separation of stereo channels.

**static region** An area in a sequence in the Timeline that you lock so that it is visible even when you scroll to see other tracks. The static area can contain audio tracks, video tracks, or both.

**stereo audio** Sound that is separated into two channels, one carrying the sounds for the right ear and one for the left ear. Stereo pairs are linked and are always edited together. Audio level changes are automatically made to both channels at the same time. A pair of audio items may have their stereo pairing enabled or disabled at any time.

**storyboard** A series of pictures that summarizes the content, action, and flow of a proposed project. When the Browser is displayed in icon view, clips can be arranged visually, like a story-board. When dragged as a group into the Timeline, the clips will be edited together in the order in which they appear in the Timeline, from left to right, and from the top line down to the bottom.

**straight cut** An edit in which both the video and audio tracks are cut together to the Timeline.

**streaming** The delivery of media over an intranet or over the Internet.

**subclip** A clip created to represent a section of a *master clip*. Subclips are saved as separate items within a bin in the Browser, but do not generate any additional media on the hard disk.

**superimpose edit** An edit in which an incoming clip is placed on top of a clip that's already in the Timeline at the position of the playhead. If no In or Out points are set in the Timeline and Canvas, the previously edited clip's In and Out points are used to define the duration of the incoming clip. Superimposed edits are used to overlay titles and text onto video, as well as to create other compositing effects.

**sweetening** The process of creating a high-quality sound mix by polishing sound levels, re-recording bad sections of dialogue, and recording and adding narration, music, and sound effects.

**sync** The simultaneous timing relationship between the video and audio portions of a clip. Maintaining sync is critical when editing dialogue.

**synthesizer** A hardware or software device used to generate sounds.

**tail** The end of a clip.

**T**

**tempo** The speed at which a piece of music is played, measured in beats per minute.

**three-point editing** The process of creating an edit by setting three edit points that determine source content, duration, and placement in the sequence. With three edit points selected, Final Cut Pro calculates the fourth.

**thumbnails** The frame of a clip, shown as a tiny picture for reference. In Final Cut Pro, the thumbnail is, by default, the first frame of a clip. You can change the frame used as that clip's thumbnail by using the Scrub Video tool.

**timecode** A numbering system of electronic signals laid onto each frame of videotape that is used to identify specific frames of video. Each frame of video is labeled with hours, minutes, seconds, and frames (01:00:00:00). Timecode can be drop frame, non-drop frame, or time of day (TOD) timecode, or EBU (European Broadcast Union) for PAL projects.

**timecode gap** An area of tape with no timecode at all. Timecode gaps usually signify the end of all recorded material on a tape, but timecode gaps may occur due to the starting and stopping of the camera or tape deck during recording.

**Timeline** A window in Final Cut Pro that displays a chronological view of an open *sequence*. Each sequence has its own tab in the Timeline. You can use the Timeline to edit and arrange a sequence. The order of the tracks in the Timeline determines the layering order when you combine multiple tracks of video. Changes you make to a sequence in the Timeline are seen when you play back that sequence in the Canvas.

**time remapping** The process of changing the speed of playback of a clip over time. The equivalent of varying the crank of a film camera.

**time signature** A numerical denotation located at the beginning of each project, which sets the rhythm. Common time signatures are 4/4 and 2/4. The first number identifies the number of notes in a measure, or bar. The second number marks the length of each beat. With a 2/4 signature, each bar has two beats and each beat is a quarter note long.

**time stretch** To change the length of an audio region without changing its pitch.

**Tool palette** A window in Final Cut Pro that contains tools for editing, zooming, cropping, and distorting items in the Timeline. All tools in the Tool palette can also be selected using keyboard shortcuts.

**tracks** Layers in the Timeline that contain the audio or video clips in a sequence. Also refers to the separate audio and video tracks on tape. Final Cut Pro allows up to 99 video and 99 audio tracks to be used in a single sequence.

**transition** A visual or audio effect applied between two edit points, such as a video cross dissolve or an audio cross fade.

**Transition Editor** A specialized editor that appears in the Viewer when you double-click a transition in the Timeline; it is used to make detailed changes to a transition's timing and effects parameters.

**Trim Edit window** A window in Final Cut Pro that displays both sides of an edit: the Out point of the outgoing clip on the left and the In point of the incoming clip on the right. You can use this window to adjust the edit point between two clips very precisely, frame by frame.

**trimming** To precisely add or subtract frames from the In or Out point of a clip. Trimming is used to fine-tune an edited sequence by carefully adjusting many edits in small ways.

**two-up display** A display in the Canvas that appears when using some type of trim or adjustment mode, such as Roll, Ripple, Slip, or Slide. Two individual frames appear to display either the frames being adjusted or the border frames.

**undo** A feature that allows you to cancel the last change made.

**variable speed** See *time remapping*.

**Viewer** A window in Final Cut Pro that acts as a source monitor. You can use the Viewer to watch individual source clips and mark In and Out points in preparation for editing them into your sequence. You can also customize transitions, modify filters, and view and edit various effects. Clips from the current sequence in the Timeline can be opened in the Viewer to refine edits, effects, and audio volume.

**Voice Over tool** Allows you to record audio in Final Cut Pro while simultaneously playing back a specified section of a sequence from the Timeline. Audio can be recorded using any compatible device, such as a USB microphone, built-in iSight microphone, or DV camcorder microphone.

**VTR / VCR** Videotape recorder/videocassette recorder. A tape machine used for recording pictures and sound on videotape.

**VU meter (Volume Unit meter)** An analog meter for monitoring audio levels.

**WAV, WAVE** The primary audio file format used by Windows-compatible computers.

**W**

**waveform** A visual representation of an audio signal.

**wireframe** A visual substitute for a clip that simply represents the outline of the clip's video frame. Clips in the Viewer and Canvas can be viewed in Wireframe mode.

**x axis** Refers to the x coordinate in Cartesian geometry. The x coordinate describes horizontal placement in motion effects.

**y axis** Refers to the y coordinate in Cartesian geometry. The y coordinate describes vertical placement in motion effects.

**z axis** Refers to the z coordinate in Cartesian geometry. The z coordinate describes perpendicular placement in motion effects.

**zero crossing** A point in an audio file where the waveform crosses the zero amplitude axis. If you cut an audio file at a zero crossing, there will be no click at the cut point.

**zoom** To change the magnification of your image or Timeline.

**zoom slider** The control that appears at the bottom of the Timeline. The zoom slider allows you to navigate throughout the total duration of the currently displayed sequence; you can use the thumb tabs on the left and right of the slider to zoom in to and out of a sequence for a more detailed view.

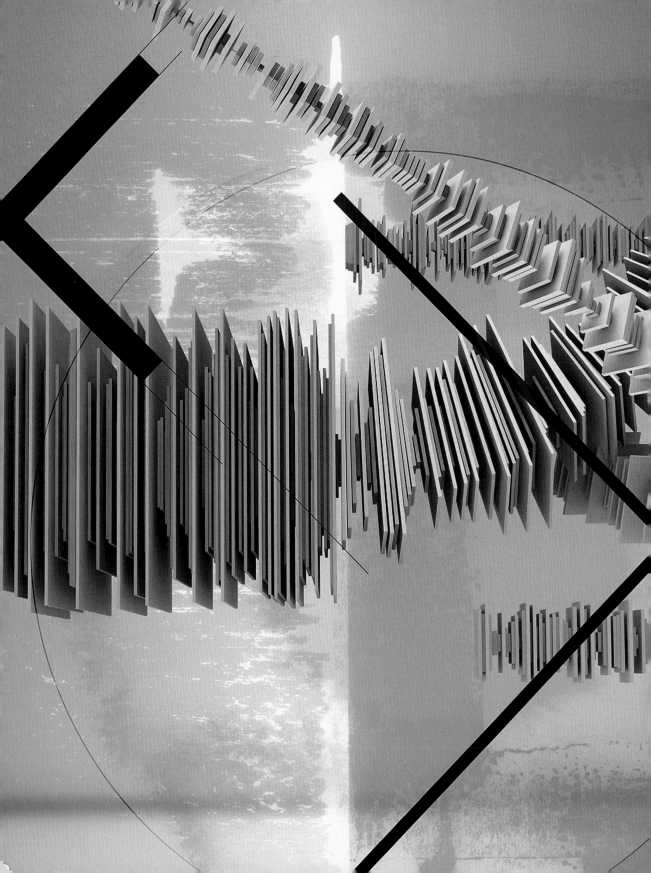

# Index

# Apple Certification
## Fuel your mind.
## Reach your potential.

Stand out from the crowd. Differentiate yourself and gain recognition for your expertise by earning Apple Certified Pro status to validate your Sound Editing skills.

This book prepares you to earn Apple Certified Pro—Sound Editing in Final Cut Studio, Level One certification. Level One certification attests to essential operational knowledge of the application. Level Two certification demonstrates mastery of advanced features and a deeper understanding of the application. Take it one step further and earn Master Pro certification.

### Three Steps to Certification

1  Choose your certification path.
   More info: training.apple.com/certification.

2  Select a location:

   **Apple Authorized Training Centers** (AATCs) offer all exams (Mac OS X, Pro Apps, iLife, iWork, and Xsan). AATC locations: training.apple.com/locations

   **Prometric Testing Centers** (1-888-275-3926) offer all Mac OS X exams, and the Final Cut Pro Level One exam. Prometric centers: www.prometric.com/apple

3  Register for and take your exam(s).

*"Now when I go out to do corporate videos and I let them know that I'm certified, I get job after job after job."*

—Chip McAllister, Final Cut Pro Editor and
Winner of The Amazing Race 2004

### Reasons to Become an Apple Certified Pro

- **Raise your earning potential.** Studies show that certified professionals can earn more than their non-certified peers.

- **Distinguish yourself from others in your industry.** Proven mastery of an application helps you stand out from the crowd.

- **Display your Apple Certification logo.** Each certification provides a logo to display on business cards, resumes and websites.

- **Publicize your Certifications.** Publish your certifications on the Apple Certified Professionals Registry to connect with schools, clients and employers.

### Training Options

Apple's comprehensive curriculum addresses your needs, whether you're an IT or creative professional, educator, or service technician. Hands-on training is available through a worldwide network of Apple Authorized Training Centers (AATCs) or in a self-paced format through the Apple Training Series and Apple Pro Training Series. Learn more about Apple's curriculum and find an AATC near you at training.apple.com.

training.apple.com/certification

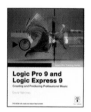